Ethical Experience

ALSO AVAILABLE FROM BLOOMSBURY

Phenomenology, Michael Lewis
Husserl's Ethics and Practical Intentionality, Susi Ferrarello
The Bloomsbury Companion to Ethics, Christian Miller
Environmental Ethics, Marion Hourdequin
The Ethics of Theory, Robert Doran
Ethics of Resistance, Drew Dalton
Posthuman Glossary, Rosi Braidotti and Maria Hlavajova

Ethical Experience: A Phenomenology

**SUSI FERRARELLO AND
NICOLLE ZAPIEN**

BLOOMSBURY ACADEMIC
LONDON • NEW YORK • OXFORD • NEW DELHI • SYDNEY

BLOOMSBURY ACADEMIC
Bloomsbury Publishing Plc
50 Bedford Square, London, WC1B 3DP, UK
1385 Broadway, New York, NY 10018, USA

BLOOMSBURY, BLOOMSBURY ACADEMIC and the Diana logo are trademarks of
Bloomsbury Publishing Plc

First published in Great Britain 2018

Copyright © Susi Ferrarello and Nicolle Zapien, 2018

Susi Ferrarello and Nicolle Zapien have asserted their right under the Copyright, Designs
and Patents Act, 1988, to be identified as Authors of this work.

For legal purposes the Acknowledgements on p. vi constitute an extension
of this copyright page.

Cover design by Toby Way
Front cover image © Getty Images
Back cover image © iStock

All rights reserved. No part of this publication may be reproduced
or transmitted in any form or by any means, electronic or mechanical,
including photocopying, recording, or any information storage or retrieval
system, without prior permission in writing from the publishers.

Bloomsbury Publishing Plc does not have any control over, or responsibility for, any
third-party websites referred to or in this book. All internet addresses given in this
book were correct at the time of going to press. The author and publisher regret any
inconvenience caused if addresses have changed or sites have ceased to exist, but can
accept no responsibility for any such changes.

A catalogue record for this book is available from the British Library.

A catalog record for this book is available from the Library of Congress.

ISBN: HB: 978-1-3500-0817-5
PB: 978-1-3500-0818-2
ePDF: 978-1-3500-0816-8
eBook: 978-1-3500-0819-9

Typeset by Newgen KnowledgeWorks Pvt. Ltd., Chennai, India

To find out more about our authors and books visit www.bloomsbury.com
and sign up for our newsletters.

Contents

Acknowledgements vi

Introduction 1

PART ONE

I.1 The phenomenological method, a theoretical 'application' 13

I.2 Husserl's ethics and psychology 29

I.3 The Trinitarian relationship of the world 49

I.4 Pathological and mystical time 67

I.5 The ethics of intimacy 81

I.6 Forced intimacy 95

PART TWO

II.1 Phenomenological research and ethical experience 111

II.2 A leadership challenge 123

II.3 A parent's ethical dilemma 141

II.4 The beginning of an affair 161

Conclusion 183

Notes 189
Bibliography 219
Index 247

Acknowledgements

First and foremost we wish to thank Dr Marc Appelbaum who originally planned to co-write this book with Dr Ferrarello but, due to a change in his circumstances and availability, had to reduce his role to editing the book. Dr Zapien was asked, as one of his former students, and a phenomenologist and psychologist to stand in and contribute to the work in his stead. The ideas and edits he offered were significant contributions and we are deeply indebted to him for his thinking and hours of detailed work on the manuscript prior to submission.

In addition, we offer gratitude to our students and clients who have taught us much about ethical experience. Our students have contributed their questions and their ideas to our philosophical understandings, against which we push and develop and crystallize our thinking. And our clients and research participants have demonstrated bravery in sharing their dilemmas that make possible our practical phenomenological research.

We wish also to thank Frankie Mace and her team at Bloomsbury for their careful and steady guidance through the publication process. Frankie is a very competent editor and an excellent project manager and her team was a delight. We thank them for seeing value in our work and supporting us through the administrative details – both large and small – smoothly.

Introduction

The genesis of this book

It is often the case that through my courses students encounter a big problem – philosophy. My psychology students, in particular, do not know how to tell me nicely that my passion for philosophy gives them vertigo. One day, Megan, a doctoral student in my class on sexuality, erupted and said that she felt as if she was sitting on the top of a tall building and that she could no longer see the facade or the structure of the building anymore. Honestly, her remark left me ambivalently happy – a combination of guilt and pride at the same time. She asked me, 'What am I supposed to do here now?' Generally, how I address this kind of anxious response to philosophy is to tell students that philosophy and psychology need each other. In fact, metaphorically speaking, we need to sit on the top of that tall building in order to approach or create theory (from Greek, *theorein* or observe, meaning to look at things as a whole) without being trapped in the reductionist view of particular details; at the same time we also need to enter the building, meet people and speak with them to fill our philosophical observations with the actual contents and details of real lives in order to be able to use philosophical understandings for practical aims. Unfortunately, despite its recent divorce from philosophy, psychology has benefited from a professional face,[1] but this early separation impoverished both.

I do not wish to diverge here to investigate the reasons that brought Stumpf[2] and others to this split, except to say that this is the root of the issue that my psychology students tend to raise. And this and similar exchanges with my students have encouraged me to pursue a project in which philosophy and psychology could be in close dialogue again. Since my love for philosophy is such that I can easily forget how long I remain sitting still on the top of that building, I decided to invite a psychologist colleague of mine to keep me company and to walk me through the whole building in order to consider experiences of real people. In this way, I hoped that the philosophical observations concerning human nature would be reflected in the lived experiences of actual human beings and would be immediately accessible to philosophers and psychologists alike.

Originally, when this volume was conceived, I invited my then husband and colleague Marc Applebaum, a phenomenologist whose support in this book is very present, most directly in his revisions of and comments on my chapters. Unfortunately, he could not continue in this project fully as was originally intended. Hence, I invited my colleague, Nicolle Zapien, whose phenomenological investigations of the lived experiences considered in this text were so intriguing to me that I felt very lucky when she accepted my invitation and decided, metaphorically speaking, to take this tour of the building together.

A general description

This volume is a phenomenological exploration of ethical lived experiences, combining philosophical and empirical studies of practical intentionality in the examination of ethical decision-making. The book is divided into two parts that are bridged together through footnotes, short commentaries at the end of each empirical study, this introduction and a conclusion. Part I is philosophical and Part II is psychological. The connecting bridge between the two is represented by the study of the ethics of lived experience. In the book the authors reflect on what constitutes reality, through consideration of many layers of reality, and how reality is built upon the ethical decisions involved in lived experiences. The method that the authors are going to use is phenomenological. In Part I of the text the approach used is merely theoretical, while in Part II, the approach is practical and involves the application of Giorgi's phenomenological research method for psychology. The authors will explore these everyday ethical experiences considering decision-making and identity through theoretical philosophical reflection in Part I in dialogue with original empirical psychological studies in Part II. Using Husserl's ethical reflection on personal narratives, the authors will present a phenomenological approach to moral psychology that hopes to offer an alternative to cognitive and neuroscientific theories.

The study of ethics is frequently framed as an exclusively technical philosophical topic, or as a domain of psychological or neuroscientific theories which, whatever their explanatory power, does not speak directly to the ways in which ethical decision-making is experienced in everyday life. In this volume these limitations will be taken up and addressed through explorations of time, identity and intimacy; time describes the essential structure of reality, and intimacy is the path through which one gains access to that reality and makes life-shaping decisions and understands the self and others.

Ethical phenomena will be viewed through the lens of Husserl's analysis of the interplay of passive and active intentionality. In this volume the authors seek to answer the following questions: What are the lived-meanings of 'values' and 'ethics' from Husserl's phenomenological perspective? What is Husserl's ethics? What is intentionality? How can we describe values as intentional objects? How does Husserl conceive the paradigm of a practical life? What is the essential structure of the experience of evaluation, or of valuing an object of perception? From a foundation in Husserl's phenomenology of ethics, the authors will explore how ethical experiences are lived and grasped through narrative, and how such narratives are both expressions of and constitutive of self-identity and the reality they experience.

The goal of the book and its main themes: Reality, time and intimacy

'Sentimental' and 'aesthetic' are two kinds of education that Flaubert and Schiller, respectively, imparted to us to illuminate a form of human growth that does not necessarily pass through a cognitive process. Understanding our position in the cosmos and being capable of looking at reality through all its layers are tasks that cannot be achieved by the means of mere logical reasoning – life needs to be involved as much as possible. As the adage says, 'Primum vivere deinde philosophari'. In this book we examined real life through practical lived experience and firsthand interviews with the hope to foster an education of reality, time and intimacy that goes beyond the limits of one's cognitive perspective and expands what is intersubjectively accepted and validated.

The book aims to flesh out the different layers of reality with the hope that professionals as well as lay people have the freedom to choose the layer of reality, time and identity in which to dwell without either undermining the actuality of the other layers or falling into relativism or nihilism. It is through appreciation of the multiplicity of views that tolerance, empathy and compassion can expand through a cognitive, sentimental and aesthetic understanding of these themes. As a scholar I can say that looking at time and intimacy from a Husserlian ethical perspective has allowed for a view of reality in a meaningful way that I think can improve the efficacy of human exchanges, and that can be considered separately from stigma and isolation.

An example of such an experience includes, in my earlier life, meeting a woman whose name was Zara, who used to work in the shop next to my parents' restaurant. I came to know later that she was treated regularly with electroshock therapy. At the time I was too young to understand the reasons for the treatment, but I recall very vividly seeing her fading away every day a little bit more. After each cycle of treatments her family used to sit her outside on a stool and at the end of the day they moved her inside along with all the other expository objects they displayed outside the shop. Although her family loved her, I find myself thinking that it is possible that she could have lived a better life if everybody (herself and all the people around her, including family and acquaintances or friends) had more understanding of her sense of reality and the ethical choices that could be made to address her presumed suffering.

For this reason, in the book we chose to look at reality and the ethical choices through the themes of time and intimacy because, emergent from my philosophical analysis, time seems to be, in its organic and spiritual quality, the most basic element of our being and intimacy seems to be the way we can gain access to all its layers and implied meanings which in turn gives us new choices. Whether we want it or not, on any level our 'we' can be afflicted by a psychological, moral or political struggle for reality – we might happen to be children of poor parents, we might be students of unusually sadistic teachers, we might be working for a very moody boss, we might be collaborating with colleagues who are in the midst of adopting a child, we might fall in love with a narcissist, we might be citizens governed by sociopaths and we might be parents of a child with learning disabilities; not to mention that we might be experiencing all of this at once! The description of reality will be very different according to these points of view. What can we do? How do we prevent ourselves from being abused by a sadistic teacher or live in the distorted reality of our narcissistic partner without either losing or imposing *our sense of reality*? And as scholars, how can we build a constructive theoretical debate around reality that is capable of defending our integrity and our right to be, even if that does not match the system of interpretations in which one should fit? How can we defend all the layers of reality?

Detailed description

To address these and other questions my colleague and I organized the book into two parts, a theoretical and a practical one. In Part I I analyse reality in relation to intimacy and time to see how they affect the ethical choices that build the layers of the human experience. In Part II, my colleague provides an analysis of these same themes through empirical phenomenological studies. Each part will be introduced by a short description of the qualitative phenomenological method used in conducting our studies. We hope this will give the reader a sense of the options that can be used in various forms of theoretical and practical phenomenology and the rationale for our approach. Each chapter of Part II will also be accompanied by a philosophical commentary that is aimed at synthesizing and enhancing the understanding of the material.

Part I of the book is composed of six chapters. In fact, each main theme (e.g. reality, time and intimacy) will be analysed according to a *construens* and *destruens pars* that characterizes the qualitative and theoretical use of the phenomenological method. Drawing upon Husserl's phenomenology this method aims towards the reactivation of meanings using Husserl's static and genetic approach. The static focuses on the eidos of the lived experience and the genetic on its actual manifestations in life. A phenomenologist who decides to apply this method can do research by a radical act of questioning meanings of the given lived experience (*destruens pars*) and by the reactivation of the old sense in a new meaningful one (*construens pars*); on the one hand this approach unveils the presuppositionlessness of science by analysing theoretical data that have been separated from their meanings and on the other reactivates the interconnectedness of sense that belongs to the lived experience that is philosophically investigated.

In Chapter I.2, I will display the main characteristics of reality as it is interpreted through Husserl's ethics and his phenomenological psychology. The overall goal of this chapter is to discover how ethics and psychology can collaborate to unfold the layers of reality, in a way that is comprehensible for us and free from moral judgements or psychological categories. In the phenomenological method the use of epoché and reduction is essential to uncover the concreteness of reality in order to see its interwoven ethical, psychological and transcendental layers. From this perspective, understanding the structure of time, being and intentionality in which phenomenology (whose region of study is the transcendental layer), psychology (whose region of study is the psychic or biological layer) and ethics (whose region of study is the volitional body) locate themselves, is utterly important for any epistemological and moral judgement we can express towards one's lived experience and one's sense of reality.

As shown in this chapter, our lives are held within a mysterious and difficult balance between at least three different layers of reality, identity and time. The major part of our lives go by in the mode of egoless, receptive matter whose time is aimed at absorbing and storing information (natural psychological life); but we live also a life of acceptances granted by a just-awoken ego who lives in the here and now (practical and ethical life). Finally, we live a life from an absolute standpoint in which we do not even exist and we are aliens witnessing our whole life (philosophical and transcendental life). None of these lives could be illuminated and described without the other; even if the transcendental life is essentially constitutive of the practical and psychological life, it would never be grasped without the commitment of the psychological ego and the awakening of the practical one. The balance we find between these three layers of reality, time and identity is what shapes our sense of goodness, normal behaviour and knowledge. Using the theoretical tools of an ethics that is grounded upon this crossroads can enhance the complexity of our understanding of human lived experiences.

Chapter I.3 compares Husserl's and Nishida's notion of time and teleology. In this chapter I will analyse ethical experience and its relationship with reality through the lenses of time comparing Eastern and Western thought: namely that of Husserl and Nishida. The goal of this chapter is to use the scholarly authority of these two important philosophers with the aim of deciding whether the meanings, in this case Eastern and Western interpretations of the phenomenon, can be reused within our lifeworld (*Lebenswelt*). If we overcome the deception of time with which both authors argue, we can see how one's reality comes from an inner reconstruction of time that knits together the concreteness of being and time with our need to encase shapeless concreteness into recognizable values and intersubjective meanings. Unfortunately, as we will see from the next chapter, those whose lives happen to dwell more in eternal, motionless time have more difficulty in synthesizing Being in a way that can be intersubjectively accepted and understood.

In Chapter I.4, I show how the layered sense of time, ego and the world can affect our constitution of reality and identity. To this end I compared and contrasted the experience of reality from the point of view of mystics and schizophrenics; from this analysis we explore the idea that schizophrenics have more problems in floating from one to another layer of reality because they seem to be dwelling in the timeless and absolute layer of time. Assuming a stigmatizing attitude towards timeless time and denying its veracity would shrink the space of intimacy that schizophrenics already struggle to have with the concreteness of their real life; whereas using a spiritual and bodily eye, or assuming a static and genetic attitude with which we look at the real as subjects and at the same time as selfless and timeless presences, might improve the chances for schizophrenics to form an onlooker who can witness the events in the timeless world in order to enhance the synchronicity of these events with the lifeworld. To conclude, I believe that an approach to the experience of timelessness that keeps both eyes open, the spiritual and corporeal, the static and genetic, would allow professionals to help schizophrenics to create an inner witness of their reality similar to the self-witnessing of mystics so that constituting meaning activity is possible. Helping people to live with the genetic eye open and a static witness present to the ongoing becoming might improve the well-being of patients and might help us to gather a better understanding of ourselves and time.

In Chapter I.5, I discuss first the lower and higher layers of the spirit to explain how the volitional body – the moral organ of our actions – validates the feelings that lead us to intimate love. In the chapter we show how this body cannot be considered to belong exclusively to material or immaterial layers; accordingly every decision it makes includes lower and higher motives. It is through these lenses that the brutal force of love and the space of intimacy that it opens up was interpreted as a vertical feeling connecting lower and higher, material and immaterial layers of us; on a lower level love is a composite of drives, instincts and desires of which we cannot have a firm hold, because we do not own them, by definition. On this level, in fact the subject is not even an ego yet but is an ongoing chain of syntheses of the passive matter. On the higher level, love is a meaning- and value-giving activity; it interprets the passive matter that is provided to it through the awakening of the I and validates it according to specific meanings and values that shed light on the identity of the person herself. The light shed on these layers form a space of intimacy through which the person can come in contact with parts of herself that were unexplored or not yet revealed. The brutal bonding force of love represents a unique opportunity for us to become closer to our factual existence. This involves that, on the one hand, intimacy will disclose a dark place where the sensuous egoless generative web of syntheses builds a concreteness that might eventually take its own shape into meanings and values constitutive for the identity and sense of reality that a person feels to live in; on the other, intimacy represents a retrospective reconstruction of the layers of the known intimate life as it appears to the sedimented in the habitual layers of an I. The former kind of intimacy lays the foundation for a valid, but yet dark, space in which the I can come into existence, the latter recognizes the interconnection between the layers that belong to that validity as a founding core around which life, the habitual one, constitutes itself as a meaningful vital flow.

In Chapter I.6, I show how sexuality defines our existence when it involves an active choice. This choice, though, being involved in a recursive teleological structure, cannot always be conscious because our factual being is usually a mystery to us, a truth whose essence speaks to us from a transcendental space. Metaphorically speaking, I named this voice intimacy. From the depth of our passive life the meanings that define us and constitute the condition of possibility for our existence come from intimacy, whose structure can be broken down into two main layers – a spontaneous and transcendental one. In our lives we are constantly called upon to choose whether we want to pay attention to the constitution of meanings that are going to shape the social category through which we will be recognized. In particular, when we encounter cases of forced intimacy, this has a negative impact on our psychological balance. If this transcendental voice remains on the layer of passivity, it is likely that our sexual existence will be foreign and meaningless to us; if we manage to attend to this voice on an active and transcendental layer and participate in the constitution of meaning, our sexual identity will be an existential one: the fruit of a choice. Our sexual identity needs to be plastic in the sense that its telos cannot be placed in one category once and for all. To fit in an existential sexuality that is meaningful for us, we need to be free from moral and social constraints and be available to entertain an honest dialogue with our facticity.

Part II of the book is dedicated to the empirical study of time, intimacy, and reality analysed through the cases of the experience of an ethical dilemma arising from an unexpected leadership challenge, a dilemma in raising a child, and the beginning of an affair. As it was in Part I, the first chapter of Part II, that is, Chapter II.1 is dedicated to the description of the method used including a discussion of the relationship between theoretical and empirical phenomenological investigations. In particular, several of the key phenomenological methods are explored and contrasted in order to justify the selection of Giorgi's phenomenological research method for psychology for the subsequent empirical investigations. This chapter in particular discusses the step-by-step process that results in the three chapters that follow and provides an orientation to the reader about empirical methods relative to the initial discussion of theoretical phenomenological methods from the second chapter.

Chapter II.2 provides an example of an original empirical phenomenological research investigation of the unexpected experience of a leadership challenge using Giorgi's (2009) method. The findings of this study suggest that leadership dilemmas that are unexpected can cause the leader to consider the role and identity of a leader and its charge anew, through the understanding of its phenomenological concreteness which can be seen only through the epoché; in fact, many possible courses of action in response to the dilemma push leaders to confront the ethics of leadership in a more general transcendental fashion – shaping their understanding of themselves, their businesses and their impact on those they serve or employ. This chapter provides both an articulated essential structure of a layered way of viewing reality and a dialogue between the findings, organizational psychological studies and Husserl's ethics including aspects of identity, intimacy (broadly understood in this case in a humanistic manner) and time.

In Chapter II.3 the results of an original and empirical investigation of the experience of a parent's dilemma in raising a child are presented. In this case, in using Giorgi's (2009) method, the issue of time becomes more evident, because the ethical choice that the parents have to make oblige them to parenthesize the daily linear sense of time in order to make choices that have actual consequences in the experiences of timeless time lived by their children. Giorgi's phenomenological research method for psychology is used in this chapter to explore six descriptions of dilemmas in whatever way the participant understands a parenting dilemma. These descriptions include different types of dilemmas and, at the same time, all of the dilemmas share some constitutive structural elements. These include the following situations: The parent first lives parenting in an organic pre-reflective manner until confronted with unanticipated negative possible outcomes for the child in the future. This then gives rise to a consideration of the meaning of several possible courses of action for both the self and the child, who has less power in the dynamic. The ethical obligation the parent has to select a course of action or to delay action gives rise to a new more generalizable meaning of parenting through which all such dilemmas can be viewed. These findings are considered in dialogue with Husserl's Trinitarian notions of time and identity and in dialogue with the self psychology and intersubjective perspectives of Kohut and Stolorow among others. Further directions for additional consideration include investigations of narcissism and parenting or other relational or self-object disturbances that may prevent the participant from accessing all layers of time and identity towards an ethical and reciprocally-beneficial decision.

Finally, in Chapter II.4, an account of loss of intimacy is given through the case of the beginning of an affair. In this chapter, an original empirical investigation of six accounts of the beginning of an extramarital affair is explored using Giorgi's (2009) phenomenological research method for psychology. These accounts do not necessarily include any similarities in the acts that transpire; yet, through the analysis, evidence is found for a unique essential structure for the phenomenon. This structure includes the following self-reinforcing constituents: The marriage or monogamous relationship is experienced as hopeless and dissatisfying. The one who has the affair feels dissatisfaction with the shared experience of passion, novelty and sexual intimacy in particular. These aspects are viewed as irreparable because the persistent view is that the partner of the one who has the affair is unable or unwilling to participate in intimacy or novel sexually passionate experiences. The one who has the affair begins to feel that there is no reason to be curious about this fixed other or the relationship and further begins to feel entitled to sexual satisfaction and intimacy. He or she reasons that he or she is a good spouse having tried to fix things but also having an intact sexual, sensuous and creative sensibility. There is no real consideration of divorce, breaking up or opening up the relationship. This unsatisfying relationship then careens towards death and boredom. The one who has an affair eventually meets someone, in the course of everyday events, with whom there is mutual curiosity. This is only passively lived rather than named the beginning of an affair, even though the curiosity fuels mutual self-reinforcing acts and experiences lived through time that build the intimacy that is lacking in the primary relationship. The affair is recognized only when it is actively grasped after a clear sexual line is crossed that cannot be passively lived anymore. In this chapter the many pivotal moments and shifts in the perspective and perceptions of the identities of the self, other and spouse as well as experiences of the different layers of time are explored and linked to ethical decision-making.

Thereafter there is a short chapter that reflects on the connections between the two sections of the book and attempts to both integrate the ideas and also to extend them into their usefulness. We propose that developing people's abilities to consider several layers of time, and therefore perspectives, at once will facilitate the development of critical and flexible thinking, empathy and may open up ethical and intimate space between others and ourselves. It is our sincere hope that this text has helped to share our goals towards this end.

Conclusions

In this book the phenomenological method and my interpretation of Husserl's ethics is used in service of understanding reality and its layers. Through the philosophical investigation we discovered how our ethical way of interacting with the lived experience is made possible through intimacy and time (broadly understood), and we used the empirical analysis of specific lived experiences to see how a more aware understanding of these notions might help to improve our ethical choices and therefore our well-being.

Reference

Giorgi, A. *The Descriptive Phenomenological Method in Psychology: A Modified Husserlian Approach*, Pittsburg, PA: Duquesne University Press, 2009.

PART ONE

I.1

The phenomenological method, a theoretical 'application'*

What is phenomenology?

Phenomenology can be defined as a disciplinary field in philosophy or as a philosophical movement initiated by the philosopher and mathematician Edmund Husserl. Before him, the term was used in different ways. Coined by the physicist Johann Heinrich Lambert (1728–1777), phenomenology initially indicated the doctrine of appearance of living phenomena; then with Kant,[1] Hegel and Peirce[2] it took the shape of a philosophical method. It was in the early twentieth century, with Husserl, Heidegger, Sartre, Merleau-Ponty and others (Spiegelberg, 1960), that phenomenology became popular in philosophy. Typical phenomenological themes like intentionality, consciousness, qualia and first-person perspective influence different fields of research today such as neuroscience, philosophy of mind and cognitive science.

The study we will pursue in this book is based on Husserl's phenomenological theory and in particular his ethical theory as an approach to investigate the psychological contents of lived experiences.

---

*It is true that when one talks about application of theory, the discourse seems to slip immediately into the field of the empirical research and any reference to pure theory seems to be misplaced – as if theory cannot be applied without losing its observational quality. Yet, from Aristotle's notion of phronesis to Husserl's archontic thesis, philosophy discussed the possibility of a pure theory that can be applied in praxis without being reduced to empirical research. This is what I am going to propose in this chapter, a practical application of a theoretical method, a grey area that can be exploited for theoretical researches in psychology and philosophy.

How many phenomenological methods in psychology?

As we know from Spiegelberg (1960), Husserl's phenomenology inspired multiple psychological theories and schools.[3] Yet, as Cairns remarked, 'it is an historical fact that Husserl's investigations of subjectivity always had a philosophical goal. Their primary goal was never psychological. The results of his investigations can nevertheless be interpreted psychologically, as he himself indicated' (Cairns, 2010, 1–2). The union of Husserl's philosophy with psychology is a difficult one because, as Cairns remarks, 'a psychological interpretation of Husserl's results is a *simplification*. The most abstruse of his methodological theories, the theory of transcendental-phenomenological reduction, is disregarded when his results are interpreted psychologically' (Cairns, 2010, 2). Despite this, Cairns maintained, this should not stop 'the psychologist who wants to discover in Husserl's writings whatever is relevant to psychology as a natural science' (Cairns, 2010, 2).

For this reason, several methods in psychology drew upon the tools offered by Husserl's phenomenological epistemology. Generally, textbooks (i.e. Creswell, 2007) mention the methods of Giorgi,[4] Moustakas, Van Manen, Smith and Colaizzi[5] as the most popular ones; the common denominator of these being the use of Husserl's phenomenology as a guidance to read psychological data regarding a collective number of people. The goal is to grasp the essence of living phenomena as they are experienced by different participants (e.g. resilience as it is universally experienced) As van Manen wrote, the goal is to 'grasp the very nature of the thing' (van Manen, 1990, 177). According to Moustakas a phenomenological investigation describes how participants lived different experiences in relation to the same phenomenon (1994). The inquirer is in fact to collect data from participants that can relate to that phenomenon and unfold the description of what makes that experience as such for all of them. The actual description consists of 'what' they experienced and 'how' they experienced it (Moustakas, 1994). The same goal prevails in Giorgi's and Colaizzi's methods; what counts in the application of the phenomenological method is the description of the meaningful essence that qualifies the phenomenon chosen as the object of the inquirer's study.

Giorgi's descriptive phenomenological method (1970, 2009), whose school is represented today by Churchill (2001), Wertz (2011), Englander (2012), Applebaum (2011) and others, articulates a method that is named 'descriptive', because it aims at a description of the phenomenon which is as free as possible from interpretation. Giorgi's method relies on the idea that *description as such is possible* and he (Giorgi, 1992) argues that interpretation, defined as the 'clarification of the meaning of experienced objects in terms of a plausible but contingently adopted theoretical perspective, assumption, hypothesis, and so on', ought not to be viewed as the exclusive possibility for qualitative research (1992, 122). According to Giorgi, ' "Objective" methods do not remove the presence of the researcher, they simply make him present in another way' (p. 166); in fact 'If the biases cannot be eliminated, they should be included' (p. 169). His method, analogous to van Manen's and Moustakas's, aims at understanding the essence[6] of the phenomenon and commits to reach this goal through the following steps: first, the inquirer gathers data through interviews; these data are divided into units of meanings; then, it is after an ongoing act of epoche that the inquirer analyses these data applying what Husserl called imaginative variation.[7] Each datum is transformed into its most essential unit. When it is not possible to proceed any further with the transformations, the inquirer makes himself available to the arising of the eidetic seeing, which normally would lead her to see the common essence among the data belonging to that phenomenon.

As Stewart and Mickunas (1990) emphasized there are four main philosophical tools in common between these different phenomenological methods.

- A reaction to scientism perceived as a limit of the empirical method and the consequent need to return to the wisdom of traditional philosophy before it became enamoured with empirical science.
- The need for a presuppositionless science that is capable of suspending all judgements about what is real – the 'natural attitude' – until they are founded on a more certain basis. This can be achieved through what Husserl called 'epoche'.
- The analysis of intentionality of consciousness. This is the point on which the theoretical method I am going to use will be mostly focused. Husserl's *Logical Investigations* (2001) described consciousness – which should not be meant as one's individual consciousness – as always directed towards an object. From this point of view the reality of an object is inextricably related to the matter of the intentionality of consciousness. Any psychological analysis should take as a starting point the lived experience.
- Consistent with the point above is 'the refusal of the subject-object dichotomy. This theme flows naturally from the intentionality of consciousness. The reality of an object is only perceived within the meaning of the experience of an individual'.

Besides the commonalities, the above-mentioned methods emphasize a specific aspect of Husserl's phenomenology; while Moustakas's phenomenological method is described as a psychological approach, van Manen's phenomenology is defined as hermeneutic, Smith's as interpretative and Giorgi's and Colaizzi's as descriptive.

Moustakas considers his phenomenology psychological because he focuses less on the interpretations of the researcher and more on a description of the experiences of participants. In addition, Moustakas's transcendental goal is to use epoche (or bracketing) in order to set aside investigators' experiences as much as possible and to achieve a wider perspective of what the phenomenon is, such that this perspective transcends the limits of the observer. Hence, for Moustakas "transcendental' means 'what is perceived freshly, as if for the first time'[8] (Moustakas, 1994, 34). Methodologically speaking, the procedures of his work can be laid out in the following steps:

1. Bracketing out one's experiences, and collecting data from several persons who have experienced the phenomenon.[9]

2. The researcher analyses the data by breaking down the information into significant statements or quotes and combining the statements into themes.

3. Finally, the researcher unfolds participants' description following what Moustakas calls a textural and structural order. First, he gives an account of what participants experienced; second, he explains how they experienced it in terms of the conditions, situations or context; third, he combines these two perspectives together with the goal to convey an overall essence of the experience.[10]

On the other hand, van Manen's phenomenology is considered hermeneutic because, according to his point of view, there is no strict distinction between facts and meanings; facts are explained to us through a narrative that continuously explicates itself before us. In his work on hermeneutical phenomenology, van Manen describes the phenomenological research as oriented towards lived experience; in this sense it is phenomenological, but with an interpretative goal whose scope is for the inquirer to read the 'texts' of life (van Manen, 1990, 4). He engages in a self-consciously interpretative discussion with the participants – there is no idea of gathering natural-attitude descriptions, everything must be self-consciously interpreted by the participants in concert with the researcher. In contrast to Moustakas and Giorgi, van Manen does not approach phenomenology with a set of rules or methods, but he discusses phenomenological research as a dynamic interplay among different research activities. Smith's[11] interpretative phenomenological analysis (IPA) aims at exploring how participants makes sense of their lived experiences and for this reason it involves a detailed investigation of the lifeworld of the participant. IPA combines an empathic hermeneutics with a questioning hermeneutics which means that the critical questions that will be addressed to the participants will be the following: What is the person trying to achieve here? Is something leaking out here that wasn't intended? Do I have a sense of something going on here that maybe the participants themselves are less aware of?

Finally, Colaizzi's method[12] begins with an examination of *approach*. The end goals and the final aims of a research project colour the undertaking from the beginning and because of this it is necessary to clarify those objectives as a first preliminary step. This clarification centres on (a) which phenomenon will be studied and why and (b) what method will be used. Colaizzi's (1978) procedural steps for phenomenological analysis involve, similar to Giorgi's method, reduction in order to bracket popular theories, scientific hypotheses and other external explanations of the data. In addition to the setting aside of preconceived ideas, the researcher must also set aside their own limited perspective to some degree. Our own position of looking, that of the researcher, is best accounted for through an explicit ownership of one's own perspective. Then, the researcher stays with the data and does not move from it with the exception of adopting a broadly psychological lens that focuses on the worldly experience of a single person. In this step, through the comparison between the knowledge withheld before the bracketing and what emerged after it, the research describes what is fully present to the participants' description.

Science and reactivation of meanings in Husserl

For the purpose of this study I will emphasize two main characteristics of the meaning of science in phenomenology: presuppositionlessness and interconnectedness. I will start with the latter – Husserl's holistic conception of science:

> The essence of science […] involves unity of foundational connections: not only isolated pieces of knowledge, but their grounded validation themselves […] and together with these, the higher interweaving of such validations that we call theories, must achieve systematic unity. (Hua XVIII, 15; Eng. trans. 18)

The essence of any science consists in a theoretical interconnection of 'pieces of knowledge', because the *quaestio juris* of scientific analysis is the reflective attitude with which the scientist assembles data in a coherent system. Science as such entails systematic, coherent understanding that grounds the scientific community's knowing. Accordingly, a theoretical investigation can be considered scientific whenever a researcher constitutes a systematic coherence around an essential core.

For Husserl this coherence lies upon the intrinsic interconnectedness of being, and it exists independently of our capacity to observe it rather than depending upon our subjective theoretical understanding of it. If the coherence depended on our capacity to observe it, we would fall into a form of psychologism for which knowledge is what the individual perceives as such. Husserl's use of Frege's famous example concerning the morning star makes the point. The fact that one understands or not that the morning star is the same as the evening star does not change anything of the nature of the star. Thinking that our psychological grasp of reality would change the structure of reality itself would impoverish the coherence of things themselves. Theoretical observation and normative definition have the task of *discovering* the (lawful) interconnection pre-existing between the parts and the whole and preserving the validity of the system through fixed norms. Therefore the goal of a theoretical analysis resides exactly in discovering this interconnectedness. That 2+2 equals 4 is a normative transliteration of my observing the recurring law of summing 2 pairs together in a 4-unit whole.

That is why 'theoretical disciplines', that is, those disciplines that, from the Greek 'theorousi', 'observe' phenomena, are in Husserl's words 'the foundation of normative disciplines' (Hua XVIII, 30; Eng. trans. 28). They found normative and interconnected disciplines because they provide a 'systematic coherence in the *theoretical sense*, which means a common ground for one's knowing, and a suitable combination of the sequence of such grounding' (Hua XVIII,15; Eng. trans. 18).

Yet, the theoretical and normative layers of a given science do not satisfy the entire structure of that science. Science – as Husserl writes – aims at the knowledge that can approximate, as much as possible, the form of the truth (Hua XVIII, 15; Eng. trans. 18). This leads to the second characteristic of science in Husserl's view: its presuppositionlessness. 'Science is not our invention' (Hua XVIII, 15; Eng. trans. 18); rather, it 'is dominated and unified by law' (Hua XVIII, 15; Eng. trans. 18). Therefore, reaching towards the greater completeness of science means approximating as much as possible this highest truth as the aim of our practical acts, as researchers.

Technology, which, differently from theory, represents the applicative side of science, arises from a teleological desire of the individual scientist to fulfil a goal; practical investigations stem exactly from this need to prove the theoretical finding right and applicable. Hence, Husserl writes, 'Where the basic norm is an end or can become an end, the normative discipline by a ready extension of its task gives rise to a technology' (Hua XVIII, 26–27; Eng. trans. 25–26). Technological or empirical approaches, differently from theoretical and normative ones, are more connected to an egoic[13] form of interest that gives directedness to our acts, whereas theoretical and normative science represent an egoless and impersonal attempt to decipher the language of nature without reference to a specific end and try to get closer to it every time.

Science is not just *art de* (*penser* in the case of logic, *agir* in the case of ethics); rather, it is a systematic unit of interconnected validations or foundational connections that approximate the essence of nature as it is given to us.[14] Phenomenological science lets things speak through their own voice in order to show their system of interconnection. In that sense pure phenomenology makes no empirical assertions, propounds no judgements that relate to objects transcending consciousness: it establishes no truths concerning natural realities (Hua XIX, 765, 862). For this reason phenomenology has to be presuppositionless because the coordination between the theoretical, normative and technological side of science is always looking for a new balance because of the difficulty in deciphering the language of nature.

As a presuppositionlessness science, phenomenology accepts that science is in an ongoing crisis (Hua VI, first part) in the sense that it is incapable of arriving at a final word around the description of the essence of a given phenomenon. Rather than viewing this lack of absolute closure as indicating a deficiency in its approach, phenomenology takes this crisis as a method of foundation, a fundamental openness. The riddle of reality is taken by the phenomenological science as a foundational call for an ongoing renewal of meaning (Hua XXVII, 3–13, 43–57). Therefore, in the phenomenological investigation one assumes that it will never be possible for a researcher to have the final word on the description of the essential core of a given phenomenon; accordingly, any research will always start from the inhibition of any previous assumptions in order to describe the phenomenon more precisely. As Husserl affirms in *Logical Investigations I*, 'the content represents what does not lie within it itself' (Hua XIX, 770; Eng. trans. 866), the scientific investigation aims at unveiling what is not given in itself yet.

In this way, each phenomenological scientific investigation unveils a layer of the essence that had not been seen yet and activates its deepest sense or functioning (*Leistung*). The scientific project of phenomenology consists of an ongoing effort of de-sedimentation and de-habituation (Hua VI, 72); it is an infinite task that Husserl locates, for example, in the re-establishment (*Nachstiftung*) of the values of classical Greek culture which he aims to revive. He writes that 'History as the vital movement of the coexistence and interweaving of construction of sense (*Sinnbildung*) and sedimentations of meanings (*Sinnsediementierung*)' (Husserl, 1970, 371) needs to be reactivated (Hua VI, 77). Scientific inquiry by means of rigorous explication (*Verdeutlichung*) enables an original Sinnbildung (construction of sense) that leads the inquirer from a condition of doxa or pre-scientific flux to episteme or determinate knowledge. This flowing constitution of meaning is possible when the researcher has adequately freed the flow of associative constructions from her habits, and is thus able to constitute new meanings and inform old meaning with new sense (Hua VI, 82, 362).

For Husserl, this scientific inquiry is to be accomplished through illuminating the meaningfulness of words, when they are authentically expressive; words belong to meanings, which necessitate repeatedly overcoming the seduction of language (Hua VI, 80, 362). Language can easily become empty and meaningless, but seductive at the same time because it gives the certainty of the direction to follow. It is a symbolic tool to indicate meanings, but in Husserl's view, language can come unmoored from meanings (Hua XIX, LI I). Language, understood as *Sprachleib* – the incarnation of meaning, should be what animates speech (Hua VI, 83) and not what closes the search for meaning with the illusion to have conquered the ultimate meaning of the essential truth. For Husserl, speech functions as the grammatical 'clothing' (Hua XIX) of fluctuating meanings.

Hence science holds always an ethical core, as Husserl writes in a letter to Metzger (Hart, 1993, 17). 'Coming back to the things themselves' with a non-naive practical and theoretical attitude is not only an epistemological goal but an ethical one as well. Only in this way can we be truly responsible for what we carry in the inevitable interconnection of our lives and for the *teloi* (goals) we unfold in our acts. As a human community we can tend infinitely towards rationality only if we take our absolute 'ought' seriously – as seriously as we take epistemological truths. In fact, absolute ought and scientific truth are two names for the same object, that is, primordial evidence. Ethics is the discipline that enables us to counteract the crystallization of meanings in meaningless words. Ethics is the science that clarifies one's daily choice to engage meaningfully in intersubjective dialogue. This dialogue relies upon the ongoing choice to renew the sense of what we are living by determining what we are passively living. Ethical clarification enables us to live this renewal through which our social and individual lives become meaningful. Renewal requires an ongoing ethical choice, consequently a volitional intention to be meaningful.

Any research in the field of humanities is strictly interwoven with an ethical goal, which explains the title of the present research: the study of any experience interlaces with an ethical goal, which consists of reactivating the passive layers of that lived experience.[15]

The phenomenological method: A theoretical approach

As stated before, the word method indicates the way (*odos*) through which (*meta*) the inquirer desires to pursue her quest. Hence, any investigation uses a method because the inquirer will always have to choose what road to take in order to achieve her goal. From a phenomenological point of view, since science is a presuppositionless and interconnected system, the inquirer has to be open to question her own steps at any moment and walk backwards, so to speak, always checking if the previous step was a meaningful one and if its sense can be linked to the other bits of sense already discovered.

Husserl's investigations used two primary methods: a static and a genetic one. Genetic analysis is a method that privileges observation from the point of view of continuous becoming, while the static one observes reality as it is given to the observer in a specific moment (Drummond, 2008).[16] While the genetic analysis digs into the facticity and the passive layers of the experience as they are in the process of continuous becoming, the static method focuses on the essential features of the given phenomenon. Yet as Biceaga (2010) and Bernet (1994) remark, genetic and static methods cannot be conceived as separate from each other, but 'as a dynamic duo'. Figuratively speaking, if we looked at an object with only one eye – the static eye, for instance – we would receive a deceiving and partial image of a stable object that stands out from its background.[17] On the other hand, if we closed the static eye and looked at things only with the genetic eye, we would have a blurred picture of what reality is, to the point that the boundary between the observing subject and its object would get lost. The static approach helps the inquirer to observe the interconnection of the pieces that make that phenomenon what it is, while the genetic approach makes the inquirer one with the flow of data that manifest themselves in the shape of the given phenomenon. In the phenomenological method both eyes, static and genetic, are to be kept open to avoid any deception. The subject and its world might seem to be given as a fixed picture, but this would be mistaken, for we know for a fact that this picture undergoes ceaseless change.[18] Being able to describe this living system is the phenomenological challenge.

For these reasons, in my theoretical research I combine both methods in a *destruens* and *construens* part. The *destruens* part, the static one, is the one in which the investigator questions the ground of her path and pledges to perform a backward investigation that is as presuppositionless and unbiased as possible. In this part of the method the inquirer challenges any previous authority and those meanings that have been accepted in previous investigations. At this level the investigator tries to parenthesize as much as possible of her theoretical assumptions and keep a committed questioning attitude. The construens part is the one in which the inquirer participates in the flow of the observation and through her own intuition[19] combines together the pieces of the analysis. Since the meaning of time changes from the static to the genetic approach (from a linear to an absolute one), and since our sense of time is linear, we would need to make an effort to keep in mind the simultaneity of both approaches and their interconnection (more on time in chapters 4 and 5).

Therefore, from a theoretical point of view the goal of the *destruens* part will consist in targeting the eidos of the phenomenon we want to question and the layers of meaning we are interested in reactivating. Once this phenomenon is delimited in a clear thesis, then it must be deconstructed into its parts in such a way that the simplest ones precede the most complex ones. Thus, the inquirer will choose the main components of the phenomenon and compare these meanings with those that have been accepted and validated by the intersubjective scholarly community. As a matter of fact this step will consist of a review of primary and secondary literature and of a description of any accepted definition of that given phenomenon within the clinical, historical, legal, political (etc.) context.

The twofold goal of the *destruens* part is to analyse the phenomenon without losing contact with the interconnected system (lifeworld-*Lebenswelt*) in which the phenomenon is located. While the inquirer is deconstructing and questioning the intersubjective network of validations, her experience is not forgotten, but is parenthesized. The overall goal is to recover the full sense of the essence of that phenomenon looking at its sedimentations from a personal (formulation of the thesis) and interpersonal (questioning review) point of view.

At both levels of investigation we need to make an ethical avowal that consists in setting aside as much as possible on our personal point of view in order to adopt a sub specie aeternitatis stance. We need to apply the epoche; that is, we need to parenthesize all the findings we gathered and the personal assumptions we might hold about the findings in order to annihilate our ego and allow it to be part of the hyletic flow with which the data present themselves. As Moran (2000) and Crowell (2013) note, the epoche is an ethical and epistemological move; one that, I would add, gives the epistemological investigation its ethical quality. If the inquirer does not commit herself to be part of an investigation in which her own beliefs and findings must be questioned, then the investigation would never be fully acceptable; the power of a free inquiry would be subverted by the researcher's narrowly personal goals and prejudices.

The authority questioned in the *destruens* part might be right and the layers of the meanings used to describe that given phenomenon might be accepted later on, but at the *destruens* stage I want to suspend my judgement and dedicate myself to a full theoretical activity. As *theorein* means 'observing', at this stage the inquirer wants to observe the data from no point of view, as if 'I' were the data and as if my 'I' would fully dissolve in them (more on this point in the next chapter). This attitude would hopefully create space for the voice of intuition to emerge louder. After the epoche the investigator can come back to that phenomenon and decide whether to integrate her previous assumptions or let them go; I can decide whether I want to reactivate meanings through what I have newly discovered, or if the layered sense of that phenomenon is still valid.

These decisions are made in the second part of the method, the *construens pars*; this consists of a number of ethical and epistemological questions and choices that the inquirer has to make in relation to the phenomenon of the analysis. The goal of the *pars construens* is to let the awakening of meaning speak through the analysis of the intentional act (more on this in the next chapter). While the *destruens* part exploits static phenomenology in such a way that it disassembles the layers of the phenomenon in their essential parts without losing their normative and axiological quality (the normative expression of the lawful interconnection mentioned above), the *construens* part collects together the pieces of the analysis using the awakening of sense that the deconstruction elicited. In the *construens* part the inquirer take a transcendental and theoretical standpoint (I will explain what that means in the next chapter) to ponder how the active meaning of the phenomenon – which flows from the previous deconstructing activity – interacts with the passive sedimented layers of sense. The inquirer will compare the just-awakened meaning with the given layers in order to decide whether it is proper to introduce a change in the way in which she understands the meaning of the eidos of that phenomenon. As I will show in the next chapter, this second methodological step is highly interwoven with ethics, since it requires an ethical decision from the inquirer, as I have addressed in my previous work (2015).

Qualitative research: Empirical and theoretical approach[20]

Research methods in psychology can be broken down into two main groups: those characterized by a quantitative approach and those by a qualitative one.[21] While quantitative approaches are concerned with quantifying (measuring and counting) data, qualitative approaches are concerned with the quality or qualities of an experience or phenomenon. Both approaches aim at gathering scientific findings, meaning results that can be generally validated.

The phenomenological methods mentioned above belong to a qualitative approach whose main features, differently from quantitative methods, consist in the opposition to scientism and objectivism. Phenomenological research does not ground meaning in measurement, instead it seeks to rigorously understand qualia and reactivate meanings. As Gadamer (1985, 239–240) remarks, the reaction against scientism carried out by qualitative approaches consists of refusing what 'the ideals of truth and liberation demand' and 'a bringing-to-light and a sloughing-off of all one's unexamined assumptions and traditional beliefs'. As Bernstein wrote, qualitative research develops a systematic and constructive philosophy that tries to redefine science as an alternative to scientism; hence any claim of validity will have to be open to cross-cultural dialogue about its claims and search not only for what is meaningful and valid but also for what is fundamental to our own culture in contrast to others. As Creswell writes: 'The procedures of qualitative research, or its methodology, are characterized as inductive, emerging, and shaped by the researcher's experience in collecting and analyzing the data. The logic that the qualitative researcher follows is inductive, from the ground up, rather than handed down entirely from a theory or from the perspectives of the inquirer. Sometimes the research questions change in the middle of the study to reflect better the types of questions needed to understand the research problem. In response, the data collection strategy, planned before the study, needs to be modified to accompany the new questions' (Creswell, 2007).

Theoretical and empirical approach in qualitative research

Any distinction between quantitative and qualitative approach does not imply that the quantitative approach only uses empirical data. As Kant taught us, a research project without experience would be as empty as its analytic a priori judgements, a research without a theoretical structure would be as blind as its synthetic a posteriori judgements. This entails that any investigation involves a theoretical and empirical effort; in fact, intuition provides the theoretical evidence around which an idea is developed[22] and perception gathers together the data that serve to make the theory come to life. Both qualitative and quantitative methods use theoretical as much as empirical information to unfold the scientific goal that is at the basis of the analysis.

In particular, the theoretical contribution to quantitative and qualitative methods is represented by the research purpose stemming from the intuition that motivates that specific direction of research and the methodological structure that is chosen in order to collect, analyse and investigate data; on the other hand the empirical contribution is represented by the actual data that are collected in the analysis. With the phenomenological method we mention the teleological interest to reactivate meanings within the framework of a presuppositionless and infinitely self-renewing science.

There is a wide number of qualitative approaches, such as narrative research, case study theory, ethnography, grounded theory, phenomenological research and so forth that balance the empirical and theoretical components of the research in different ways, emphasizing both the theoretical and hermeneutic intuition that lies at the basis of the study (narrative research), the voice of the empirical data as they present themselves within a specific context (ethnography), and the meanings emerging from the analysis of a given phenomenon (phenomenology).

This close combination of theoretical and empirical contributions in the research could hopefully involve a tight collaboration of philosophical and psychological expertise; while philosophy offers the inquirer a wide range of theoretical concepts useful for the analysis, psychology provides the investigation with a number of data that pinpoint the investigation in real life. On the one hand, philosophical papers[23] are often fruitful investigations that in different measures challenge the authority of a specific theoretical approach; but their disadvantage is the lack of a clear methodology, precisely because often they are challenging it and at the same time therefore not following it. On the other hand, psychological papers are expected to use a clear methodology, but they might not dig sufficiently into the theoretical change and reactivation of meaning that the research purports because they are accepting the authority of the method they use in order to conduct the analysis. In the worst-case scenario, philosophical papers appear as a form of arbitrary and fascinating stroll into the land of abstract ideas, while psychological papers might leave the reader with a sense of duplication of reality, in the sense that the theory is taken for granted so it is as if the researcher is just describing the 'real world' using a naïve attitude.

Hence, what I think is needed in the investigations concerning human studies is to become aware of the theoretical and empirical layers involved in the study and exploit their functioning at best so that the infamous gap between philosophical and psychological, theoretical and empirical analysis can be filled.

A theoretical standpoint according to Husserl's phenomenology

What do we mean by theoretical[24] investigation? This section will discuss the idea according to which the main goal of theoretical research is to reactivate meanings whose actual essence became increasingly overshadowed by an empty authority. In fact, theoretical research often investigates and challenges authoritative data with the aim of bringing forth a meaningful change within the structure-system in which the investigation took place.[25]

Some scholars[26] have suggested that building theory involves showing 'how the variables are connected, how they influence each other (. . .)' in a sort of 'ladder of abstraction' (Carney, 1990). Theoretical observation has the aim of delineating the 'deep structure' of a phenomenon and then integrating its data into an explanatory framework that produces 'data transformation' (Gherardi & Turner, 1999). In that sense, Rein and Schon (1977) view theory as a map that generalizes an explanatory story (p. 91).

This procedure cannot be confused with a paradigm shift, literature review (Wilber, 1998, 27), or the method used for the research. If one confuses theory with any of these terms (i.e. method, paradigm, description of literary review), she might miss the actual reactivation of meaning that that research endeavour is designed to accomplish. In fact, a theory differs from paradigms, as Kuhn (1962) wrote, because a paradigm is used to denote 'both the established and admired solutions that serve as models of how to practice the science, and also for the social structure that keeps those standards in place by teaching, rewards, and the like' (p. 23). Accordingly, a paradigm is 'the practical component, a set of exemplars or experiments or injunctions' (Wilber, 1998, 30) or social practices implied by a discipline.[27] In that sense it might happen that a theoretical research uses a paradigm, without addressing it explicitly; In other words, a paradigm is 'a technique taken as an exemplar for generating data' (Wilber, 1998, 158), not a theory.[28] A method, instead, from the Greek *meta* (through) and *odos* (road), indicates the route one decides to take in order to arrive at its goal and the literary review represents the information we decided to gather in order to get ready for the journey.

As Husserl proved in the *Prolegomena*, theories precede paradigms and precede science (I will focus on this last point in Part II). While a normative system states what is necessary (Hua XVIII, 42; Eng. trans. 36) – that is, the ought (*Sollen*) contemplated by the theory into another form of necessity, a must (*Müssen*). 'It tells us on what basic standard or basic value all normativization must be conducted' (Hua XVIII, 42; Eng. trans. 36). Every norm is grounded in a theoretical core, a *Sollen* whose necessity is translated in a paradigmatic system, a *Müssen* (Hua XVIII, § 16).

The most relevant goal of a theoretical investigation is to clarify that theoretical core – the ought of the analysis (e.g. a clinical definition of depression) – through critical analysis and clarification of the logical implications, assumptions, inconsistencies involved by that core. According to Greening (1984) and Pilisuk (2008), good theoretical research 'explains how this theory is better, different from, and/or more useful than other theories in explaining data, in predicting events, in integrating other theories', or in 'facilitating effective action' (Collen). The object targeted by theoretical research are the concepts, meanings, ideas that have been accepted by the authority and yet need to be restored, reactivated, or simply changed meaningfully.

The goal of a piece of theoretical research is 'description and critique of theory that accounts for the subject domain studied, *theoretical* analysis, synthesis, explication, interpretation, and exegesis of constructs, their meaning, and [their] relevance to advancing theory' (Collen, 2010, para. 5).

Differently from empirical qualitative research, the theoretical component of theoretical research is wider and works with textual data coming from, as Clingan noticed (2008), textual authorities. According to Clingan (2008), when a theoretical research is conducted theoretical, philosophical, historical, and/or literary textual information (primary and secondary literature), rather than primary empirical ones are employed. Thus, they use a review of the literature and the intellectual skills – that are required to gather textual data, analyse it, hypothesize critically and apply the theory in a manner appropriate in the scholar's field.

As Higgins (2009) remarked, differently from literary review, theoretical research goes through the existing literature(s) in a subject area(s), but with the goal to add something new to that literature; from my point of view the newness is represented by the individuation of a meaning that is more loyal to the essence of that phenomenon than others. The overall aim is to look for gaps, weaknesses, problems or biases in the existing literature that hide the essential components in order to lay the ground for future research (para. 4, 6). In that sense, as Higgins (2009), 76, 78) have stressed, the crucial function of critical analysis is of documentary analysis. 'The process of generating findings from the detailed examination of printed materials [secondary data sources] … [is] documentary analysis … .The qualitative interpretation of secondary sources [is] one of your main methods of both developing an advanced understanding of theoretical concerns and of introducing an empirical component' (Higgins, 2009, pp. 118, 157–158). In theoretical research the argumentative purpose that guides the quest is oriented to achieve findings whose status is as scientific as the results achieved by more heavily empiric studies.[29]

Summary

This chapter gives an overview of the qualitative methods that are currently used in phenomenology. While these qualitative methods are used to conduct empirical research, discussed more deeply in Part II, this chapter proposes a method to a theoretical application of the phenomenological research that, drawing upon Husserl's phenomenology, aims at the reactivation of meanings. Using Husserl's static and genetic method, the phenomenologist can do research using a *destruens* and *construens pars* that on one hand unveils the presuppositionlessness of science by analysing theoretical data that lost their meanings and on the other reactivates the interconnectedness of sense that belongs to the lived experience that is philosophically investigated.

I.2

Husserl's ethics and psychology

Introduction

In this chapter, I will expand on the key concepts mentioned in the previous chapter, such as transcendental intentionality and the static versus genetic method, in order to understand how a phenomenological approach operates and provides the researcher with theoretical tools for the analysis of the layers of reality. The goal of this approach is to avoid a polarizing description of reality that too neatly distinguishes the real from the unreal, and instead offer a description of the multiple layers of the real that is faithful to the complex, even contradictory, facets of psychological experience.

Often psychological, social, political or moral conflicts flow into concrete, brutal struggles about what view of reality dominates: In other words, who has the power to dictate what reality is? Who decides the reality principle around which my experience should revolve? Who is going to narrate reality? And, what space is left to those left out of that narration of reality? In our practical life we may avoid or resolve these conflicts through empathy, which helps us to see life through the eyes of the Other. However the academic style of writing and research can neglect to exercise empathy in the observation and description of reality[1] – resulting in an emotionally colourless facsimile of reality that does not register with us as real, because we see reality through the colours of our emotions.

Whether we want it or not, on any level our life can be afflicted by a psychological, moral and political struggle for reality: we might happen to be children of unbalanced parents, we might be students of unusually sadistic teachers, we might be working for a very moody boss, we might be collaborating with borderline colleagues, we might fall in love with a narcissist, we might be citizens governed by sociopaths and we might be parents of depressed children. The description of reality will be very different according to each of these points of view. What can we do? How do we prevent ourselves from being abused by a sadistic teacher or live in the distorted reality of unbalanced parents without either losing or imposing *our sense of reality*? Or as scholars, how can we build a constructive theoretical debate around reality that is capable of defending our integrity and our right to be, even if that does not match the system of interpretations in which one should fit? How can we defend all the layers of reality?

I think that Husserl's ethics and in particular the concepts we are going to examine here can address these problems. In fact, since the phenomenological method as a descriptive approach to lived experience offers a way to describe reality as *real* (intentional content) and *reel* (immanent reality),[2] this approach can help to overcome the human natural temptation to polarize reality in the face of conflict.

Epoché, reduction, real and reel

In this section I will explore the meanings of epoché and reduction in phenomenology, psychology and ethics as a means of penetrating the reality of the world we live in, in order to describe its multiple layers. To remind the reader, epoché and reduction are two phenomenological devices introduced by Husserl in order to suspend the natural way in which we look at reality. While the epoché entails that we suspend the attitude through which we take reality for granted as a network of meanings that stand there for us, the reduction leads the phenomenological actor to assume a questioning attitude towards the suspended reality, and it is thanks to this attitude that one has the chance to grasp the essential, unshakable truth of what is experienced.

In a beautiful article written in defence of Husserl's phenomenology, Fink addresses these and other relevant issues. Fink was Husserl's last assistant before the outbreak of the Second World War when as a 'non-Aryan' Husserl was forced into early retirement due to Nazi-promulgated laws. During the years the two became very close to each other and gradually, Husserl recognized his assistant as his academic voice[3] (1970, 75). Hence, here I will use Fink's voice to discuss some of the key points of Husserl's phenomenology throughout its development.[4]

In the article Fink presents phenomenology as 'a revolution of thought' that has for the most part been misunderstood (1970, 74). While Husserl's detractors read *Ideas* (Hua III, 1913) as a sign of betrayal of the foundations laid out in *Logical Investigations* (Hua XIX, 1900), Fink reads Husserl's work as a continuum. He considers the phenomenological motto – 'back to the things themselves' – as an exhortation to penetrate the concreteness of things and unfold their meanings – by concreteness here he means the portion of reality that is not formalized yet in any words or logical meanings.[5] Both in *Ideas* and

Logical Investigations, phenomenology's goal is to clarify 'everything which can be brought to the point of manifesting itself as it is, be it real or ideal' (1970, 85).

The way in which phenomenology cracks through matter's concreteness is by means of the reduction and epoché. These two phenomenological devices give us access to a double reality: the intentional reality (real) of what is believed as true by the experiencing subject, and the immanent reality (reel) which is conceived of as existing independently of our experiencing of it. On the one hand we have the real world as it is per se and on the other we have the world as it is experienced by us – these two forms of reality are of course very different from each other. Genuine phenomenological inquiry begins with 'the awakening of an immeasurable wonder over the mysteriousness of the state of affairs [*Sachlage*] confronting philosophy at its beginning [*das Erwachen einer maßlosen Verwunderung über die Rätselhaftigkeit dieser Sachlage*]' (Fink 1970, KS 115f/109).

What occurs in the awakening invited by the reduction and epoché? In its everyday, 'natural attitude', the ego that lives a daily normal life awakens from the state of certainty and full acceptance in which it was previously merged, and wonders about its own being and all the beings around it.

The awakening which the phenomenological inquiry initiates is made possible thanks to the actual existence of what Husserl terms the 'psychological ego'. The psychological ego, as Fink remarks, points to 'the human being who is preoccupied with the world' (p. 115). Through its awakening, in fact, it changes its natural attitude – in which it accepts life unquestioningly – into an attitude in which its actions and their contents are subject to ongoing questioning in the light of reflective reasoning. The psychological ego lives a natural life in which a reflecting and questioning transcendental ego stands out and takes a reflecting position that clarifies the concreteness of what is being lived by means of its own being (1970, 93). The transcendental ego, meaning the layer of the ego which reflects on the conditions of possibility of its own being, tries to grasp the meaning of its own concreteness through the epoché and reduction, which themselves are set in motion by the psychological ego. In that sense Fink writes that while the epoché and reduction are triggered due to transcendental motives and by ego's wakefulness, they originate in a psychological act (1970, 111). Through the reduction 'consciousness as continuing life of activity' awakens from its 'concrete life' and disconnects itself from the real (intentionally meant) in order to investigate the reel and the real at the same time: 'To perform the phenomenological reduction is to disconnect the belief in the world of the depths of its transcendental primordiality' (1970, 110).

The motivation for epoché and reduction is transcendental in the sense that it is guided by the necessity of reflecting on the conditions of possibility of its own being, but the departure point is psychological[6] because the epoché and then the reduction are performed from a natural attitude. Reflecting on one's own transcendental being presents itself to us as a vocational call that we can hardly escape and generally we explicate through the various activities and occupations we choose to do in life in order to fulfil ourselves: 'His initial point of departure is psychological. The world which we know and within which we know ourselves is given as a universe of acceptances' (1970, 107). The human being in its natural life puts in epoché (in brackets) the natural flowing of the concrete life and discovers the world as a unity of beliefs that have been thus far accepted as fully valid – what we call the real life (real). The phenomenological epoché has as its goal disconnecting the real from what is believed as real in order to seek the concreteness that presupposes it (reel). Hence, it is through the epoché that what we took for granted in our normal life is willingly detached from what is actually supposed to be our life; the goal of this operation is to recover and clarify the meaning (meant as sense) of what makes our life as we perceive it in that moment. It is only through this clarification that then our psychological daily life acquires a new more fitting meaning again and it can flow in a way that is more consistent with what we essentially are. In that sense the psychological epoché prepares the way for a phenomenological one, and in turn the phenomenological epoché enables the transcendental one, because it shows 'the world as a universe of transcendental acceptances' (p. 110); finally, the transcendental reduction discovers the absolute concrete stream of experience (p. 114). It is in fact through the reflection on our transcendental being as other from the unquestioned being of our daily life that the stream of our original experiences is opened up to us. We come in contact with the original stream of life as it is for us before we make decisions about its truthfulness and meanings; we come in contact with the originary streaming of life as it is for us apart from the meanings we had assigned to that streaming, within a natural attitude, as an expression of our psychical life.

Through the application of epoché and reduction in the phenomenological method the inquirer should be able to move with awareness through these different layers of reality and engage an observation of the same lived experience from different perspectives. There is a learning process implied here – in other words, just knowing about these attitudes theoretically is not the same thing as learning how to inhabit them. It is not possible to shift attitudes at will from psychological to transcendental attitudes because that shift requires an actual effort and commitment to look at reality with different eyes.

Phenomenology and psychology

As Fink writes 'phenomenology does not disconnect the world in order to withdraw from it and occupy itself with some other philosophical thematic, but (...) in order ultimately to know the world' (p. 115) in its full concreteness and pre-predicative meanings.[7] For this reason Husserl, according to Fink, remains loyal to the phenomenological motto even after the transcendental turn. As we saw above, the transcendental turn takes place thanks to the phenomenological epoché and reduction which are initiated on a psychological level. This means that if the psychological ego is not willing to commit to shedding light on its lifeworld and to suspending its beliefs in order to seek the ultimate essence of its lived experience, the backward analysis typical of the phenomenological investigation will not take place and no transcendental dimension will be uncovered. The access to the transcendental dimension is strongly grounded in the lifeworld and in the psychological subject who decides to undertake this kind of search. The transcendental realm is the realm to be clarified in phenomenological analysis. For this reason, 'the phenomenological reduction is not primarily a method of simply disconnecting, but one for leading back. It leads, through the most extreme radicalism of self-reflection, the philosophizing back through itself to the transcendental life of belief whose acceptance-correlate, the world is. In other words, it is the method for discovering and exposing a knowledge-thematic which is in principle nonworldly: the dimension of the origin of the world' (1970, 126).

In this sense phenomenological and psychological reductions cooperate in reaching a single goal, although within two distinct types of natural attitudes. While the phenomenological reduction sheds light on the absolute interconnection of the world, the psychological one illuminates only a region of the interconnectedness, that is, the psychical or animalistic one (*Ideas* II, 118).

> Psychology is a science which rests upon the basis of the natural attitude and which is thematically directed toward the psychical, that is the level of psychical animal life, and primarily that of human life. (1970, 118)

The psychological reduction discloses a region of consciousness that is conducive to the phenomenological exploration: 'the sphere of my own immanence, as well as the spheres of immanence belonging to other psyches which come to be identified through empathy' (p. 118).[8] The psychological epoché delimits 'an area within the world, but is rather a method for going beyond the world by removing limits' (p. 119), and differently from psychologism 'it does not dissolve the world into mere being-for-us in the sense of psychical subjectivity but maintains the existence of things as independent of human knowledge' (Fink, 1988, 187).[9] Phenomenology comprehends the psychological region, using it as a basis for human exploration, while expanding beyond this region and reaching through the spiritual layers[10] that constitute it.

One can gain access to these two regions of Being through the different positions the ego can take in relation to the concreteness of a given matter.

The psychological ego who performs the psychological epoché and reduction cannot be fully equated with the transcendental ego that is discovered through the disconnection of beliefs put in practice by the epoché and reduction. The former is located within the psychic layer of consciousness; the latter is located within the spiritual one. 'If we make the identity of the ego which believes in the world and the ego which disconnects the belief in the world' (1970, 115), we would run into an inescapable problem, because any observation of the world would be flattened to just one layer and would not provide any entrance to the multilayered reality. For this reason whenever we are doing practical or theoretical research we need to start thinking of our egos as simultaneously occupying multiple, different positions in varied layers of reality and observe what kind of sense each position has to offer.[11]

In fact, the epoché plays the important role of elucidating the triadic structure of the ego (psychological, reflexive and transcendental), whose identity remains the same even though it occupies different positions in time and space. As I noted above, the psychological ego is 'the human being who is preoccupied with the world' (p. 115). When the reflexive ego, practising the epoché, suspends the psychological ego's natural belief in the world, it invites the transcendental ego to reflect on the previously taken-for-granted acceptances of the world through ongoing awakenings. The epoché itself, in fact, is part of the egoic structure as a reflexive answer to awakening; as Fink writes the epoché is 'a structural moment of the transcendental reflection', 'a reflexive moment of refraining from belief on the part of the reflecting observer' (p. 115). This triad does not imply an actual change within the life of the subject, but an actual repositioning in relation to the meanings it can grasp and clarify; the state of affairs, philosophically speaking, has not changed.

The triadic structures and the meontic Absolute

The epoché and reduction disclose a triadic structure of the ego comprised of the psychological ego, the transcendental ego and the practical or awake ego – or as Fink called it, the onlooker. This structure should be taken as a layered identity of the same ego which can simultaneously open to a threefold view of the world, a threefold reality and time–space. The epoché in fact cracks open the system of acceptances through which we live our natural lives and shows crossroads of beings. This leads Fink to distinguish three modes of intentionality as shown next.

'The psychical intention of the psychological ego is essentially receptive; in terms of its own self-illumination, it is performed as a means of gaining access to being which is in itself independent of its intention' (1970, 134); the intentionality of the practical ego, which Fink calls transcendental-act intentionality, indicates the intentionality through which the ego awakens from the ongoing flow of its natural life and reflexively performs the epoché; finally, the transcendental-constitutive intention is the intentionality of the transcendental ego; a description from this standpoint is doomed to appear paradoxical to us because it speaks from a layer of time and space that is not aligned with our normative embodied self-experience as psychological subjects (more on this point in the next two chapters).

The first two forms of intentionality, the natural life and reflexive awakening, involve a sense of time–space that is conceivable for human beings. The former is an ego-intention situated in a linear sense of time; the latter is situated in an eternal now. In contrast, the third sense of time, the transcendental one, is situated in an absolute space–time fully disconnected from our beliefs as psychological egos. It can be absolute precisely because it is disconnected from our existence as psychological entities. 'Both the hyle, which is first exhibited as the act's nonintentional moment and the totality-form of the act itself are constituted within the depths of the intentional self-constitution of phenomenological time, a constitution which, however, does not proceed by means of act' (1970, 136, 137).

The transcendental layer of the ego is not actual because it does not locate itself within a mundane time–space, but is an absolute whole whose primordiality can be perceived only through awakenings. Since the transcendental layer is motionless, the awakenings originate from within another egoic layer: the practical ego. The directedness of this egoic layer is always alternating between the psychological and the transcendental directions because its nows knit together the two different dimensions of time, linear time and absolute time. The threefold nature of time is such that 'the phenomenologist who desires to communicate has only worldly concepts at his disposal'; that is, the concept of the psychological ego made available through the awakening of the practical ego. 'The mundane meaning of the worlds available to her [the phenomenologist] cannot be entirely removed, for their meaning can be limited only by the use of other mundane words (...). The inadequacy of all phenomenological reports caused by the use of nonworldly meaning also cannot be eliminated by the invention of a technical language (...). Phenomenological statements contain an internal conflict between a word's mundane meaning and the transcendental meaning which it serves to indicate' (p. 144). Application of the phenomenological method has to take into account this stratification of time and the tensions it yields.

The real challenge of phenomenology is the Absolute, understood as 'not ... a homogeneous universal unity of that which is existent ... but precisely the comprehensive unity of the existent as such and the pre-existent' (SCM 157/143).

Despite the fact that we encounter the Absolute in our daily lives as the core of certain experiences such as intense emotions, meditations, prayers and so forth, our words to explain it are always biased by the limits of our mundane life. The phenomenologist, as a human being does not have words to describe the sense of concreteness, but she might have the eyes to see what that core of reality actually is. Since the transcendental embedded in this concreteness is an Absolute that is itself beyond any linear being graspable in a logical shape, Fink characterizes this form of Absolute as meontic (Bruzina, 1995, lv–lvii; 2004, 366f), meaning a being (*on*) that is not (*me*) yet.

What phenomenology can do in relation to the meontic Absolute is to enable the 'transformation [*Verwandlung*] of the "self"': the reductive performance 'doubles' the human ego by bringing its transcendental ground to self-evidence, and transcendental reflection reunites these at a 'higher' level by realizing in self-consciousness the 'identity' of the whole (Fink, 1970, KS 123/117). Thus, the '"concrete" concept of the "phenomenologizing subject"' is the 'dialectical unity' of the two 'antithetic moments' – that is, 'transcendental subjectivity "appearing" in the world' (SCM 127/116; cf. 147, 157, 163/134, 142, 147). Retracing the path back to the things themselves, the phenomenologist can activate the transcendental layer of the ego and let it speak through the psychological egoic layer. The three egoic layers can, in turn, become aware of the concreteness of the transcendental layer through the awakenings of the practical ego. These three layers are deeply interconnected and all of them actively operating in the phenomenological and psychological analyses.[12]

Phenomenology's bias and the two eyes open

It is evident from the preceding discussion that reality is a difficult concept to grasp and a difficult dimension in which to fully dwell. According to Hussserl's phenomenology, the two poles of reality (real and reel), reality as it is and reality as it is grasped, are always intertwined with each other and distorted by the limits of our biology which shapes our psychological answers to the experience of the world. This biological and organic shape constitutes a bias for anyone who wants to pursue a radical analysis of direct experience.[13] In order to lessen the effects of this limit and in order to get as close as possible to the view of the threefold layers that comprise reality, Husserl's phenomenology uses the combination of static and genetic methods that grasps both poles of reality simultaneously and sees them as operating within the triadic structure mentioned above.[14] Neither the static nor the genetic method are sufficient, in isolation, to do justice to these interrelated aspects of reality.[15] In other words, I cannot give an account of ethical issues and their psychological implications from a solely static eye alone because, in this case, the unsaid will never be brought to the surface and the ethical problems I grasp will amount to merely my interpretation of the present facts as I present them in the here and now. On the other hand, I cannot gain a full grasp of an ethical issue from a solely genetic eye, describing the inner motives that brought about a given action, because I would lose sight of the ethical fact, as it would disappear in the linear time and passive syntheses (I will say more on time as a passive syntheses in the last section of this chapter and in the next two chapters). Using one of the two eyes at a time would be equivalent to giving a partial account of the ethical phenomenon.[16] In fact, we would see the volitional body first with the right, then with the left eye, but without both eyes open together – without the depth of seeing the phenomenon as it is lived.[17] We cannot say that the reality of schizophrenics is not real while our reality is;[18] this would equate to denying someone the right to be because her view differs from that of the majority of people. The challenge of research conducted using this approach is to keep both eyes open and to be able to discern the data provided from every layer of time, space and intention. Being an ethical subject means being able to reflect in a wakeful manner on what we are living as embodied, biological creatures, and arriving at reasoned decisions in this midst of embodied life.

Husserl's ethics and the triadic structure of Being

This second part of the chapter will describe how Husserl's ethics and psychology interact with this triadic structures of time, reality and egos, while Part II of the book will explore in an applicative way the same triadic structure.[19]

Indeed, the foundational ground on which Husserl's ethics is based is the triadic structure described above; without the awakenings of the practical ego there would be neither ethical awareness nor an actual effort to become responsibly self-reflectively aware of our deeds. In this sense the foundational ground of ethics is situated between the psychological receptive material layer (*Natur*) and the active transcendental egoic layer (*Geist*).[20] For this reason, the first distinction I proposed in my (*Husserl's Ethics and Practical Intentionality*, 2016) systematization of Husserl's ethical thought is between *ethics as a practice* and *ethics as a theoretical science*. Ethics is an embodied, practical response to a situation, and is simultaneously a reflective – hence theoretical – analysis of our decisions in response to that situation. Much the same as psychological phenomenology, this phenomenological ethics does not purport to clarify the full, interconnectedness range of being, but only the region of volitional bodies which includes the psychological layer (the animalistic psychic body). This ethics adds, in fact, the thin additional layer of volitions which connects the living body with the spiritual-reflective body. Volitional receptive being and volitional reflective spirit represent two basic poles that give shape to the ethical human being. The two poles 'speak' different languages: one is a passive, receptive language that displays itself through linear time and passive syntheses, the other one is the language of the absolute that becomes visible to us in the living present and the active effort of reflecting on it through our intentional activity. These two poles are unified within a triadic structure through the awoken practical ego, which functions in the living present as a here and now. The awoken ego connects the passive selfless matter of the syntheses with the active one that just awoke through its activity. An example is discovering oneself to be hungry. The ego who just awoke due to its hunger takes ownership of the body (matter) that felt hungry and decides (activity in linear time) whether to do something or not about that hunger.[21]

In fact, despite the fact that these poles speak different spatial, temporal and psychological languages, they need each other and cannot exist without each other. The volitional reflective spirit needs a body with an appropriate neurological structure in order to be able to think and the volitional receptive being needs a spirit in order to be able to receive and store information. The awoken psychological ego, which decides what to accept and negate, is the practical connection between the two. The receptive side awakens through the awakening of the practical ego, the reflective, transcendental layer begins the process of constituting meanings from the same point of awakening. From this consideration, it follows that Husserl's ethics must be described in accordance with a triadic structure. On the one hand, Husserl's ethics is the ethics of our receptive bodies which are continuously *in fieri* – I (2016) named that ethics *practical intentionality*. On the other hand, Husserl's ethics is the ethics of reflective spirit, a meta-ethics that I (ibid.) referred to as *ethical science*. Differently from phenomenology, this science does not encompass the whole of being, but discloses and clarifies one specific region of being, the *volitional body* which is described by Husserl as the connecting bridge between body and mind, nature and spirit, being and absolute. The volitional body is the embodiment of the awoken ego, which makes decisions about receptive matter and provides the ground for the constituting meanings of the reflective spirit. In this book the volitional body and its relation to time and to the reality of its own self will be the object of my investigations and will be the object to which I will refer for a phenomenological description of reality.

For Husserl, this region of being can serve as the ground for a science because the ethical scientist commits herself to a never-ending clarification of the ontological roots of ethical being which, as we saw before, also comprises psychical being. Hence, in the analysis that will follow in these chapters, we will focus on that region of being as it relates to the threefold structure of ego and time. This is the reason why it is difficult, if not pointless, to neatly separate psychology from ethics, and this is the reason why in this book we decided to investigate the ethics of lived experience. As psychology helps phenomenology to disclose the transcendental layer through the psychological epoché, so psychology helps ethics to clarify the receptive layers of the volitional body. While each of the three disciplines has a character of its own, they are strictly interconnected with each other.

A difficulty that we need to bear in mind from a psychological, ethical and philosophical perspective is that each discipline has to do with layered meanings of time, space and intention. The receptive matter within which the transcendental concreteness of being is enclosed is – so to speak – egoless, because the ego, as the leading motor of actions, is not yet awoken, and its motionless time is given through a number of passive syntheses. The awoken ego, the practical one, is an ego that knits together the receptive and reflective matter by validating the passive syntheses as they take place in the here and now within the linear flow of time and the natural life of the psychological ego. Despite the fact that these three layers are independent of each other, our organic functioning is such that, for us, reality results from their combination; the absolute can manifest itself to us only through awakenings that we can understand in the semantic continuum of our brain.

Body–Mind and intentionalities

In Husserl the body is described as an aesthesiological unit (Hua-Mat IV, 281), an original field of possibilities (*Urfeld de koennen*) in which undifferentiated matter that is not yet owned by a subject *becomes* a living thing, and then a living body and bearer of sensations (Hua IV, 183).

The way in which the subject perceives her body and comes to own it is described by Husserl through layers. Unlike Carman's (1999), interpretation, these layers do not refer to a static cognitive equilibrium, but instead describe the corporeal functioning of the subject as a whole. For this reason, looking at a body from a static perspective would not be sufficient, but requires an integration of a genetic perspective as well. The thing becomes an organic body (*Koerper*) because it can move and it is through this movement that the body realizes that it can perceive itself in space and time. This realization comes through an *Ich will* (I want) that mediates between the *Ich kann* (I can) and the *Ich tue* (I do). There is an 'I want' that translates the perceptual information gathered by the body and gives, or denies, the fiat to proceed to an action. In that sense, motility is the first intention. The 'volitional body' is the 'connecting bridge between nature and spirit' (Hua-Mat IV, 186), which facilitates the process of becoming a subject within a material body. In fact, the volitional body – the embodied, awoken I – on the one hand mediates between the varied physiological and perceptual syntheses coming from the organic body and allows on the other hand the act of meaning giving to these syntheses. The awoken I mediates between the syntheses and the acts of meaning given to these syntheses.[22]

Each of these three layers, organic (in whose concreteness the transcendental ego dwells), volitional (whose awakenings are lived by the practical ego) and living body (whose natural life corresponds to the psychological ego) are characterized by a different form of intentionality which I recognized as simultaneously passive, practical and active; each of them can be understood as one station of the same intentional activity. In *Analyses Concerning Active and Passive Synthesis* (2001), Husserl writes extensively about all three. We can summarize the content of his writing in this way: passive intentionality represents an ego-less form of intention that is expressed through a complex combination of spontaneous and non-spontaneous syntheses. The first layer of synthesis, that of *Sinnlichkeit*, is the layer in which *esse* and *percipi* (being and being perceived) arise together; matter constitutes itself through a constant rhythm without the participation of the ego (1920, 204) and organizes itself in a dynamic combination of affectant and affected. In this duo the matter is fused together (*Logical Investigations*, II, VI, 47) and comes to association. The spontaneous sensuous association is organized around a principle of homogeneity; matter tends to associate with similar matter and to organize itself around a homogeneous core of meanings. On the second associative layer, which is not spontaneous because it involves the predicative effort of an ego that is not fully there yet, this homogenous sensuous cluster becomes the thematic object of an ego. Yet, before the ego becomes fully active there is a process of validation in which the ego accepts or refuses the hyletic syntheses. On this level we have the combination of two forms of intentionalities: practical and active.

The words *acceptance* and *refusal* here indicate the range of the practical intention and should be taken in a very wide sense, occurring on multiple levels. The first form of acceptance concerns the acceptance of sensuous information as being *yours*. Imagine the case of a person with an artificial limb versus the case of a person with a numb limb: their volitional bodies will come to accept the information provided from their limbs at different speeds and with different degrees of certainty; but yet the steps involved in the process of recognition will remain the same. Becoming an active subject requires first of all the acceptance of being bound to that specific body. After that, the volitional body has to decide if what the syntheses of the organic body are demanding from the body are things that can be done, and on a more refined level, the body must choose whether or not it is acceptable to do them. For example, I feel that my body is demanding food (first level). I realize that I have a mouth and I have food available, so my volitional body accepts the possibility of my body eating food (second level); yet while I am vetting the possibility of eating I realize that it would not be acceptable for me to begin eating because I am lecturing in front of a class (third level). This is what I would call practical intentionality – the awakening of receptive matter into a decisional and reflective matter. This form of intentionality is at a crossroads between the two other forms of intentionality – active and passive. In fact, practical intentionality stems from the here and now, a point in time in which the ego awakens (Hua-Mat IX, 128–129, 133) and owns the concreteness of its receptive matter by constituting meanings from it. On the other hand, active intentionality is that form of intention that gives meaning to what has been decided upon and done.

One thing that is important to note here is that these three forms of intentionality and accompanying egoic stances happen simultaneously due to the time–space structure that I will describe in more detail in the last section of this chapter.

> We find, as *the originally and specifically subjective, the Ego in the proper sense,* the Ego of 'freedom', the attending, considering, comparing, distinguishing, judging, valuing, attracted, repulsed, inclined, disinclined, desiring and willing Ego: the Ego that in any sense is '*active*' and *takes a position.* This, however, is only one side. Opposed to the active Ego stands the passive, and the Ego is always *passive* at the same time whenever it is active, in the sense of being affected as well as being receptive, which of course does not exclude the possibility of its being sheer passivity. (Hua I, 224–225)

This means that the active intention, the ego stance through which we constitute meanings, can never completely cover all the passive syntheses of receptive matter. The ego, as Husserl wrote, is always accompanied by a non-ego; passivity and activity, matter and reflection, nature and spirit, psychological and transcendental ego always coexist. Subjective life is constitutively made by a passive undifferentiated nucleus that strives to be awake and take a new shape. 'In the conscious life of the concrete ego there is an abiding hyletic core of non-ego yet belonging essentially to the ego. Without a realm of pre-givenness, a realm of unities constituted as non-ego, no ego is possible' (Husserl, 1973, 379).

Awakening of the I and passive syntheses

In order to better understand how this co-presence of layers works we need to explain the structure of the awakenings that knit together transcendental and psychological reality. Reality is given to us as a systematic association of parts comprising a whole; this association functions because of a systematic affective awakening (Hua XXXI, 230) – an accomplishment of Being that, while hidden, explains the mystery of givens. The concreteness of Being is hidden and at the same time given to us through transcendental evidence and psychological understanding. As explained above, any unit arises necessarily independently of the ego as a homogenous compound of hyletic concrete data that relate to each other within a percept (Hua XXXI, 482–483). In passive syntheses, this homogeneous compound arises through a primordial association that functions by means of similarity, contrast and contiguity (Hua III, 112). Every homogeneous matter given in the now-phase of the flow of consciousness is integrated into a 'system of referential implication' (Hua XXXII, 42). Undifferentiated matter becomes something in a moment in time because of the association of its parts revolving around a core and through the awoken subject's recognition.

Instead of being simultaneously present, the material receptive flow is synthesized and diffused for us only by means of presenting egoic activities such as memory, phantasy and empathy. My ego is present in my acts of remembering or phantasizing about the matter on which it is reflecting. Such presentifications enable the subject to transform undifferentiated matter into sedimentations that establish 'the unity of world-certainty' and disclose the possibility of reproductive activity (Hua XXXI, 152). The primordial ego irradiates affective awakenings; the awake ego re-*acts* and opens its horizon to a chain of other possible fusions or primordial homogeneous associations of hyletic matter.

For Husserl (Hua XXXI, 123), while primordial association is independent of the psychological and transcendental ego, it awakens both egos.[23] At first the necessary lawfulness of given data is recognized by an egoless affection, then this egoless affection secures the given data within a system of interrelated data, while awakening the structure of something different from and yet relating to the data. Husserl writes: 'We can secure decisive insights into the essence of association when we comprehend the (...) structure pertaining to the function of affection, its peculiarity, and its dependence on essential conditions' (Hua XXXI, 211).

Awakening to its subject-hood, this locus of awakening recognizes itself as a living body or an *Ich kann* (I can) and an *Ich tue* (I do) who wants to act and be in a persistent temporal flow (Hua-Mat IX, 128–129). This I as a *wache Ich* (awoken I) in a moment of time (*Zeitpunkt*) functions in time (Hua-Mat IX, 133), which means it decides to acknowledge its ownership over the hyletic layers that constitute its being with its momentous choice (*jetzigen Wahl*) (Husserl, 2012: 133). '*So tue ich!*' (Hua-Mat IX, 133) – 'Then I act'. The I responds to a specific number of stimuli in a point of time (Husserl, 2012: 133, passim) and the decision of the primordial I guides any direction it takes.

> Every awakening proceeds from an impressional flow or from an already non intuitively reproduced present toward another reproduced present, whose movement presupposes a 'bridge element', that synthesizes what is given and leads toward the next coincidence (*Deckung*). (Hua XXXI, 123)

The synthesis initiated by this retentional power becomes a protentional synthetic activity in which all the data of hyletic matter are gathered together and given to the subject as a form of alien rhythm. The impression leaves its mark in the past and protends towards a future creating a rhythmic chain of associations. This rhythm repeatedly affects and reveals to the ego the contents of the 'now' in the ego's flowing life. We can describe this flow as waves of ego-less matter that becomes egoic and then falls back upon egolessness.

Although not completely a-subjective, the hyle remains nevertheless foreign to the ego in the sense that the hyletic field organizes itself without the ego's participation (*Ichbeteiligung*) (Hua XXXI, 478). Every 'now' that is more than a 'now point' (*Jetzpoint*) is a living presence that organizes itself on the basis of this rhythmic encounter between past and future. Rhythmatizations generate coherent hyletic patterns in which the manifold of future impressions affectively resonate with the present impressions and ignite associative syntheses in which the psychological I discovers itself as an affected I; the psychological I discovers itself as an 'already-affected I'. Husserl terms that which affects the ego a 'prominence' (*Abgehobenheit*). Prominences are sensible unities (Husserl, 2001, 527), which depend directly upon hyletic contrast and conflict (Husserl, 2001, 196–197). By contrast and conflict Husserl means the kind of force that drives matter to a synthesis.

For Husserl (Hua-Mat IX, 131–133), the I stems from a *jetzigen Wahl*, a 'momentous choice' that responds to the impetus of hyletic data. As Husserl writes, what guides the act to its realization is the will (*das Wille*) (Hua-Mat IX,125–126) that aims at its fulfilment as desideratum (Hua-Mat IX, 125). It is sensing will in time that triggers the constitution of the subject.

The triad of time and intentions

As mentioned above, Husserl's phenomenology elucidates a threefold structure of time.[24] In Hua 33 and Hua 10 4Husserl distinguishes three senses of time (Hua 33, Hua 10): in the first sense, time is connected to a pre-temporal and egoless absolute – the time in which nothing changes, but just is. In the second sense, time stands for the stream of immanent experience such as hyletic data and passive experience – that is, the time of the matter as it is experienced by our body before the body's mind starts reflecting upon it. In the third sense, time is meant as a world-time constituted through the acts, in which everything streams – that is, the time that we organize using clocks. The primordial absolute layer of time discloses itself in the third stream through the transcendental ego's questioning-back and through a reflexive act directed upon the stream (Mohanty, 1970; Lohmar, 2010).[25] World-time is mostly characterized by cognitive, conventional world-time of 'before and after' and causal connections. In contrast, the first kind of time does not allow for any form of movement since it is an absolute time. In the Latin sense, *ab-solutus* (loose, 'untied' or freed from our mind) indicates something that is not fully for us since it is untied from our minds. In other words, whenever we seek to explain the data we perceive, the fullness of the data escapes us because we are constrained to the second and third form of streaming time. Hence, this form of time presupposes what Fink (Hart, 2009; Bruzina, 1997) termed a meontology of the questioning transcendental I. 'Meontology' (science of non-being) means that the actual being on which our reflection is grounded is a non-being (Greek: *me on*), a being that by definition has not yet come to existence for us because it is 'absolute' for us, in the sense that it belongs to a level of time and being that we can experience only if we abandon the linear and hyletic way of explaining time. In this respect, we are absolute, but as we begin reflecting on it and trying to make sense of its meaning we lose contact with its real meaning.

Indeed, this first original stream is not yet an I but is the original presence, the living presence as a 'standing-steaming present' (C3, III 88) from which my being-for-myself is constituted as *my* living self-presence. This pre-temporal stream is not yet intentional; rather, it is the stream that 'awakes' or 'irritates' the ego and makes it a '*wache Ich*', an awoken I, ready for any intentional activity.

It is within the second stream that we find the first form of intentionality that we name *practical* and *operating* in relation to the I (Hua VIII, 34; Hua XI, 61; Hua XIV, 172). On this level the stream of hyletic concrete data that relates to the ego in the form of stimuli (*Reize*) generates a number of egoless affections, drives and reactions connected to each other in a chain of here-nows. At this stage the flow of the world is absolute and not yet interrupted by *my* presence in the stream. It is only when the absolute presence of consciousness interacts with the passive stream of hyletic data and stimulates my ego that the third stream, that of the lifeworld, is finally disclosed. Linguistic description of the interrelation between these three streams is absolutely inadequate because our language too is enslaved to world-time. As neurology shows us (Chan, Fox, Scahill et al. 2001), we need to order our knowledge according to a before and after, a cause and an effect, while events themselves are just *e-venientes* ('coming-from'), occurring in our lives from a nowhere.[26]

Practical intentionality often serves as a bridge between awakening in time and the absolute without time. The horizon of passive possible awakening in the nows, of continuing memories and attentional modifications of what is apprehended (the second layer of the stream) can interact with the newly awoken horizon of the ego (third layer) due to a *substratum* (first layer) that is there for that interaction. In this crossroad the I discovers its primordial ethical core: that is, its ability to decide and then act in the world. In the connection between this second and third layer the I finds itself as an *Ich-fremd* (other than my Ego's own) because the hyletic is foreign to it, but at the same time awakens it and compels it to pursue with full awareness the intentional force that determines it as intentional.

The I and the other than the I (*Ichfremd*) are inseparable and both are alive and intentional (C16, VI, I, VII). What is pre-I (*vor-Ich*) is nameless but operating (*fungierende*) and always engaging with the world (Hua XXXIII, text 15, 277–8). This remarkable difference between the different layers of time, which are deeply entangled with our identity and our capacity to make a decision, shows that moral and psychological discourse requires identifying the specific type of temporality with one's decisional identity, and thus grasping how one's temporality affects one's sense of reality. Once an autistic student half jokingly told me 'professor, it's all a matter of time. They do know it, but every second of mine is like an eternity for me. It's an ongoing struggle for me to keep up with your sense of time'. I will expand on this point in the next chapters; at this stage what I want to emphasize is the intimate connection between time, Being and identity as time seems to be a layered medium of Being on which our identity relies.

As Dodd (2010) pointed out the absolute sense of time might correspond to the presence of time (*Weltgegenwart*; Lohmar, 2010, 54), that is, the moment in which I am oriented towards the now. It is a kind of time that depends on the accomplishments of life. The subject experiences a linearity of time in virtue of a *Sonderheit*, a particularity of what is happening here as located between a before and after, but in fact the person is experiencing time and her own life from a no-space-and-time because of its absoluteness. Yet, the person enters in time because of the peculiarity of this moment (*Sonderheit*) which enables her to locate herself in the second longitudinal sense of time, the systatical[27] one: this standing streaming presence has often been compared to Bergson's (1965) *durée*, a form of here-now whose phenomenological structure at each segment is such that it simultaneously looks at the future (protention) while retaining the past (retention). Yet, as Simenov's (2015) critique points out, if time ended here, it would assume the role of being only a spatial category whose function is to order in space things according to a before and after. The great richness of Husserl's approach is that he acknowledges that this here-now has a synthetic quality. Indeed, this second sense of time is systatical and categorical. As it emerges from the combination of genetic and static method, time is not only a spatial category but also a genetic synthesis whose functioning is to bring formless matter into existence.

In that sense I disagree with those who criticize Husserl for supposedly forgetting existence. Husserl often refers to *Dasein* (Being here) and *Sosein* (Being thus) in order to name the primal manifestation of the concreteness of Being that comes into existence through time. The systatical quality of time opens to a generative (Steinbock, 1995) way of seeing existence as a dynamic stability, 'Die dynamische Stabilitaet' (Bergmann & Hoffman, 1989), which combines becoming and being, the flow of passive receptive matter, and the given meaning with which it comes into existence for us. This is the kind of reality that the phenomenological method should be able to grasp.

In that sense, static and genetic methods allow phenomenology to describe Being from both perspectives; as a given and as a becoming, as an object in space and as a synthesis of the same object coming to space.[28]

Summary

In this chapter I displayed the main characteristics of reality as it can be interpreted through Husserl's ethics and his phenomenological psychology.

The overall goal of this chapter is to discover how ethics and psychology can collaborate together in order to provide a way to unfold the layers of reality that is comprehensible for us and free from moral judgements or psychological categories. In the phenomenological method the use of epoché and reduction is essential to uncover the concreteness of reality and see its interwoven ethical, psychological and transcendental layers.

From this perspective, understanding the crossroad of triads in which phenomenology (whose region of study is the transcendental layer), psychology (whose region of study is the psychic or biological layer) and ethics (whose region of study is the volitional body) locate themselves is utterly important for any epistemological and moral judgement we can express towards one's lived experience and one's sense of reality.

As shown in this chapter, our lives are held within a mysterious and difficult balance between at least three different layers of reality, identity and time. The major part of our lives go by in the mode of egoless, receptive matter whose time is aimed at absorbing and storing information (natural psychological life); but we live also a life of acceptances granted by a just-awoken ego who lives in the here and now (practical and ethical life). Finally, we live a life from an absolute standpoint in which we do not even exist and we are aliens witnessing our whole life (philosophical and transcendental life). None of these lives could be illuminated and described without the other; even if the transcendental life is essentially constitutive of the practical and psychological life, it would never be grasped without the commitment of the psychological ego and the awakening of the practical one. The balance we find between these three layers of reality, times and identity is what shapes our sense of goodness, normal behaviour and knowledge. Using the theoretical tools of an ethics that is grounded upon this crossroads can enhance the complexity of our understanding of human lived experiences.

I.3

The Trinitarian relationship of the world

Introduction

This chapter and the following one will focus on the interconnection between ethical, religious and psychological experience. The issue we will investigate revolves around the source of morality and its temporal boundaries with religion and psychology. As it appears evident both religion and morality[1] provide human beings with values through which they interpret and give structure to their lives and to the overarching sense of the real.[2] In moments of psychological distress, this axiological structure might mutate and lead to a view of reality that becomes detached from the accepted intersubjective understanding of it within one's surrounding community.

The way in which I intend to proceed in the *pars destruens* is to first target the eidos of the phenomenon I want to investigate – in this instance, the ethical experience of reality as one detached from that validated by one's surrounding, intersubjective community. Second, I will investigate how the meaning of this experience can be reactivated within an intersubjective community through a proper understanding of its layers such as time, being and teleology. I argue that the multilayered nature of time entails an organization of ethical and psychological reality that cannot be explained through an exclusively epistemological point of view: rather, a unique form of teleology is required that bridges epistemology and ontology. Third, I will clarify how ethical experience and its way of processing reality has its source in a mode of spiritual belief that we may call religious. Finally, I will explain how this religious source reflects a teleological manner of experiencing time.

In this chapter I will analyse ethical experience and its relationship with reality through the lenses of time comparing Eastern and Western thought: namely that of Husserl and Nishida. My goal is to use the scholarly authority of these two important philosophers with the aim of deciding whether the meanings, in this case Eastern and Western interpretations of the phenomenon, can be reused within our lifeworld (*Lebenswelt*). In a nutshell, does the meaning that we assign to ethical experience make sense to us? What kind of tradition are we relying upon when we vet the existing relationship between ethics and reality?

While in the *pars destruens* of the method I disassemble the phenomenon in all its layers and keep it related to the intersubjective system to which it belongs, in the *construens pars* I reorganize the layers belonging to this phenomenon in order to recover the full sense of its sedimentations both from a personal point of view (the verification of my thesis) and from the intersubjective point of view (the verification of validated authorities like Husserl and Nishida). I will unfold the meaning of Nishida's conception of the Trinitarian relationship of the world and 'logic[3] of topos' using Husserl's theory of intentionalities. Hence, in my analysis I will tackle Husserl's and Nishida's notions of teleology as they interlace with theology and time; and Hartmann's (2010) critique of Husserl's teleology as well.

This analysis will be primarily theoretical, using the data emerging from my reading of Husserl's and Nishida's ontologies. In the following chapter I will investigate the same phenomenon using interviews provided from a study of clinical cases.

Title of the chapter: The Trinitarian relationship of the world

This chapter's title, 'The Trinitarian relationship of the world', comes from Nishida Kitaro's beautiful book *The Logic of Topos and the Religious Worldview* (*ashoteki ronri to shūkyōteki sekaikan*). Surprisingly, the author is not even remotely Christian; rather, he was a Japanese philosopher and Zen practitioner whose path-breaking work bridged Eastern and Western philosophy. In his book Nishida does not explicitly mention Husserl's phenomenology, although he was influenced by him and lectured extensively on phenomenology. In this chapter I will use this philosophical bridge that connects Eastern and Western philosophical tradition to shed light on the common source of morality and its relationship with theology and time.

The chapter is divided into two main sections. The first compares Husserl's theory of intentionality with Nishida's logic (The Logic of Topos), while the second discusses Hartmann's critique of teleology as it relates to Husserl's and Nishida's use of teleology. In the following chapter the theoretical findings emerging from this analysis will be used as a tool to interpret the relationship with time and divinity as lived by mystics and schizophrenics.

On Nishida and Husserl: Bridging Western and Eastern interpretation of reality

Nishida, the founder of the Kyoto school, had the unprecedented merit of bridging the depths of Western and Eastern philosophical traditions.[4]

The 'Logic of Topos (*basho*) and the Religious Worldview' is one of Nishida's last books and represents a dense summary of the main tenets of his philosophical research and meditative Zen practice.[5] About his logic he wrote: 'The problems that have been unthinkable in former logics because of their form have become thinkable [in mine]' (NKZ, 12, 266; NKZ refers to the Complete Works of Nishida Kitarō, in nineteen volumes, cited as NKZ followed by volume and page number. New Edition 2002–2009, twenty-four volumes, edited by A. Takeda, K. Riesenhueber, K. Kosaka and M. Fujita, Tokyo: Iwanami Shoten). As Arisaka noted 'the logic of place (*basho no ronri*) is an ambitious hybrid of "systematic philosophy" and "phenomenological ontology"' (2000, 41). 'The Trinitarian relationship of the world' (Nishida, 1945, 23) is an expression that Nishida uses in his logic in order to describe the ontological relationship between the world and our understanding of it:

> The world, the contradictory self-identity of the many and the one, moves from that which is formed to that which forms. (1945, 4)

These dense two lines offer an overview of the main issues we are going to discuss in this chapter, that is, the problem of the contingent order of the world, namely the problem of movement and its teleology, the multiplicity of the self and the source of its formal identity. In the following sections I will tackle these issues through a comparative analysis of Husserl's phenomenology and Nishida's logic in order to explicate the religious source of morality.

The logic of topos and religious worldview

At the very beginning of his book Nishida writes: 'Suffice it to say that we cannot discuss religious reality from the standpoint of objective logic, and that religious questions cannot even emerge at this level' (1945, 2). Yet, the title of this meditation connects religion and logic, why?

The answer is that for Nishida, logic and religion are ontologically but not epistemologically related: both are rooted in Being and are determinations of Being. Although logic and religion are formally determined in different ways, the content-matter around which their determination revolves is the same, that is Being itself. If we remain at the level of formal logic, the religious question will not emerge, but if we dig into the ontological matter that informs the shape of Being, then it will become evident that logic and religion are intimately correlated in an ontological circle – the description of which will be the task of this chapter.

A case in point is this passage in which Nishida writes: 'Logic must reflect upon itself. The self-realization of logic itself is necessary (. . .) Logic is not an abstract thought apart from reality, but rather it can be said to be a self-formation of historical reality itself. Logic emerges when historical reality undergoes a self realization of its own reality' (NKZ, 10, 448, 458).[6] It is only when logic becomes reality through self-formation that its connection with religion becomes apparent. Self-realization (*jikaku*) is here a keyword linked to negation, world and time, terms which I will address in the next section.

Negation of negation and self-affirmation

According to Nishida, self-realization is a necessary means to allow the self-formation of reality. As Arisaka wrote 'self-realization denotes our fundamental relation to reality' (1999, 50). The act of self-realization passes through the logic of self-affirmation or 'logic of contradictory self-identity'.[7] The way in which logic becomes reality, that is ontologically standing, is through self-affirmation, that is negation of negation. Nishida explains this basic point as follows: 'Two things stand in opposition and their mutual negation is simultaneously their mutual affirmation'[8] (1945, 3). Naming something stems from the affirmation of the self as different from what is going to be named, or otherwise put, from the negation of what is not the same as the naming itself. For two opposite things to affirm their individual uniqueness, they need to negate what they are not; their identity is affirmed through mutual negation. Using Nishida's poetic words, we can explain the logic of contradictory self-identity as 'seeing the shape of the shapeless, hearing the voice of the voiceless'[9] (NKZ, 4, 6). Naming Being passes through self-affirmation, which means the mutual negation of what is going to be named. To affirm what we are, we need to negate what we are not and this negation will be always referential; I can negate what I am not only if I know that there is something else I cannot be. Negation is a way to break through the limits of an ungraspable immanence and move towards an endless chain of self-affirming acts, which assign a form to what is still ungraspable.[10]

The leap from Being to meaning

As noted above, self-realization is the act through which logic shows its ontological roots. In fact, the epistemological act of negation of negation implies two ontological evidences: movement and action.

> Action arises in, and from, a mutual relationship between things. Action presupposes a relationship of mutual negation, wherein one negates the other and the other negates the first. This mutual negation is simultaneously a mutual affirmation. Each thing realizes its own uniqueness. That is, each thing becomes itself. That two things maintain their uniqueness as they stand opposed to each other and negate each other means that they are mutually conjoined and compose one form. (1945, 4)

Negation of negation describes an ontological and epistemological circularity in which the meaning of self-negating Being is determined by the Being that discloses itself through *the act of* negation, and the Being that discloses itself through the act of negation is determined by *the meaning of* the self-negating Being.[11] This circularity involves an epistemological and ontological level, which is crucial for the self-realization of the things in the world. Clearly, Being and meaning belong to two different levels of reality: using one to explain the other involves a leap that needs to be justified; Nishida addresses this problem through his Trinitarian view of world and time which I will describe in the next section.

The Trinitarian view of world and time

According to Nishida, movements and actions are illusions, or at best they are a form of perception arising from a human linear sense of time within the lifeworld. In fact, Nishida claims that there are three kinds of worlds: material, lifeworld and creating world which can be described as follows.

'In the material[12] world there are no active things. To conceive active things, we need time' (Nishida, 1945, 3). As Kopf remarks (2002, 233), 'Nishida's theory of Basho suggests three layers of the human experience: the abstract world of knowledge, the lived world of activity, and self-awareness qua self-contradictorily identity'. In our human experience, first we encounter the opposition between the first and the second world, what I will call the material and the life world, following Nishida's language. Then we encounter the second world, the lifeworld, within which we are able to conceive of activity, through acts of self-awareness; this encounter happens in a different kind of time according to the layer from which one would observe it. In fact, it is a synchronic encounter in the first world and a linear one in the second world; which means that as human beings we experience time and reality as a sub specie aeternitatis encounter and as a Being that can be organized according to a before and after. In fact, while in the material world any form of activity would be inconceivable because the 'time' of this world is properly time-less and accordingly any change of state would be impossible, in the lifeworld 'the eternal present temporalizes time (. . .); time forms as the self-determination of the eternal now' (NKZ 6, 188). In the lifeworld eternity temporalizes itself through logical negation. In this latter layer of the world, activity is essentially conceived of as a declension of eternal time by virtue of which human beings are allowed to understand Being as a flow from a state A to a state B. Accordingly, what was conceived of as Being in the material world becomes the multiplicity of beings in the lifeworld. This encounter is possible through the third world, the creating one.

In fact, these two worlds are bridged by a third world, namely the creating world or world of awareness, in which activity in the form of Being[13] realizes itself by discovering to be directed towards its self-affirmation. This third world is the world of circular or dialectical time[14] which revolves around the axis of the material world. On this layer linearity collapses upon eternity in the attempt to determine it and creates an ongoing dialectical circle in which eternity and linearity coexist. In this circularity 'time reverses itself forever' (NKZ 6, 204). Nishida figuratively imagines these three worlds in Pascal's terms: 'like a sphere with no circumference and whose center is everywhere' (1945, 6).[15] As Kopf remarks 'Nishida collapses past and future in the dynamic self-determination of the present or material world to signify the paradox of personal continuity (. . .). He rejects a linear model of continuity (. . .) describing the continuity (. . .) as a progression from the created to the creating' (2002, 228). The lifeworld revolves as a 'world of momentary self-determination of the absolute presence which has its direction of self-forming focal point' (1945, 6).

The material world, the world of the absolute present constitutes the axis around which the lifeworld revolves itself:

> The term 'world' (. . .) does not mean, as it is usually the case when people think about the world, this world that stands in opposition (*tairitsu*) to us as selves. It is used for nothing else than expressing an absolute place-like existence; therefore one could also call it 'the absolute'. When I discussed mathematics, I called it 'the system of contradictory self-identity.' (1945, 6)

The (first) world is the material world, that is the world of what is created; grasping the essence of this world creates the meaning through which we perceive the difference between our self and the essence around which our self revolves. In this world physical phenomena are modifications of field forces,[16] which means that they are the field of force and at the same time they determine themselves as differentiated physical phenomena. Things appear as different because we know them through a linear sense of time, which operates through the self-contradictory logic I described above. In the lifeworld the self-contradictory logic comes to know Being according to a before and after, that is, first, it operates through the act of negating the identity between the knowing Being and Being and then it creates the multiplicity of Being by the very act of negation. From a human point of view the three worlds are strictly interwoven and we would not be able to conceive of one without the other.

In the 'material world' time is reversible because there is no movement and, in fact, no time in the way in which humans are used to conceive of it. On this level time is made of absolute nows, while when we come to the lifeworld, time becomes irreversible because it goes through a line of befores-afters. As Nishida wrote in his essay "Life" (*Seimei*), the lifeworld, differently from the material world, also includes within the individual self its self-expression, and because the inside of the self is its own reflection, in this world action proceeds from the created to the creator, in balance between the inside and the outside (NKZ, 11, 375). 'Negating itself, the created creates the creating' (NKZ, 9, 160).

It is in reference to this created-creating-created qua creating unity that Nishida mentions the Trinitarian relationship of the world:

> The world of the absolute present, the absolutely contradictory self-identity, mirrors itself within itself; it has its focal point in itself, and forms itself while it revolves around this dynamic focal point. A Trinitarian relationship between the Father, the Son, and the Holy Spirit may be found in this dynamism. We, creative elements of the creative world, form the creative world. In this way, one can see that we as persons are grounded on such a Trinitarian relationship of the world. Therefore, the absolutely contradictorily self-identical world as topological being is not an emanative world nor is it a merely productive, generative world. (1945, 23)

It is not in my aim to engage with Christian theological doctrines regarding the Trinity; however, what I find remarkable is the proposition of a paradigm that informs different geographical, historical and cultural areas in a similar way.[17] This Trinitarian view of the world explains Being as a dynamic yet static whole, and conveys a complex sense of time that actually illuminates the linearity with which we perceive it from a different perspective and helps us to bracket its absoluteness. While linear time tricks us into conceiving life as an irreversible movement, which generates multiplicity and separation, the material sense of time in its absolute presence allows us to discover the absolute present as the ground on which we stand.

Teleology and morality, religion[18] and the topos of logic

While the lifeworld is the world in which actions, changes and linear time are conceivable through the negation of negation, the material world is the world of uniformity, continuity and eternal time. From this distinction it follows that it is the lifeworld that provides the ground for morality, while the material world lays the foundation for religion. The lifeworld is the realm in which because of the multiplicity of Being and movement we can conceive goals and personal choices, while the material world is the living present of the absolute in which any action would not be even possible. Yet, as we understood from the previous section, these worlds cannot be envisioned as separate from one another because the material world is the axis around which the lifeworld revolves and this movement (lifeworld's movement), which we called self-realization, is the creative act through which we become aware and awake.

> When things are acting, this action is directed towards the self-formation of the world. All activities must have some direction. Time must have its own content. This direction is the end, *telos*. Certainly, time has its own property even in the material world (. . .) time negates itself. (1945, 4)

In the material world time is an absolute present, while in the lifeworld time acquires a moral quality because it has a goal, that is directed towards the self-formation of the world. While in the material world time simply is and is the place where the being is in existence, in the lifeworld that same material time becomes the moral goal of the self-forming being. While in the material world there are no individuals, the lifeworld Being understands itself through multiplicity; it is in this multiplicity that action and hence its direction build the foundation for choices that constitute individuals' moral world. In the lifeworld the self or momentary self-determination of absolute present revolves around an axis whose goal is self-forming. Without the absolute present, though, that is, the religious ground of Being the multiplicity of Being would not be conceivable. '*The moral order of the world*' (1945, 6) *represents this synchronistic interconnection of goals whose ontological axis is spatial time, that is, the locus of the absolute present.* 'By the word world I designate' – Nishida writes – 'absolute topological being' (1945, 23). The movement of the lifeworld goes in the direction of the self-forming and the determination.

The individual's self is a topological being revolving around this absolute axis. Morality and religion, the acting world and the absolute present are strictly interconnected with each other in accruing self-awareness. The logic of topos is the expression of this place of eternal presence within the movement of self-determination. 'The contradictorily self-identical world expresses itself within itself, and in so doing forms itself' (1945, 23). In negating the negation we self-realize the goal of our own movement whose content is the eternal presence. At some point during our life each human being experiences the truthfulness of this eternity around which our life revolves; the self-evident essence of the absolute Being discloses itself through Being and in front of our beings giving sense to what we are.[19] Morality, religion and logic are the scientific description of the Trinitarian relationship of the world.[20]

One world cannot be conceived without the other; the material world *is* without the lifeworld, but its being would be unconceivable (for us) without the lifeworld. The moral world, the world whose teleological movement is morally (ought) directed towards self-determination, is the world in which the topos of being comes to a form for us. In my opinion, even Nishida's style of writing this book evokes the dialectic structure of these synchronistically interwoven worlds. As Walter Ong (1982) pointed out Nishida's style is repetitive and sometimes formulaic; in fact, it appears to me that the argument moves towards a new direction and enters in a new stanza, while remaining always in the same place in order to determine its own content.

From my point of view reading and meditating upon Nishida's text is itself a way of embodying the same ontological whole that Nishida is pointing towards, in which epistemology and ontology, meaning and being, theory and praxis are embedded and interrelated. It is thanks to Nishida's introduction of dialectical time (Kopf, 2002, 288) that the actuality of these three worlds can be conceived as a whole, despite their different layers. In this sense the interrelatedness of religion, morality and logic mirrors the Trinitarian relationship of the material, creating and lifeworlds. Without the eternal presence of material being there would be no self-affirming consciousness; without time there would be no logic of self-contradiction. In the same way, without religion, that is, the fact of our existence, morality would have no ground on which it can break through its own limits and move towards the determination of its own Being. As Nishida wrote, morality is based on its own negation (1945, 17). Necessity and freedom, being and ought are intrinsically interwoven with each other in this 'sphere with no circumference and whose center is everywhere'.

Husserl's theory of intentionality

As mentioned in the previous chapter, now that Husserl's writings are almost completely published in the Husserliana, it is becoming more and more evident that his theory of intentionality cannot be limited to his *Logical Investigations* and *Ideas*. For example, in his *Analyses Concerning Active and*

Passive Syntheses, we see Husserl analysing a wide range of intentionalities such as feeling, affective, passive, instinct and so forth.

In my *Husserl's Ethics and Practical Intentionality* (2015) I organized these forms of intentionalities in a system that I argued is the ground of Husserl's ethical science. This system became a particularly helpful framework through which to examine psychological phenomena.

In my reading of Husserl's theory of intentionalities I distinguished at least three categories of intentionality: active, passive and practical intentionality, which respectively correspond to Nishida's life, material and creating worlds. While active intentionality entails position-taking (*Stellungnahme*) and meaning-giving (*Sinngebung*) activity (Hua III, 207), passive intentionality is a synthetic process that takes place mainly on two ego-less layers: those of spontaneous and non-spontaneous syntheses (Hua XXXIII). The spontaneous syntheses bring together the percepta of our experience according to a principle of homogeneity, while the non-spontaneous one names these data. Through the layers formed by these syntheses we constitute the material core around which the meaning-giving activity of active intentionality revolves. The transition from ego-less synthetic processes to egoic meaning-giving (*Sinngebung*) activity is characterized by practical intention. In fact, the sphere of irritability (Hua XXXIII, text 1), the layer of affections and reactions, represents the lowest level of affections from which the ego emerges and reacts to the irritating affecting matter by deciding what position it is going to take (Hua XXXIII, text 1, 5, 6, 9, 10). This reactive emergence is rooted in the volitional body (Hua-Mat IV, 186) which bridges nature (passive syntheses) and spirit (active intention). The ego reacts to matter by deciding whether to accept and validate that matter as its own. Some of the material content provided to the ego will remain in the form of passive syntheses, others will be organized through values and meanings. While the realm of passivity provides heretofore formless matter with a logical or graspable form, the realm of activity is the constitutive pole through which a given number of synthetic layers are comprised in a graspable meaning. The practical intention is that phronetic act through which the subject decides to move towards a self-constituting act in recognizing the interconnection between passive syntheses and its own activity as a self-reflecting subject.[21] The bridge between active intention and passive synthesis is represented by practical intentionality, the 'Ich will und Ich tue' which operates by means of the volitional body in order to awaken (Hua-Mat IX, 128–129, 133) the ego to its present matter.

Husserl's Trinitarian relationship of the world[22]

I argue that the relationship between passive, active and practical intentionality describes a Trinitarian relationship to the world very close to Nishida's created-creating-created qua creating one. Even if Husserl does not use the expression Trinitarian, the similarity with Nishida's world view is startling. The material world – the world that stands as eternal present matter that is still ungraspable but yet present–is interwoven with the lifeworld (here Nishida's and Husserl's language overlap): namely, the world of movement in which the subject creates meanings. The layer of matter is the '*founding* stratum' (Hua I, §44) around which the awoken ego gravitates in order to realize itself, that is, determining the matter in a graspable meaning.

Similar to Nishida's view, this foundation cannot be thought in terms of a before-after but as a noetic-noematic core that entertains a threefold relationship with time and teleology; notions that I will discuss in this and the following sections.

While in Nishida we have timeless, linear and circular or dialectic time,[23] similarly in Husserl we recognize timeless, linear and phenomenological time. Similar to Nishida, Husserl's notion of time cannot be reduced to the mundane linear version; the time that knits together the passive syntheses of the material world is a living present, the eternal moment whose structure is explained in the series of protentions and retentions. This living present of consciousness is the *substratum*, the original flow or the light through which what comes to evidence is luminous (Hua XIV, 45, 301). This '*lebendige Gegenwart*' (living present) is an impressional stream[24] which continuously fills intentions/protentions. 'It is a creative primal presenting' (Hart, 1959, 25 26). This form of time constitutes the core for immanent, hyletic time[25] that organizes itself in the mundane form of time perceived by the subject in a chain of before-afters. Both in Husserl and Nishida time is not a category or a predicate, but is a *systatical*[26] *function*. Systatical, a term borrowed from physics, indicates a synthetic activity. I think that from Husserl's and Nishida's points of view human time synthetizes its eternity in a linear time which coexists with eternity; time brings formless matter to existence in an ongoing synthesis of being and meanings.

Time, like the three forms of intentionality, can be said to possess a three-fold structure that allows us to have a synchronistic relationship with the material and lifeworlds;[27] eternal, linear and dialectic time coexist because of time's systatical property.

I argue that both philosophers invite us to overcome the limits of our own immanent time in order to make contact with the eternal core through which flow our ongoing decisions, recognized or unrecognized, whereby we determine our own matter. The primordial I is first of all an *Ich kann–Ich tue* (I can–I do) that can decide to act in many different and teleologically directed ways (Hua-Mat IX, 128–129). This I as *wache Ich* (awoken I) in a moment of time (*Zeitpunkt*) functions in time (Hua-Mat IX, 133), which means it decides to renew the source of its habits or the horizon of its being with its momentous choice, *jetzigen Wahl* (Hua XXXIII: 133). As a matter of fact the subject and its world are given as a fixed picture, but one which is at the same time living and changing.[28]

In the next section I will examine what Husserl means by teleology and I will discuss how teleology can bridge for him epistemology and ontology and what consequence this has for ethics and its interpretation of reality.

Teleology in Husserl

Hartmann's critique of teleology can serve as an excellent point of departure for an investigation of Husserl's notion of teleology and the religious source of morality. Despite the fact that current debate on teleology is very complex, I will seek to summarize the debate's main positions in the following way: using teleological arguments involves at least a two-layered problem, ontological and theological. If ontological matter is teleological, then it follows that we encase the world in a theological category because the goal of this Being would revolve around a final end, God. In doing so we commit the mistake of confusing ontology (the matter) with epistemology (what we know about it) and axiology (the value we assign to that final goal).[29] In fact, if matter is teleological, then its being is explained by axiological and epistemological arguments, that is by the value that we know we assign to that arguments.

To use Hartmann's words (2002): 'teleology is the peculiarity of human nature', (*Ethics*, I, 282) and 'a choice must be made between a teleology of nature and existence in general, and a teleology of man (...). The alternative is a complete and genuine disjunction (...) On one side of the alternative stands a theory; on the other, a phenomenon (...) a philosopher (...) must give up teleological metaphysics in favor of the ethical phenomenon' (*Ethics*, I, 288). According to Hartmann if philosophers want to examine thoroughly the ethical phenomenon, they must look at existence as such and give up on using teleology as a psychological human need to make sense of the worlds. Taking sides in relation to teleology implies a choice in which the philosopher has to declare her intentions, whether to favour a theological world view or an ethical realistic one.

In *Teleologisches Denken* (1951) Hartmann distinguishes three forms of teleology. The first is the teleology of process and indicates the form of action for which the question 'why' precedes 'the what'. It is a form of teleology that Husserl rejected and resembles the Aristotelian way of conceiving teleology. A second form of teleology deals with relation of forms and is that kind of teleology that considers forms of all forms as a productive principle. Finally, there is a third kind of teleology, that is the teleology of totality in which theological or half-theological forms become the most popular form of the ultimate picture of the world (*Weltbild*). This form of teleology seems to be the most relevant for Husserl and seems the most criticized by Hartmann.

According to Hartmann (1872) this form of teleology is problematic because it confuses ontology with axiology such that 'any argument from teleologism cannot be valid, but only a flight from the horror of meaningless and contingency' (1951, 128). For Hartmann this third sense of teleology is a way of assigning values and accordingly meanings to the ontological confused mass with which the world gives itself to us. Therefore, for Hartmann this form of teleology stretches psychological demands to a historical and ontological contingency of the world operating confusion between what is ontological and what is merely axiological and psychological. This is so because the philosopher assigns matter with a value that is not intrinsic to the matter itself but to the philosopher's human need to make sense of it.

Hartmann's critique is sharp and undeniably crucial; yet, I think that his critique can be addressed using Nishida's and Husserl's view of the Trinitarian relationship of the world.

In relation to teleology Husserl wrote: 'I call teleology the form of all forms' (Ms E III, 9). In stating so Husserl seems to agree with Hartmann's second form of teleology according to which teleology is a productive principle, or in Nishida's terms a creating principle, whose action is directed to the generation of the form that determines itself while revolving around its own material axis. This second form of teleology seems to operate only on the creating (Nishida's terms) or meaning-giving (Husserl's terms) layer.

Nevertheless, in the same passage, Husserl continues, this form of teleology 'is the latest for us and the first in itself. Why? It must be the totality as totality already disclosed in its whole system of particular forms' (Ms E III, 9). This form is the latest for us because we are capable of perceiving the form of chaotic matter and recognize its value only at the very end of its unfolding process; yet it is the first in itself because without this unfolding nothing would be given to us. Once again Husserl's way of explaining teleology is very close to Nishida's and describes a triangular contingency of the world. According to this form of teleology, which corresponds to the third kind of teleology indicated by Hartmann, the level of formation is the latest for us because it requires the logic of self-contradictory identity; namely, in Husserl's terms, it requires for our egos to awaken from the state of undifferentiated matter, thereby overcoming the limits of our own contingency, and actively assigning meanings to it by means of specific, mostly logical, forms. The whole system of forms that we actively create is a way through which the totality of being discloses itself and makes itself visible to us in a 'system of particular forms'. To conclude Husserl's quote 'teleology is what makes all Being possible' for us.[30] Reality discloses itself to us through a system of forms that interpret and explain concrete Being.

Third form of teleology and time

In Husserl and Nishida, teleology explicates itself as a movement that unfolds itself through forms that mutually negate their identity; this movement is only formal because of the role played by time. In fact, eternity is synthetized by the lifeworld in a way that humans organize according to befores and afters. In Husserl and Nishida teleology is another way of explaining the interconnectedness of the material world and the lifeworld: the material world, which is given to us in a chain of nows through passive syntheses awakens us to its axiological meaning and invites us to assign an axiological and epistemological sense to matter in the shape of a linear form that is understandable for us (Hua XXI,). Reality is time – or better, reality is our epistemological and axiological interpretation of time. As mentioned before, these interwoven layers arise because time is 'an acategorical element, which cannot be registered systematically, i.e. spatially, but only systatically, when related to a combination or synthesis (systatics)' (Gebser, 2011, 51); the passive syntheses of the material world are appreciated by us in a linear time that cyclically collapses upon itself. In life individuals try to make sense of this synthesis of eternity through values first, that is the acknowledgement of the Being of that given and through meanings that explicate the sense of that eternal core. If we observe reality from the standpoint of eternal, linear and cyclical time, it might be easier to understand and accept interpretations of the real that do not conform to previously validated, intersubjective patterns.[31] To come back to what is stated in Chapter II.2, it would be easier to understand and accept reality as *real*, the intentional content, rather than *reel*, the immanent and unquestionable reality.[32]

If time is reality, teleology can be defined as an actual unfolding movement directed towards a goal only if we look at it from the point of view of lineartime. If instead we look at the actual movement from the point of view of the eternal present we would only see Being eternally disclosing itself in what the Orphics called the cosmic egg. In trying to see both layers of time we discover a dialectic or cyclical sense of time within which eternity and time coexist.

Looking at the three layers of time we realize that the leap from the ontological to the axiological and accordingly, the epistemological layer never actually takes place, because originally they are the fruit of a temporal deception. In order to investigate epistemological, axiological and ontological matter one should keep a dialectic mind open to see the operating synthesis (*Aufhebung*), which seems to comprise in itself ontological and epistemological matter.[33] Primordially teleology represents an original stillness because at its core is the eternal presence of matter; then it is also a movement whenever on the mundane level this movement awakes the self to its self-forming activity.

As Husserl writes 'If Being as transcendental Being, accordingly absolute subjectivity, is only thinkable to be in ontic universality and in a universal will related to the ideal telos, respectively to the ideal progress of teleological infinity' – in Nishida's terms if the shapeless can acquire a shape in its temporal and spatial form through an always moving action directed towards the telos of self-knowing – 'then it has to be borne in mind that this will is creative, world-creative, but in a certain sense is a creation out of nothing'[34](Ms E III, 9). Here Nishida's and Husserl's language overlap completely; the movement of creation is a creating or creative moment because it produces epistemological and axiological forms. Yet, it is a creation out of nothing (or formless Being),[35] namely a creation out of what is already created but not yet intelligible in the life world, although already synchronistically woven to it.

In that sense Hartmann's critique is correct, there is a confusion between the ontological and psychological levels. However it is a structural confusion[36] that using the radical realism of Nishida's philosophy[37] and Husserl's phenomenology, I would call the dialectic contingency of the world.

Morality and religion

The Trinitarian way of explaining the contingency of the world points to an ontological source of morality that shows morality as hardly distinguishable from other disciplines. From Husserl's and Nishida's perspectives absolute Being discloses itself to us in a teleological way and since this teleology can only be grasped through the values and the meanings we assign to it, we cannot strictly separate ethics from axiology, epistemology, theology and the psychological interpretation of all of it. Separating being from meaning would be as desperate an attempt as seeking to separate matter from form; it might be theoretically conceivable but practically impossible for our minds. The teleological form that we register in axiological and then translate in epistemological terms is inseparable from Being as it discloses itself to us.

The material world, that is, the world of the factuality of being is the world of absolute presence that reveals itself through a teleological movement. The atemporal core of Being around which the temporal self revolves in its movements of self-determinations encounters its temporal self in the religious, if not even mystical experience.

That is the reason why Husserl writes:

I also want what the churches want: to lead humanity to the Aeternitas. My task is to try to do this through philosophy. Everything that I have written up to now is only preparatory; it is only a development [Aufstellen] of methods. In the course of one's life, one unfortunately does not arrive at the core, at what is essential. It is so important for philosophy (…) to be led once more to what is essential, to truth. The question concerning ultimate reality, truth, must be the object of every true philosophy. This is my life's work. (Ms E III 11, 1934, 3b: in conversation with E. H. 1931–38)

Leading humanity to this encounter, namely the encounter with the eternal self is the teleological goal of Husserlian phenomenology. Nishida's and Husserl's Trinitarian way to explain the contingency of the world would not allow us to conceive any actual founding difference between disciplines because they all find their roots in Being as it discloses itself. On the formal level, instead, what we can actually distinguish is a deceiving difference between forms. Hence the source of morality, as much as the source of philosophy, is in Being and its absolute manifestation as eternal presence and facticity; this manifestation in the real world can speak to us and be organized by us in different ways, moral, epistemological, axiological and the like. When we encounter this absolute, our life is charged with meanings which suddenly we feel responsible for. The self-formation of those meanings is the teleological ground of morality in which axiology and ontology are joined together.

Summary

In his introduction to the translation of Nishida's works, Dilworth (1978) concludes that Husserl is an essentialist, while Nishida an existentialist. I think that in proposing such a distinction Dilworth flattens the dialectic contingency of the worlds that is presented by the two authors; essence and existence can be theoretically conceived as separate but they are ontologically interdependent in their facticity. I think that this contingency is the very core of human understanding of reality; becoming aware of it might enhance the quality of our lives. The gap between matter and form, being and existing, essence and existence are with each other in the same relationship as material world and lifeworld. One cannot separate the two without losing something essential.

In that sense, to address Vandevelde's remark (2016)[38] in relation to my analysis of Husserl's theology (Ferrarello, 2015), I would say that it is possible for Husserl to conceive of an ethics that is separate from theology, as much as it is possible to distinguish political science from ethics, or physics from mathematics. Nevertheless, it is evident, as well, that there is a foundational continuity between disciplines. The self-forming acts are aimed at different spheres of meanings and values which all revolve around the same material axis. The third sense of teleology, which as we saw influences Husserl's ethics the most in a theological direction, offers a way to explain how one can escape the deception of separating time, meanings and values.[39]

If we overcome this deception we can see how one's reality comes from an inner reconstruction of time that knits together the concreteness of being and time with our need to encase shapeless concreteness into recognizable values and intersubjective meanings. Unfortunately, as we will see from the next chapter, those whose lives happen to dwell more in eternal, motionless time have more difficulty in synthesizing Being in a way that can be intersubjectively accepted and understood.

I.4

Pathological and mystical time*

Introduction

While the previous chapter described the layers of the ethical experience (i.e. time, religious feelings, identity) from a theoretical point of view by means of a comparative reading of Husserl and Nishida, in this chapter I will explore how these theoretical findings can be applied to lived experience. The goal remains the same; namely, to understand how ethical experiences structure our view of reality and reactivate the meaning of its layers. In this chapter, I will contrast two views of reality, the schizophrenic and mystical one, which are often viewed as resembling each other, the difference being that schizophrenic experience is often considered pathological or at best hypernormal.[1]

In the previous chapter a description of reality as an intuition of oneness in all ('identity in difference') emerged as an original, creative, unifying activity, also called force of life.[2] In this chapter I will explore this primal flow and the way in which it shapes the experiences of reality reported by schizophrenics and mystics. In particular, I will expound how the triadic structure of time, which makes possible this form of intuition, conditions the way in which we relate to reality and assigns meanings and values to it. As Merleau-Ponty remarks, primary delusions and hallucinations in schizophrenia seem to be not part of this world (1962, 395) and yet they happen in this world. The main challenge a therapist has to face in working with the reported experiences of schizophrenics is how to handle the relationship between the different layers of the lifeworld, and whether or not to accept the actuality of the schizophrenics' experiences.

---

*Of course, I am aware of Heidegger's 'Being and Time'. I decided not to cite him here because it would have taken too much space for two reasons: (1) It would have required an in-depth explanation of his work which would have inevitably framed the conversation within an hermeneutic perspective that I have no interest in developing here; (2) Introducing Heidegger would have demanded a further clarification of his debt towards Husserl's notion of Dasein and Zeit.

Thus, this chapter will be divided into three sections. First, I will compare and contrast the pathological and non-pathological ways through which we gain access to the timelessness of the world. Next, I will address the way in which psychology treats the pathological access to the experience of timelessness, in particular those of schizophrenics, and I will offer my interpretation of their positionality in relation to time. Finally, I will present a view of time and reality that combines static and genetic phenomenological methods. Since these goals will demand attention and space, but at the same time the body of literature dedicated to this topic is wide, I decided to leave a footnote that illustrates the main critical positions taken in relation to the problem.[3]

Access to the other's reality

How do we practically inhabit the different layers of reality in our daily life? How can we verify for our psychological selves that the claims of physics (Carroll, 1966) or philosophy (Husserl or Nishida) regarding timelessness is true? How can we agree upon different versions of reality?

One way to address these questions is by comparing religious experiences described by mystics with hyper-normal experiences described by people diagnosed with schizophrenia. Although these two modalities of experiencing reality seem to offer a glimpse of what it really means to gain access to the absolute layer of timelessness, often described as the 'heart of reality' (Parnas & Henriksen, 2016), I agree with Steinbock (2007), Parnas and Henriksen (2016), and Zahavi (2014) when they write that these two forms of experience ought not be conflated. There is no reason for mystical experience to be labelled as pathological; in fact, while mystical experience conveys deep meanings for those who report it, what schizophrenics experience seems to be incommunicable and generate occasionally personal psychological disequilibrium.

For example, in this passage a schizophrenic patient describes her way of seeing and experiencing reality:

> There are two worlds. There is the unreal world, which is the world I am in and we are in. And then there is the real world. *The only thing that is real in the unreal world is my own self.* Everything else – buildings, trees, houses – is unreal. All other humans are extras. My body is part of the charade. There is a real world somewhere and from there someone or something is trying to control me by putting thoughts into my head or by creating (...) screaming voices inside my head. (Cited in Parnas & Henriksen, 2016, emphasis mine)

I live in a sort of bubble, where the world does not matter. *I lack synchrony* with the people around me. (Cited in Henriksen & Nordgaard, 2014, 437, emphasis mine)

In these two passages what the intersubjective 'normal' community would consider real is experienced as a 'charade' or even 'a sort of a bubble'. In this fake reality one thing at least seems real, the self and this reality seems to be the source of the suffering. In this clash of realities the individual feels alone and trapped in an asynchronous reality; reality can arrive to her only as an echo. Being human in that world does not have the same meaning as being human in the intersubjective 'normal' world, because in that fake reality the patient does not see herself as an individual, but feels 'fused with the surroundings'.[4]

Schizophrenic experience seems to happen sub specie aeternitatis, that is, it seems to be an experience in which no differences, multiplicity and segments of time actually exist. While those living in the intersubjective normal world[5] experience time in a linear way and perceive individuals as separate from each other and undertaking activities aimed at specific purposes, the schizophrenic seems to dwell in the motionless layer of reality where 'everything is unreal except for their own self'. In the previous chapter, Nishida and Husserl named these two layers of reality as lifeworld and creating (Nishida) or transcendental (Husserl) world. While this latter, the transcendental or creating one, is motionless and at the same time provides the core for what is real, the former one, the lifeworld, seems to be the world where the intersubjective community dwells. What is interesting to notice is that both mystics and schizophrenics seem to have access to the former world, though the meaning of that access for them differs. As shown in the excerpts above, schizophrenics seem to dwell in the creating world, where no time, movement and actual differences have reason to be; whereas mystics live in the lifeworld, but have occasional and meaningful glimpses of the transcendental world. While schizophrenics 'lack synchrony', mystics learn a way to gain a synchronic access to both world-layers.

As Chittick shows, mystics experience an actual meaningful dialogue between these two worlds and they sense the different quality of time that the two worlds imply. In his essay on Ibn al-Arabi's view of temporal unfolding he describes the view *sub specie aeternitatis* as a view from nowhere: 'Hudūth means to arrive newly, to come to be, to happen, to occur. It is contrasted with qidam, which means to precede, to be old, to be ancient. In technical language, Hudūth means to have an origin and to enter into time; qidam means to have no origin, to be outside of time, to be eternal' (Chittick, 2007, 3–10).[6] Yet, in Malami mystical tradition (Hanif, 2002, 424), the access to the timeless layer of reality is disciplined by the principle of sobriety in witnessing that does not equate with losing meaning (Ibn al-Arabi as read in Chodkiewicz, 1993); gaining an access to that reality and losing the meaning of it is not the actual goal of the mystical practice. What should be pursued is the achievement of a sense that can increase the well-being of human community.

Thus, schizophrenics and mystics seem to share a related experience of time and reality but in two different ways: first, while for mystics linear time and lifeworld seem to be exceptional, for schizophrenics the exceptionality equates to a timeless normality within the creating world; second, these reversed positions are such that for mystics their experience of the creating world is meaningful, for schizophrenics the experience of the creating world is the norm while the lifeworld is alienating and profoundly disorienting. In the next section I will start from a description of the commonalities recurring between these two forms of experiences with the hope that the non-pathological experience of timelessness might bring some clarity in understanding the pathological one. The overall goal is to see if by using the knowledge offered by mystics, it is possible to find a way to revert the process and use it theoretically as a way to envision the schizophrenic's experience as meaningful rather than meaningless.

'Into the Heart of Reality': Analogies

Both mystics and schizophrenics claim that the reality they experience is 'the heart of reality' (Stace, 1960, 72); this seems to be the first strong commonality between the two. Both believe to have attained a profound and penetrating insight into *another dimension of reality* that is more meaningful, from an ethical and psychological point of view, than the reality that is commonly defined as real. Becoming aware of the heart of reality shows an axiological core of Being around which a deepest sense of identity can be shaped by the rupture from the worlds and the self that they knew. Even though, in both cases, those involved in this kind of experience are aware of being witnessing an essential truth that resides outside the realm of ordinary experience, language and rules of logic – as Conrad puts it, 'outside the categories of comprehensibility' (Conrad, 2002, 110) – they know that this essential truth is more meaningful than any other truth attainable in the ordinary world. The mystic looks at the world of the natural attitude as veiled, and contrasts it with the more real experience of the world, while schizophrenics would not make such a distinction, because what they are seeing or hearing (like 'auditory' or 'visual hallucinations') is just self-evidently real to them, it is not contrasted with another view of the world.

In the passage cited earlier, the patient thinks that people behave politely towards her, even if they know that she is an alien. Her sense of self is stationed on multiple layers – the same layers I was describing in Chapter I.2 – there is an onlooker, which observes herself from a distance and sees how the real self is trapped in the fake dimension that most people call reality and there are three more competing egos, the transcendental, the psychological and awake ego, that do not seem to find a fluid synthesis and interaction with each other. In fact, the psychological ego seems to awake in a transcendental dimension rather than in a psychological one and from that layer it cannot encounter the intersubjective view of reality in which other psychological egos dwell. Consequently, it finds itself isolated and asynchronous with respect to other people.

The layers of reality with which mystics and schizophrenics report contact coincide with the theoretical findings I discussed in chapters I.2 and I.3. In Chapter I.2 I named these layers transcendental, practical and passive,[7] and I described how they correspond to the transcendental, awake and psychological ego respectively, and to the three layers of time: timeless, here-and-now and linear time.[8] In Chapter I.3 these layers were examined in the light of Nishida's radical analysis of pure experience and Husserl's phenomenology in order to illuminate the relationship between passive receptive matter and lifeworld. Passive receptive matter is a reality in which neither time nor individuality have yet come to be grasped; that reality can be compared to the transcendental reality since it represents a layer for which reality is possible. The lifeworld is the concreteness of reality that is shaped and grasped through the awakening of the practical ego, which synthesizes the concreteness into understandable values and meanings.

Stace (1960, 148) names this exceptional interaction between layers of reality as *transsubjective*; the term refers to the fact that the layers involved in this kind of experience are not located in one ego position (as described in Chapter I.2), but instead they represent a *sub specie aeternitatis* stance that can be contemplated by the self only in terms of subjective (and bodily) limits that it can witness but not overcome. As Stace remarks, transubjective experience yields a disclosure of the Real accompanied by a greater sense of certainty because, in contrast to natural experience, transubjective experience is lived on multiple rather than just one layer of reality. On this point, Stace cites an interview in which a mystical experience is expressed in these terms:

> I experienced a complete certainty that at that moment I saw things as they really were [N.M.]; I saw no new thing but I saw all the usual things in a miraculous new light – in what I believe is their true light (...). *I have looked into the heart of reality*; I have witnessed the truth. (Montague, quoted in Stace, 1960, 72, p. 83f.)

Even if, as Merleau-Ponty wrote, objective reality is an abstraction (1945),[9] the lines cited by Stace point to the fact that, for the mystic, reality entails a form of objectivity; yet this objectivity emerges from a radical self-reflection and self-transformation, which is a constituent of the experience itself. Both mystics and schizophrenics have the certainty that what they experience is the truth, while what is commonly accepted as true in the intersubjective lifeworld is only an opaque image of it.[10] They can look at the heart of reality which, as Stace writes, represents the transcendental layer of the real, that is, the condition of possibility for the real to be as such. Unfortunately, because of our biological limits, this layer of reality is the most difficult one to reach for us.

The second strong affinity between the pathological and non-pathological sense of reality is the experience of timelessness which is attained through a *self-distancing attitude*.[11] In both cases distancing from and being disinterested towards the lifeworld involve the application of what phenomenology recognizes as epoche, that is, a suspension of common assumptions (Overgaard, 2015) which opens the doors to a place of spiritual solitude from which one's sense of self is weakened and the ego desists to be itself (*désistement de soi meme*; Depraz, 2001). On the basis of mystics' self-reports, Steinbock (2007) remarked how this attitude would facilitate the emergence of a mystical view of reality as absolute comeliness of time. To cite Chittick (2007, 3), the constitution of the Real seems to manifest itself to us as an 'absolute comeliness'.[12] From the point of view of mystical traditions, as Chittick remarks, new arrival is the name that one can use to fully explain the reality situation that makes time manifest itself as a being. Being comes to space as a transformation of absolute timelessness in time.

'It is the pervasive and collective capacity of the events [read 'new arrivals', hawādith] of the world to transform continuously, that is the actual meaning of time (…) The soul, however, has no essential limits tying it to one form or another, even though its very essence demands that it arrive newly forever', (2007, 13, 14 passim). The way in which our sense of being an individual attaches to the experience of the true reality is synthesized through and by time. It is through the coming of time in the actual being that I can find myself as a segment of the new arrival occupying my own place in the continuum of the events; in timelessness instead, the ego is not even a segment yet and it cannot be, otherwise he would be immediately back in time. In timelessness the ego can exist only as an onlooker, that is, only if it applies the epoche, and witnesses its being from the outside. As an onlooker it would not perceive its mundane individuality,[13] but it would be capable to sense the absolute indifference and stillness of timelessness in which its core is merged. Apparently, schizophrenics and mystics can gain a privileged access to this standpoint;[14] yet, as I will describe in more detail in the next section, schizophrenics seem to have more issues in allowing the transition back to the natural and psychological ego. In fact, it seems that their onlooker awakens in a practical ego that communicates with the transcendental and not with the psychological ego. For this reason the 'absolute comeliness' that the onlooker witnesses cannot find an adequate language and cannot be satisfactorily translated in meanings, forms, or numbers that the psychological ego can share with the intersubjective reality.

To summarize, both in schizophrenic and mystical experience there is an emergent contact with timelessness and the truth that on the one hand requires a particular way of self-disposing in an absolute 'place' (e.g. isolation, denial of place [dépaysement], prayer), and on the other this kind of experience enables the individual to look at a layer of reality that is felt immediately as a bearer of meaningful truths and values that they recognize as the heart of reality. In the case of mystics, the experience might be organized according to a principle of sobriety whose goal is to make the content of experience available to a higher understanding of the human condition; whereas for schizophrenics, since this form of experience does not originate from an actual change of state, there is no actual principle they can use to preserve a meaningful contact with the intersubjective world. As Parnas (2007) noticed, both mystics and schizophrenics may suffer from a failing sense of being one with oneself (automatic, pre-reflective self-coincidence or 'radical self-recognition' [Parnas, 2007]), but in the case of mystics, by practicing occasionally a reflective self-identification, they can recover a more solid sense of self.

'Into the heart of reality': Differences

It is in relation to the problem of self-recognition and self-identification that a wide gap seems to emerge between mystical and schizophrenic experience of reality.

As mentioned above, while mystics preserve a form of witnessing that allow them to give meaning to the annihilating experience they go through, schizophrenics do not seem to hold a sense of self because they seem to live their life from the station of timelessness – from which they derive a sense of estrangement. Hence they seem to fully identify themselves with a reality that differs from the one accepted by the intersubjective community. Moreover, since their sense of self is very thin and always threatened by the absoluteness of reality, they cannot assume any self-distancing attitude and witness their own reality from the onlooker position. Differently from schizophrenics, mystics seem to be able to integrate their sense of extraordinary insights into a mundane-spiritual existence because their access to the absolute is not fully caught in the motionless absolute but is witnessed by an onlooker; this allows them to switch more easily from one to another layer of reality. On the other hand, the life of many people affected with schizophrenia seems to be motionless, that is, their main sense of temporality seems to be in the now, an eternal present with a fixed, immutable past and seemingly no openness and projects for the future.[15]

Consequently, schizophrenia has been proposed to be a specific disturbance of 'ipseity' or 'minimal self'[16] (Cermolacce, Naudin, & Parnas, 2007; Nelson, Parnas, & Sass, 2014; Sass & Parnas, 2003) because it destabilizes the very sense of self-presence and of being a self-coinciding subject of experience and action. Moreover, I would say that this disturbance more than the cause is the consequence of the way in which they synthesize time. By necessity the disturbance of ipseity originates from the timeless layer of reality in which they seem to dwell for most of their life; this layer of reality does not allow for the constitution of a thick self or for the presence of an onlooker because the absolute by definition cannot tolerate differences.

Accordingly, schizophrenics do not seem to hold a minimal sense of self because the layer of reality in which they normally conduct their lives is timeless and absolute. In that space there is no room for a minimal self.[17] Generally, the first-person perspective arises as an act of active intention of the psychological ego, which interprets the passive matter (in this case, 'I-me-myself') of acts through meanings and values. Inhabiting a first person involves an affective presence that connects passive receptive matter to the meaning-giving activities of one's awakening I. In this triad, the minimal self is, according to Hart, an affective sense of self-presence, self-familiarity or self-intimacy that persists across time and changes of modalities of consciousness that permeate any particular intentional act (Hart, 2009). Accordingly, the minimal self would allow for that affective constancy that would explain the interconnection between the passive ego-less self and the active ego.[18] The minimal self participates with the awoken ego in order to enable an understanding of pre-predicative receptive matter and its combination with the basic structures of consciousness.[19]

In the pre-reflective milieu, the very alterity or the 'me-not me' (self-other) that is just awoken from the passive receptive matter normally articulates itself as a platform for the formation of meanings that transcend the limits of the temporality of the minimal self. At the level of passivity the primordial, tacit threads of practical intentionality anchor us to the lifeworld through the formation of 'passive syntheses' (Husserl, 1973), 'common sense', 'natural self-evidence' (Blankenburg, 1971, 2001) or pre-reflective immersion in the world ('Being-in'; Heidegger, 2007). Then, the awakening of the I along with its transcendental activity enable the constitution of meanings and values that shape timeless matter into a graspable form.

Apparently, some schizophrenics cannot fully close this circle for two reasons, a structural and an environmental one. First, as explained before they seem to be dwelling in the absolute layer of reality and second, the treatment they receive seems to reinforce the idea that what they live is delusional. While this negation might help them avoid self-harming, it does not help them to create a space of intimacy with *their* lifeworld (on intimacy more in chapters I.5 and I.6) – which is lived mostly as a nightmare in which they are stuck. As Hart noticed (2009), the lack of minimal self equates to a lack of self-intimacy and self-familiarity that resist the foundation of the identity (Hart, 2009). In their experience the layer of lifeworld reality that should be conducive to the constitution of meanings and values capable of interpreting primal matter do not find any outlet, and people affected with this disorder are not given the possibility of establishing a space of intimacy with their passive and receptive matter; instead, primal matter is voided of meanings and values and thus ceases to be consistent with their experience.

Since schizophrenics are told not to confirm their version of reality, their relationship with the pre-reflective matter seems to be empty of affective tonality. They are not helped to establish any intimacy with their pre-reflective life and therefore the minimal self or ipseity becomes even thinner and weakened because its roots are cut.

Taking Husserl's and Nishida's point of view we can say that our sense of self is grounded in Nothingness, a rich nothingness that encompasses timelessness and passive receptive matter. If the materiality of that nothingness is disconnected from our meaning activity layer, no living self can emerge because the self would be missing the contents that foster its meanings and values. In these cases, the challenge the self faces is to create a connection with a frightening, timeless nothingness and the world of meanings and values that that nothingness might assume.

Stigmatizing time

To expand on the interesting connection between time and psychopathology,[20] there is an interesting study conducted by Minkowski in which he raises an important and simple question: 'Where exactly is the discordance between psyche (the schizophrenic's one) and our own?'(1958, 131). The answer that the author gives lies, in fact, in time. Minkowski had the opportunity to work very closely, night and day, with a client who was affected with schizophrenia; in relation to him he wrote: 'I now knew that he would continue to go on, day after day, swearing that he was to be tortured to death that night (...). Our thinking is essentially empirical; we are interested in facts insofar as we can use them as a basis for planning the future. This carry-over from past and present was completely lacking in him' (1958, 132).

According to Minkowski, his client's basic problem resulted from the way in which he conceived of temporality. Minkowski wrote: 'Could we not suppose that the more basic disorder is the distorted attitude toward the future, whereas the delusion is only one of its manifestations?' (1958, 132). According to his findings, schizophrenics do not have the sense of future, past and present as segments separated from each other in a linear way. For them time is a homogeneous compound in which no sense of self and moral growth can actually emerge, because there is no reason to differentiate between them. All the threats that undermine the schizophrenic's stability seem to come from what is outside that compound, as a distant echoing world that continuously throws off balance the actuality of the other world one. For this reason Mikowski concludes that schizophrenics lack a proper sense of time (1958, 132).

While the study as a whole is engaging, I find this conclusion stigmatizing towards time and schizophrenic patients as well. In fact, as we saw above and in the previous chapter, schizophrenics' and mystics' way of seeing time is in one sense closer to the essence of time itself than the linear way of interpreting it. It does seem that schizophrenics experience time and along with it the reality that is synthesized through time in a way that is qualitatively different from most people; but I would not call it delusional because it adheres to the reality of time much more than our linear intersubjective perception of it does. It would be unfair towards the sense of intimacy that they need to establish with their own roots. We cannot claim that our way of thinking is empirical because it is fact based, while their way is delusional because it is not grounded in any factuality. Both ways are based on facts, even though they are synthesized in different ways. What they are experiencing is as factual as our experience is, but it is rooted in a concreteness that escapes our way of ordering the events. Denying the actuality of that reality equates to stigmatizing time (the time that physics can explain in fact, the reversible one) and to cutting the roots of the passive syntheses on which individuals can build a space of intimacy with their sense of identity and meanings. By stigmatizing time I mean the stigma that we put on the kind of time that we cannot immediately understand, which we dismiss as pure fantasy or, at times, delusion.

Hence, I think that Minkowski's strategy to deny the consistency of that reality is an unfair treatment of schizophrenics' experience of time.[21] While I understand that the goal of such strategy is to reassure the patients and help them ground themselves in an intersubjective shared reality, I do not think it can actually be reassuring. Personally, in a reversed situation, I would be frightened if I were surrounded by people who want to convince me that there are aliens waiting to kidnap me and bring me on their spaceship; instead if there were someone open to meet me in the middle, maybe that person would win my trust and I might feel willing to share my view of reality with hers.[22] This is even truer, if we know for a fact that in physics and in neurology[23] non-linearity is easier to explain than linearity. It would be intellectually disloyal to the schizophrenics to negate the truthfulness of their sense of reality and time, especially if we know that science agrees with them and accordingly, the intersubjective way of experiencing reality does not seem to be the only one. I named this chapter pathological and mystical time and I decided to include it in this collection because we have an ethical responsibility in relation to the understanding of time and the sense we make of it. Our identity and the meanings that our life can take in relation to time can change drastically according to the relationship we entertain with it. Certainly, the way in which schizophrenics live time is unaligned with the time as it is intersubjectively validated in our world and that makes this world-time unable to fulfil their function. Yet, human imagination and fantasy are such that, if attached to a loyal sense of reality, they can offer many creative ways to organize the different layers of reality.

Minkowski reports having the following dialogue with the same patient and he was trying to convince him of the inactuality of his experience: 'Look here, you can believe me when I assure you that nothing is threatening you (...).' The patient answers: 'I have to admit that so far you've always been right, but that doesn't mean that you'll be right tomorrow.' To that Minkowski's remark is '(...) this reasoning indicated a profound disorder in his general attitude toward the future; that time which we normally integrate into a progressive whole was here split into isolated fragments' (1958, 132).

I agree with Minkowski's conclusions about schizophrenics' sense of time; their sense of time does not allow for any completion into a progressive whole, but this does not mean that we should deny the truthfulness of that sense of time or oblige them to stay in our stream of time because, as we saw in the previous chapter, our reality too is at its core grounded in that same timeless time. As he noticed in relation to this patient, 'The future was blocked by the certainty of a terrifying and destructive event' (1958, 133); this meant 'that his life-impetus could not spring from the present toward such a distorted future' (1958, 133). Hence, 'delusions and depressions come from the inability to become better person in the future, to evolve as human beings. Our entire evolution consists in trying to surpass that which has already been done. When our mental life dims, the future closes in front of us, while at the same time the feeling of positive actions of the past disappears' (1958, 138).

Rather than coming from the failure of being better persons in the future, I believe that delusions and depressions come from a stigmatizing attitude towards time and its layers; this stigmatization closes for them the doors to any possible experience of intimacy towards their inner world of concrete passive syntheses. Since the matter of their lived experience is not fully acknowledged in its actuality, its sense is lost. This entails the loss of the space of intimacy too[24] because they cannot reconnect with the matter of their passive experience and accordingly gather a fulfilling meaning for their lives. If the space of concrete experience is precluded to them as something bad and delusional, their sense of reality will be rarefied and floating, nothing would acquire meanings because nothing would be, since everything would be a lie. In Conrad's description of psychotic episodes he refers to the missing connection to the passive affective matter in this way: 'The revelatory articulation of delusion is often preceded by an increase of basic affective tone (*erhöhte Bodenaffektivität*).' Before a psychotic episode the person tries to reconnect to the affections that belong to the passive realm of his/her life and convey their meanings; but since this meaning and value transformation is not possible, this effort is 'followed by an atmosphere of apprehension, free-floating anxiety or insecurity (occasionally of elation or ecstasy), perhaps of something impending, "something in the air" (*Wahnstimmung*). The patient increasingly feels as if he is at the very center of what is happening (incipient "anastrophic" experience)'. I believe that the anxiety is triggered by the impending sense of frustration due to the impossibility of formalizing and transforming into graspable meanings the concreteness of their lives.[25] 'However, in this state of uncertainty, the sense of uncertainty is itself "absolutely certain"' (Müller-Suur, 1950, 45; our translation). The patient may be feeling uncertain about what is going on but he has absolutely no doubt that something is happening. As stated above, they are looking at the heart of reality – denying that reality would be as useless as harmful.

Defending time and its ways

In relation to time Gebser (2011) writes, 'Time has us because we are not yet aware of its entire reality'.[26] In fact, according to Gebser, our limits in understanding time impairs, to a certain extent, our sense of reality and the quality of our life. '"I have no time" – this million-fold remark by man today is symptomatic. Time, even in this still negative form is his overriding preoccupation; but when speaking of time, man today still thinks of clock time. How shocked he would be if he were to realize that he is also saying "I have no soul" and "I have no life"!'[27] Our soul is our time – if we deny time one of its dimensions, we are denying our soul the opportunity to breath, or more simply to exist. Gebser, of course, is not the only one to have proposed a connection between time and soul;[28] whether in a philosophical and poetic way with

Augustine's Confessions where time is explained as *distentio animi* (*Conf.* XI, 24, 31, 28, 37), or in another way with James where time is connected to the feeling of the now,[29] the distinctive connection of time and soul has always been apparent. Yet, curiously, we seem to forget how deeply an alteration of our sense of time can affect the sense of reality, values and meanings upon which we build our sense of self. As Ey (1973) remarked, in schizophrenia the fluidity of the experience of a delusional mood condenses into a sense of an insidious or more sudden alien presence (co-presence), a sentiment of anonymous, intrusive, otherness or alterity in the midst of the patient's self-intimacy or 'sphere of ownness' (*l'experience d'alterité*) (Ey, 1973). In this case reality emerges as an alterity, as a missing connection with the passive syntheses – the affective matter organized in the timeless time of a now. This missing connection constitutes, I believe, the noematic substratum for that which appear to us as psychotic projections, but are for them the expression of what is real.

Any viewpoint one decides to adopt on time affects strongly the view of reality; as Huw Price (1996, 4) argued, one should assume a 'view from nowhen', an Archimedean viewpoint *outside* time, in order to pay adequate attention to the temporal character of the world. We are creatures *in* time, and this has a very important effect on how we think *about* time and the temporal aspects of reality. Many schizophrenic-type patients do not seem to live in 'a flesh-and-blood world of shared action and risk but a "mind's-eye world"' (1994, 46), in the world of another time. As remarked by Parnas (1993), the 'mind's eye' (Schreber, 2000) or in Nishida's terms the 'reversed eye' do not refer to an act of introspection or imagination, but it indicates another ontological dimension, the absolute one. Schreber (2000) compares, in fact, the notion of seeing with the 'mind's eye' (*geistigen Auge*) to the 'bodily eye' (*körperlichen Auge*). He writes: 'I use here the expression "seeing with the mind's eye" (...) because I cannot find a more suitable one in our human language. We are used to thinking all impressions we receive from the outer world are mediated through the five senses, particularly that all light and sound sensations are mediated through eye and ear. This may be correct in normal circumstances' (Schreber, 2000, 120). Schreber used these terms in order to articulate his experience of continual communication, through 'nerve-contact' and 'rays', with God. Schreber's notion of the 'mind's-eye' seems to echo Böhme's and Nishida's notion of the 'reversed eye', which reflects a breakthrough into the ultimate ground of a temporal reality, that is, the experience of the primal flow of reality as an original, creative meta-noetic activity.

Geistiges and *körperlichen Auge* (spiritual and bodily eye) are a useful image to keep in mind the, at least twofold, layers of time through which we screen our view on reality and to remind us how that view can differ from the intersubjective common one.

The spiritual and bodily eye can be comparable to the static and genetic eye mentioned in Chapter I.1. The static eye is the lens through which we see our presence in time throughout the constitution of the real, while the genetic one represents the regard from the nowhen point of view. In static phenomenology constitution is explained from the viewpoint of an I whose descriptions are based upon the observation of static objects. In contrast, for genetic phenomenology the I is not regarded as pre-given but rather as emergent;[30] hence the arising of objects for an "I" is not distinguished from the constituted arising of the I itself. While the static approach describes phenomena as they appear in the present, in the genetic approach phenomena are seen in the context of their history of sedimentation, a history that contributes to the constitution of their matter. A way to help schizophrenics to introduce an onlooker to their world would be for us to keep both eyes open and appreciate both layers of time (even if the sense of one of these layers would completely escape us) and check our sense of reality from both points of view.

Summary

In this chapter I showed how the layered sense of time, ego and world can affect our ethical constitution of reality and identity. To this purpose I compared and contrasted the experience of reality from the point of view of mystics and schizophrenics; from this analysis it emerged that schizophrenics have more problems in shifting from one to another layer of reality because they seem to be dwelling in the timeless and absolute layer of time. Assuming a stigmatizing attitude towards time, or more precisely their experience of timeless time and denying its veracity would shrink the space of intimacy that schizophrenics already struggle to have with the concreteness of their real life; while using a spiritual and bodily eye, or assuming a static and genetic attitude with which we look at the real as subjects and at the same time as selfless and timeless presences might improve the chances for schizophrenics to form an onlooker that can witness the events in the timeless world and enhance the synchronicity of these events with the lifeworld. To conclude I believe that an approach to the experience of timelessness that keeps both eyes open, the spiritual and corporeal, the static and genetic, would allow professionals to help schizophrenics to create a self-witness of their reality similar to the self-witnessing of mystics in a way in which a constituting meaning activity is possible. Helping people to live with the genetic and a static eye open in order to witness the ongoing becoming might improve the well-being of patients and might help us to gather a better understanding of our self and time.

I.5

The ethics of intimacy

Introduction

Is an intimate experience something to which we give consent? Do intimate bonds allow us to discover something new about ourselves? If so, is that which we discover something we really want to know about ourselves? This chapter will investigate the lived experience of intimacy and its ethical implications with respect to the problem of consent, within the constitution of our psychological and moral identity.

In order to investigate this phenomenon, I will focus on what Husserl calls lower spirit, higher spirit and wakeful ego. I will then describe the genetic constitution of intimate bonds as well as the generative web of instincts, habits and values in which intimate love, in particular, expresses itself as a bond-forming force.

The method I will use, as in earlier chapters, is composed of a *destruens* and *construens pars* and will make use of both theoretical and practical data. The goal remains the same as in the other chapters: to analyse the phenomenon of intimacy in order to reactivate its meaning. For this to happen we need to explore the psychological and ethical layers of the phenomenon as they impact our sense of reality. Once again, in considering this phenomenon I will combine the static and genetic viewpoint so that the complexity of intimacy generative and static structure can be grasped. Hence, these two chapters, chapters I.5 and I.6, complement each other. In Chapter I.5 I will explore the theoretical findings concerning intimacy and in Chapter I.6 I will turn to the related practical data. In both cases I will deconstruct the phenomenon into its most essential parts in order to name its layers and reassemble them with the hope that new active meanings will present themselves.

Lower and higher spirit

For Husserl the volitional body (Hua-Mat IV, 186) is a multilayered unit comprised of strata, including both the material and immaterial, which can be categorized into three supersets: material things, living body and the spiritual I (*Ideas* II and *Ideas* I, 1989, chapters 1 to 3; Husserl, 2002, 185–186). According to this structure the volitional body cannot be considered exclusively either a spiritual or a material whole;[1] thereby, if one wants to understand how an ethical subject engages with the world, one needs to inquire into the realm of the 'material spirit', that is several degrees from the most material to the most ethereal to explain how the spirit engages with its natural layers.

To clarify this point it is helpful to refer to the sixth chapter of volume 37 of Husserliana in which Husserl describes Geist (the spirit) as characterized by inferior and superior qualities (Hua XXXVII, 107). The inferior spirit represents the layer of lower affection, which I will describe in the second part of the chapter as the generative web of drives, desires, instincts and habits. On this level the spirit is not yet an ego; instead, it is the flow of that which is primitive and original. This is the level of the spirit that is the closest to Nature. Nature here signifies an underlying whole that expresses an ontological lawfulness (Hua XXXVII, 103)[2] and a universal interconnectedness that cannot be intellectually understood but only felt through the sphere of affections or sensations (*Gemüt*).

On this level spirit is a whole of primal affections and instincts that is continuously in a process of being sedimented as habitus[3] in the realm of passivity or subpersonal spirit (Hua XXXIX, 422, 483). As Moran (2011) remarks it is through habits that meaning (as in *Sinnhaftigkeit*) and sense (Husserl's *Sinnesgestalten*) can be constituted, and therefore the personal characteristics can be determined and sedimented on many different levels. Motivations, interests and volitions flow from this sedimentation. In *Ideas* II, §§54–56, Husserl connects 'habit' (*Gewohnheit*) with 'the fundamental lawfulness of spiritual life' (*Die Motivation als Grundgesetz der geistigen Welt*). Indeed, habit functions as a form of primitive 'association' (*Assoziation*) through which the lower spirit sediments its basic character and accordingly the core of its motivational life. 'The similar motivates the similar under similar circumstances' (quoted in Moran, Hua IV, 225; Eng. trans. 236).

Motivation is not something originally connected to volition or desire or an ego's ends, because original motivation is egoless and grounded in the organic material level. As a matter of fact, motivation is a passive force that irrationally or pre-rationally moves the hyletic flow, affecting the biological body and turning it into a subject. It is through this motivation that we come to experience desire which gives birth to the subject.[4]

'The first law' (Hua IV, 222; Eng. trans. 234) of motivation is rooted in this continuous tendency to be. We are motivated because our biological body (*Körper*, i.e. a body that is not ours yet) is constantly encountering nature and feeling evidence that is the ground of axiological, aesthetic, practical and theoretical values. Struck by this flow, the Body (Hua XXXVII, 114) feels an immediate rightness that it experiences as truthful. This bodily (*Leibhaftig*) encountered truthfulness founds the value itself – or what is believed to be true – as an immediate hyletic datum. The beliefs, habits, affections do not entail any active position-taking because they are the original core for the constitution of the ego. The encounter represents the birth of emotional consciousness (Hua XXXVII, 117), that is, the a priori condition and eidetic laws (Hua XXXVII, 118, 115) for any correct act.

The superior spirit is the layer of spirit that constitutes itself as an I and participates in the constitution of its meaning. On this level, hyletic matter becomes an I that infinitely clarifies its core of habitus and action (Hua XXXVII, 104). In the *Analyses* Husserl writes:

> The part 'demands' the whole – something uniform awakens something else that is uniform, which is not yet at all constituted as a unity explicitly for itself; and it does not demand the whole by a pure and simple awakening, but rather by a co-connected 'expectation', by the demand as coexisting as co-belonging to the unity. Even the force of this apperceptive expectation increases with the number of 'instances' – or with habit, which amounts to the same thing. (Hua XI, 190; Eng. trans. 240)

On this level motivations interweave with the egoic sphere. According to Husserl there are essential laws that order matter into a uniform and homogeneous core; this natural necessity or immediate sense of rightness strikes the body and triggers its reaction. In this way the body transforms a flow of indistinct hyletic data into a homogeneous unit (Hua XXXVII, 102). On this level subjective bodies are motivated in the sense that they are mere functions for varied forms of consciousness (Hua XXXVII, 101): emotive, logical and practical (*et alia*) consciousness. For example, while logical consciousness determines its awakening through reflectively grasped meanings, practical consciousness does through decisions, aesthetic consciousness through perceptions, and so forth (Hua XXXVII, 117). The varying hyletic demands that impinge upon the ego shape it functionally, prompting the ego to constitute itself in these varied modes.

Every act carries a sense that Husserl calls *propositions*. Every proposition is an attempt to recover and clarify the felt sense of immediate evidence (what I will later call values) and truthfulness felt by the consciousness in a previous encounter (Hua XXXVII, 118). At this level motivation has to do with what the ego considers it right to do. In the hyletic encounter there is a felt sense that is later recovered and clarified in the form of a value. The lawfulness is determined in an intelligible sense through which the motivational force turns from something hyletic and egoless into something reflexive and personal.

In the next section I will first describe how love runs through the lower and higher spirit in connecting the degrees of our material and spiritual life; then I will describe the space of intimacy that love discloses.

Love and the constitution of the spirit

According to Husserl, among all the sentiments love is the one that entails a true awakening (Husserl Ms E III 4, 12b). From Husserl's perspective it is through love that we can gather a privileged access to our lower and higher spirit; hence to our ego-less and egoic life.

Through love lower and higher levels can be awoken and connected to each other, first through desires, then through a volitional acknowledgment of their meanings and values. On the lower level Husserl describes desires as not simply a 'turning toward' but a 'striving after' (*Analyses*, Ibid., 282). 'Desire', he writes, 'is a tendency that occurs in the way that both passivity as well as activity are carried out, everywhere an intentionality of feeling in the mode of striving [and] has its positivity and negativity, like feeling in general. Its fulfillment is a relaxation that results from realizing [the striving, etc.], in the change into the corresponding joy of fulfillment: At root, joy lies in the arrival of what was lacking' (Ibid., 282). Desire is a tendency that connects passive and active layers of our actions; in this sense it is considered as belonging to the intentionality of feeling.[5] The fulfilment of this intentional striving (or the lack of it) leads to a sense of joy that gives (or subtracts) meanings and values to the experiential goal that was felt as desirable to us. This shows us desire represents one of the vessels that leads our lower drives to the shores of our higher spirit. A better understanding of the intentional structure of this tendency can be attained if we look at the crossroads of intentionalities discussed in Chapter I.2: the intersection between passive syntheses and active intentionality as they are informed by practical intentionality. Husserl in fact calls intentionality of feeling (affective intentionality) the mode of striving that aims to connect passivity, that is, what is not yet subjective, with activity, that is, the meaning-giving activity through which we discover our being-a-subject.[67] In this encounter joy arises as the outcome of two intentions, whose structure is different from one another. On the one hand, passive syntheses are egoless material fusions of affectant and affected which take place according to a principle of homogeneity.⁸ Their 'hidden teleology' (C, 70; K, 71) moves towards a sense that needs to be recognized and unfolded. On the other hand, when the subject is awoken by these syntheses, it activates itself in giving a meaning to this already-present sense. Oftentimes, the problematic aspect of this process lies in the communication between lower (passive syntheses) and higher spirit (meaning activity position). The awakening (practical intention) in fact invites the almost-awake organic body still involved in the ongoing activity of the passive syntheses to take responsibility for its passive syntheses and interpret them in the right way; since the synthetic process is an unstoppable one, which continues even when our organic life transforms in something else, the ideal of actively taking responsibility for the fullness of passive syntheses transcends the capacity of the personal ego – therefore, the proper attitude of the personal ego in relation to its passive ground is one of respect and humility. As Hart noticed (1992, 231), through the active recognition of passive syntheses we displace our self within a territory that we do not yet know and in principle can never know exhaustively. Our self is seen as a first Other that we want (or not) to recognize and let harmonize with the space of world in which we have just awoken. This first encounter between passive syntheses and active intentionality is what I call intimacy, and it is this intimacy which opens the individual to the vertical stream of love. The first intimate bond we create is with our passive selves and then others; this connection is established through our ability to be awake and create a contact between our lower and higher spirit.⁹ The next section will focus on the structure of wakefulness and the ego's volitional stance in relation to it.

Wakefulness and consent[10]

Since love among all the sentiments involves a true awakening (Husserl Ms E III 4, 12b), love is also that connecting force that brings matter to unity; this unity can be interpreted as individuals' or groups' identity. Through the gradual (Hua 42, 36) awakening my I is affected by passive syntheses and starts acquiring knowledge in relation to its lower matter. On this level the volitional body is called to take a position of validation that results in the acceptance or rejection of what is offered to it. This is the subject's most primitive act of moral identity.

> Issuing from the passive perceptual situation, letting oneself be determined such that one has a judicative position and then has a judicative determination. Thus, we also understand why in practice, judging and conviction become equivalent expressions. We will see shortly that this position-taking

> or this group of position-takings that occur here are completely non-independent from the standpoint of intentionality, namely, insofar as they presuppose the occurrences of passive doxa. Let us note in advance that these position-takings, this validation and its transformations, further, are not to be confounded with other modes of comportment by the ego that belong to the sphere of judgment, especially not with active explication, colligation, comparison, differentiation, and the like – all of the operations to which we are indebted for the logical forms of different state-of-affairs. (*Analyses*, 93/53)

As evident in this passage, validations are the most primitive acts through which one allows oneself to take a specific shape as a person. Whenever we take a position that validates or invalidates the passive syntheses of affections, whether this validation results in the acceptance of external interpretation of our character or in the refusal of the values projected upon us, every validation is going to shape our sense of self. In the next sections I will expand upon the discussion of how instincts and habits interact with this act of validation, acceptance and consent. It is important here to note that the volitional body allows the transition between lower and higher spirit, passive and active intentionality through an act of consent, 'a yes or no' that meaningfully shapes what we are in relation to ourselves and the society in which we live. As Husserl writes 'the realm of activity is *eo ipso* a realm of free volitional activity' (*Analyses*, 283/11). On the level of active volitions we decide how our living body will interact with its matter and give a meaning to it, on the level of passive volitions our body decides which passive matter will affect our awakening and how it will do so, and if so, how to handle that responsibility. The psychical ego's reflective choice to say 'yes' to a given content of passive intentionality, through practical intentionality, is what Husserl terms 'consent'.

> The noetic Yes and No, however, arise from taking a position specifically as judging. (...) Here, of course, this correlate is the noematic 'valid' or 'invalid' arising in the objective sense; it occurs in the objective sense with the character of being declared valid or invalid by the ego. (*Analyses*, 94)

Consent (*Zustimmung, Einverständnis*)[11] occurs at a level of volitional activity in which the just-awoken ego recognizes the values and meanings that were passively motivating its acts as material syntheses.[12] The mark of interest – that which is intrinsically compelling, which I was discussing above – that characterizes a powerful sentiment like love consists exactly in the ability of the I to be in that flow that connects lower and higher spirit. The organic syntheses through the active participation of the volitional body transform into values, judgements, and finally a social stance the interest mark proper to their subjective presence (Hua 42, 192).

Love, consent and its ambiguity

This description provides some clues as to how difficult it can be to define consent from the part of the volitional body.[13] In fact, the ownership we can claim over our body will be always limited to the point of awakening in which our ego finds itself whenever the irritations arise; our awakening always uncovers a limited space of passive matter.

For example, education, habits, the geographic and social map of our life tend to generate in us an habitual form of awakening that does not cause too much distress because it always takes place in the same area of our life and in a similar manner – this is what describes psychical habitualities or the psychical ego's habitus. Yet, when something extra-ordinary happens to us, such as falling in love, our ordinary space of awakening is expanded to something new, which seems familiar, intriguing and frightening at the same time.

The famous Ovidian 'amo et odi' (love and hate) summarizes this universal feeling for which love forces us to awake to something new and often hideous about us because it sheds light on parts of us that we are not always willing to visit or simply do not want to know.

Hence, the consent that follows any validation generates in us a sense of responsibility that is proportional to the matter that we decide to own; its meanings and values will always be limited to the level of understanding we can hold in relation to that space of awakening. There are cases in which people fall in love because the beloved one is capable of making her free to attend to an unknown, new area of her life. Whether this area is full of darkness and flaws or light and good qualities, this new understanding will in any case be valuable to her because it will provide the possibility of mending previous wounds that otherwise would remain buried in the sedimented layers of her passive life. Love is a vital and somewhat brutal force that awakens us in a place that is not familiar to us, but at the same time is particularly important because it can foster our spiritual (lower and higher) growth. It is in fact through this force that we are given a larger view of who we are. On the other hand, the feeling of love shows us that our degree of consent to it as a disclosure to an intimate space will never be fully informed and weary of its consequences. We can only sense what is important for us and what we want to be respected in us, but mostly our consent will be a process of ongoing discovery that can even lead to a direction that conflicts with our physical or psychological well-being (not to mention the disorientation that can occur when the habitualities, that is, the psychical ego's familiar self-image, is challenged by conflicting disclosures).

The next chapter will be entirely focused on the problem of forced intimacy and validations. Unfortunately, there are numerous stories of sexual violations, especially perpetrated by people close to the habitual surrounding of the victim, a colleague at work, family members, or partners, in which the first most common reaction reported is to freeze or to minimize the effects of the event.[14] The ego awakens in a place that is totally new and yet still habitual because of the familiar background shared with the aggressor. This gives way to a chain of validations that might involve problematic consequences with the intimacy of the person involved. Full consent always evolves through an arc of time that cannot be synchronistic to the event that takes place; it often involves a long and sometimes painful process of discovery that will necessarily be asynchronous to the event of awakening (if interpreted through the lifeworld stream of time). The value/meaning-giving activity, in fact, will never be exhausted in the moment itself because the synthetic matter is generally too wide to be comprised in only one validation.

Instincts, habits and brutal love

As explored in the previous section, the primal bond of intimate love that bridges lower and higher spirit is due to a primal brutal force that we call love; this connecting force opens a space of intimacy through which the human being can regain a contact with their passive matter. In this section, I will examine the genetic and generative[15] components that belong to this force. As Hart noticed Husserl once claimed that 'love is a chief problem of phenomenology', by which he meant that love 'is a universal problem for phenomenology because it embraces the depths and heights of intentionality as a driving and productive force' (1992, 225).

In this analysis love is not taken as merely a static category but also as a genetic and transformative one. As mentioned above, the lowest sensuous roots of love comprise desires, instincts,[16] impulses[17] and drives while the heights of love comprise meanings, values and higher feelings. The lowest and highest roots of love tend to move in two opposite directions since the former tend to irritate the ego to the point of its awakening, and the latter builds around the ego a psychic armour that we might call personality that turns the ego into a semi-sleeping static being. Both sides of this force are a necessary bridge to connect the lower and higher spirit. As Lee remarks (1993, 166), the lowest roots of our being are original affections (*Uraffektionen* that originally awaken us and call us to be). They are the organic matter that manifests itself as being there for the ego (Hua-Mat VIII, 351). 'Original affection is an instinct, thus a kind of empty striving still lacking the presentation of a goal' (Hua-Mat VIII, 253). These affections present a hidden kind of intentionality, which has its direction but is not yet cognitively explicit. As Husserl writes:

> Here the word 'instinct' is used in an unusually broad sense, first of all for each drive-intentionality [*Triebintention*], which originally is not yet disclosed in its sense. Instincts in the usual sense relate to remote, originally hidden goals, in a chain of partial drives aiming at these goals and serving the preservation of the species, or, as the case may be, the self preservation of the individual of the species. (E III 10, 6a)

The lowest roots of love have an intention that is not known to the subject and is not yet owned by it.[18] That is why love is often described in poetry as a force that takes us – Dante for example writes, 'Love, so swift to grasp a tender heart'.[19] We do not choose to love, it is love that chooses us and moves us towards directions that we cannot know immediately and even less control. The intentional movement of this sensuousness seems to be aimed at self-preservation; whenever we love someone we confide in eternity or as Sartre put it we hope that our thinghood can finally come to existence through the regard of the Other. In that sense instincts are our deeper connection to the hidden goal that regulates our survival. Husserl assigns to instincts an intentional quality which, even if not comparable to the active intentionality described in his *Logical Investigations* or *Ideas*, while lacking a referring quality (*Beziehung auf*), is still intentional, since it forms a tension towards something through associations. Husserl describes the instinctive intention in these terms:

> Unity of the process of filling of intention, and this itself is the telos, namely, that the instinctive intention which in a unified way from the start heads towards this interpenetration of intentionality and its releasement and is fulfilled as something unified not in a single phase but in an ongoing achievement (Tun). (*C* 16 IV, 14; see Lee, 109)

Instinctive intentionality triggers a process of ongoing achievements for which the *telos* (goal) that moves the affectant and the affected of the synthesis can be fulfilled through the act that the subject awoken by those syntheses decides to take. Instincts thus have the strength to move upwards from the depth of our organic life to the activity of our decisions.

It is when our instinct emerges to the surface of our active decision-making that an opposite force takes shape, that of the habits. Indeed, when instincts tend to emerge always in the same locus and to drive us towards the same validation, they can easily become habitualized and constitute a stable layer;

an example of it can be the instinct of hunger that arises always around lunch time.

On this level instincts and habits compete with each other. The repetition of validated instincts become habits; while the directionality of instinct opens to new territories and draws a vertical trajectory because it starts from the lower primordial affections and travel up to higher feelings, the directionality of habits is horizontal and tends to fix fleeting instincts into stable sense-meanings. When habits and instincts conflict in love, Husserl warns us: 'There is indeed a danger here. Because an absolute ought and an absolute value is only what it is as an absolute statement, in absolute love; and a love which would be mechanized, is no love. Although love becomes habitualized, it is only real and actual in active exertion' (Husserl, Ms E III 4, 12b).

Real love is actual only in active exertion; when love is mechanized, constrained and shaped by habits, love ceases to be that absolute ought that defines its essence. Naturally, love, like any other lower feeling, can be habitualized; when that happens part of its brutal force is lessened. Yet, since love 'embraces the depths and heights of intentionality', it cannot dwell in only one of two positions for too long if it is actively exerted; so if it gets stuck on the lower or higher level it means that its power is not fully exerted. Whenever habits inevitably emerge from the repetition of instincts, love frees itself through breaking those habits and freeing new sensuous lower matter; whenever instincts repeatedly erupt without allowing the constitution of stable patterns, love normalizes the instincts through affections and constancy needs Chaos and order, poros and penia; Apollonian and Dyonisiac seem to be the two extremes that describe the polarity that contains the force of love. Love needs chaos in order to keep intimacy with passive matter alive and open to interpretations, but it also needs order and harmony in order to establish that continuity in which the psychical ego can observe its passive life and build a web of meanings. For example, controlling mechanisms are never successful in love because they force the life of the partners on a sphere of active meaning-activity that loses touch with the hyletic passive matter (that is generally chaotic and unpredictable). Uncaring behaviours and avoidant attitudes do not work either because they do not help the constitution of meaningful positions from which the psychical ego can observe its life and give a meaning to it. Love is actual when it shocks and awakes the ego to a new intimate bond within the richness of its sensuous matter. Any ego lives a necessary double life between free instincts and sedimented habits; on the one hand, instincts awaken its being to the matter that the ego needs to own in that given moment as a responsible being within a community; on the other, habits shape its personality according to the content of its sensuous matter and it is through that personality that it can live in the real world. As Husserl recognizes, I am not only the I that awakens in that moment of time under the irritating pressure of its drives but I am is also a cycle of habitualities that start building out of awakenings. The habits have the goal to actualize my ability to be and allow me to come into existence by fulfilling my qualities and fine-tuning my capabilities. On the other hand they prevent me from exploring all the drives that are blossoming in different directions.

As we can see from what Husserl wrote below:

> The personal Ego constitutes itself not only as a person determined by *drives* (...) but *also as a higher, autonomous, freely acting* Ego, in particular one guided by *rational motives* (...) Habits are necessarily formed, just as much with regard to originally instinctive behavior (...) as with regard to free behavior. To yield to a drive establishes the drive to yield: habitually. Likewise, to let oneself be determined by a value-motive and to resist a drive establishes a tendency (a 'drive') to let oneself be determined once again by such a value-motive (...) and to resist these drives. (Hua IV, 255; Eng. trans. 267)

As this passage shows, at the level of passive syntheses the most effective motives might be those to which we do not attend and do not become habits (see Hua XI, 178 and Lee, 55). Whether we want it or not, our personality is determined by drives through our pre-reflective bodily and affective directedness, and on a reflective level, the choices that we make in response to them. Hence, on a higher level the intimate bond that is established through love runs through validations that involve our volitional body, while on a lower level through instincts that escape our ability to consent. When an intimate bond is established, then our primary I emerges from the whole of instincts and drives that we decide to accept and explore; this whole of lower affections become recognizable through habitualizations and then active meanings that we decide to assign to the bundle of instincts that became visible through habits.[20] In this always new I, we can see a number of capacities that we can accept or not and it is through this acceptance that we participate in the flow of life as persons.[21] The very primal bond is between instinctive matter and ego. From there the crossroads of intentionalities (which I described in Chapter I.2) is the structure that builds the personality of a subject and generates an intimate space with others; the passive flow of syntheses, in fact, combines together lower instincts and active intentionality which provide the passive matter with meanings and values that the awoken volition decides to validate. As Husserl writes, 'As feeling is founded in the hyletic or the affective tonality [*Gefühlsmässigen*] of the hyle so the conative as response-form of the I is founded in the affective tonal' (E III 9, 16b).

While the intimacy disclosed by the lower level of instincts sheds light on the dark area of validity and consent, we can never be fully aware of all our instincts. The higher level of love assigns meanings and values to the passive matter while bringing awareness and a sense of interconnection. The interconnection is first between the lower and higher level of spirit and then between individuals. It is in this dimension of interconnectedness that the I comes to existence as a person. Human beings are in fact places of validity from which intimacy stems as the founding force which interconnects different points of owning matter (the awoken ego) through acts of validation (Hua I, 54, 55, 62). In Husserl we can distinguish primordialness (*Urtümlichkeit*) as the primordialness of my, the mature, self-reflecting I (higher level), and the primordialness that, through the process of 'questioning back' (*Rückfrage*) in which the genesis of meanings is uncovered, becomes reconstructed habitual primordialness (lower level), the primordialness of the 'beginning' of constitutive genesis.

When I decide[22] to be intimate with someone, first of all myself, I discover myself as being interconnected with another and since I am a living system I keep interpreting what am I in relation to the other. Hence, intimacy is never given, created or discovered once and for all, but it is a generative, recursive and participative concept (I will write more about these characteristics in the next chapter); this means that my hidden past will always stand out in a dark horizon as impediment for true intimacy and at the same time a resource for its generative quality (C 13 III, 7; Lee, 28).

Human beings (*Menschen*) are in fact defined by Husserl as organic functioning elements (Hua-Mat IX, 170, 176) that do not belong solely to their monads but are parts of a larger whole. My genetic and lower life is not primordially mine because it is made of passive matter that my psychical ego did not make mine yet through any act of recognition and ownership; the awakening of my ego makes that life mine. The space of intimacy that that awakening unfolds makes my own functioning and validating system part of other systems. For Husserl, individuals are units of goals, values and certitudes (Hua-Mat IX, 171) that relate to each other in a social community. I can grasp the interconnection of my space of intimacy with other spaces through my habitual I who can sediment layers that allow the reflecting I to grasp its own being. Human beings are concreta that relate to the whole of society as parts to a whole, and these parts are a whole on its turn. They can function independently of the whole-society, but as they explicate their task they form a whole with the society to which they belong. The way in which the wholes are formed is through love and the way in which these wholes are kept together is through a fluid access to intimacy. Hence the individual is not an isolated monad in society. Everyone is responsible for what part of herself she brings into 'one single universal coherence'. The goals and the values that move each personal subject to action are inevitably interconnected to the values of others.

Summary

This chapter discussed first the lower and higher layers of the spirit in order to explain how the volitional body – the moral organ of our actions – validates the feelings that lead us to intimate love. In the chapter we showed how this body cannot be considered as belonging exclusively to material or immaterial layers; accordingly every decision it makes participate of lower and higher motives. It is under these lenses that the brutal force of love and the space of intimacy that it opens up was interpreted as a vertical feeling connecting lower and higher, our material and immaterial layers; on a lower level love is a whole of drives, instincts, desires of which we cannot have a firm hold because we do not own them. On this level, in fact the subject is not even an ego yet, but is an ongoing chain of syntheses of the passive matter. On the higher level, love is a meaning and value giving activity; it interprets the passive matter that is provided to it through the awakening of the I and validates it according to specific meanings and values that shed light on what that person actually is. The light shed on these layers form a space of intimacy through which the person can come in contact with parts of itself that were unexplored or not yet revealed. The brutal bonding force of love represents a unique opportunity for us to become closer to our factual existence. This involves that on the one hand intimacy will disclose a dark place where the sensuous egoless generative web of syntheses build a concreteness that might eventually take its own shape into meanings and values constitutive for the identity and sense of reality that a person feels to live in; on the other hand intimacy represents a retrospective reconstruction of the layers of the known intimate life as it appears to the sedimented in the habitual layers of an I. The former kind of intimacy lays the foundation for a valid, but yet dark, space in which the I can come into existence, the latter recognizes the interconnection between the layers that belong to that validity as a founding core around which life, the habitual one, constitutes itself as a meaningful vital flow.

I.6
Forced intimacy

Introduction

This chapter will reactivate the meaning of intimacy by applying Husserl's genetic method on what Koestenbaum calls 'existential sexuality'. The chapter will be divided into two parts. The first part will follow up on the description of practical intentionality and the genesis of intimacy provided in the previous chapters. The second part will analyse the link between sexuality and intimacy to show how the genetic character of intimacy informs the passive and active choices that constitute sexual identity. The goal of this 'construens' chapter is to describe how and why intimacy can become a space that opens to us despite our consent and unfolds uncontrollable meanings.

Existential sexuality

This section will investigate the teleological and recursive structure of existential sexuality, which I will read as being defined by the passive and active layers of the decisions people habitually make in their intimate lives. In my opinion, existential intimacy is the most relevant characteristic of the recursive structure of existential sexuality because its fluid nature provides the key to understanding our sexual facticity and the meaning we assign to it.

I borrowed the term *existential sexuality* from Koestenbaum, whose therapeutic approach is openly influenced by existentialism and Husserl's phenomenology. In *Existential Sexuality* he defines existential sex as the 'chosen sex; it is the sex life that an individual has chosen authentically ... There's no law that says life must include love ... Our freedom is total' (1974, 10).

According to Koestenbaum, our sexuality is existential in the moment in which it acquires a meaning for us; the meaning comes from the awareness of our decision. Love is not the law around which we build sexual identity; we have absolute freedom in our sexual facticity. He continues: 'Meaning stands for integration, meaning refers to total life and to the fulfillment of its potential ... [E]xistential or meaningful sex is sex experienced as an integral part of a beautiful life' (1974, 8). 'Choosing to cope' (1974, 12) is the first step that leads to the meaning and the beauty of our sexual existence.

The recursive structure of sexual existence

The problem that any existential choice entails is directly connected to the structure of our being. As Sartre remarks (1942), we are factual beings, meaning that we are part of a reality that we do not fully understand and at the same time we are meanings that we continuously construct. Making a choice about our existence means, as Koestenbaum writes, 'being awake to each situation' (1974, 13). Our receptivity, as McDowell (1996) and Husserl (2001) remarked, is such that we often construct meanings without being able to attend to them consciously; the meanings that define our lives are often meaningless and even invasive for us. Although these meanings represent who we factually are, usually we are not fully aware of the determining power they have on our lives.

For example, as Zapien will show in the second part of the book, people involved in extramarital affairs realize that they are in an affair only when the latter relationship negatively affects the harmony of the former one. Before that realization they would not feel they were part of the category 'affair' because the decisions they made were grounded mostly in their passive and receptive life. Their new sexual identity was shaped without their being aware of it. Being awake to one's meaning is an important step towards the constitution of a meaningful existential construct that can shape one's facticity in a way that can be recognized as authentic. In *The Transformation of Intimacy*, Giddens states that 'a pure relationship is one in which external criteria have become dissolved: the relationship exists solely for whatever rewards that relationship can deliver. In the context of the pure relationship, trust can be mobilised only by a process of mutual disclosure' (1992, 40). An intimate relationship is a relationship of an active choice of intimacy that is made by partners who decide to be close to themselves as individuals and to each other as related individuals.

Sexual existential freedom lies exactly in the decision of being awake and attending to the constitution of one's sexual identity. As Koestenbaum notes: 'In reality a human being is a free consciousness; activity and passivity are free role choices. The meaning of sexual activity is not pre-ordained by human anatomy but is created by free choices of liberated men and women'

(1974, 93). Realizing that we are free from inappropriate moral constraints and social constructions would enable us to meaningfully shape a passive life into an active one.[1]

Koestenbaum calls the space of this absolute freedom *transcendental*. By that the author is referring to the space of the original constitution of meanings. It is in this space in fact that 'consciousness is prior to sex and that consciousness is asexual. The sexualization of consciousness is a free decision and a free construction' (1974, 86). In this space the asexual free consciousness decides to become meaningful. According to Koestenbaum, 'A therapeutic relationship, like existential love, is "transcendental." It is a relationship that exists on the level of pure consciousness ... It is a mind-to-mind encounter and not solely a feeling or emotional experience ... He perceives his love now as an object that must be lived. That distance from an emotion is a key to understanding existential love' (1974, 25). Transcendental is the space opened up by the encounter of practical, passive and active intention. As a space that describes the condition of the possibility for the sexual experience to be such, this space can be grasped through the awakening of the passive matter into a now that acquires a meaning through active intention. This space is what I called intimacy and one that I will describe soon. As we saw from Chapter I.5, the practical intention is that intention in which the subject as a just awoken ego decides to own in a now the passive contents of its body and validates that content matter of active meaning giving. Transcendental is exactly the space disclosed by the crossing of these three different qualities of intentions; one operates in a space of absolute freedom in which it discovers the matter and accordingly the meanings that determine the sense of its own facticity. This space of transcendental (i.e. condition of possibility for a meaning) freedom is the space in which real intimacy between the subject and its own world is disclosed.

In a beautiful passage in *Being and Nothingness*, Sartre writes: 'As soon as I am referred to myself because I must await myself in the future, then I discover myself suddenly as the one who gives the meaning to the alarm clock ... the one finally who makes the values exist in order to determine his action by their demands. I emerge alone and in anguish confronting the unique and original project which constitutes my being ... I do not have nor can I have recourse to any value against the fact that it is I who sustains values in being. Nothing can ensure me against myself ... I have to realize the meaning of the world and of my own essence' (1942, 39). According to Sartre, one discovers one's facticity through the free awakening of the I rising from the nothingness of Being.

I would call the dimension that both Koestenbaum and Sartre described in these passages intimacy. It is in this space disclosed by an act of transcendental freedom that one acquires a space of absolute closeness with oneself and anyone whom one encounters in this original realm. This space of constitution of meanings connects one's passive layers of facticity with active existential ones. Indeed, it is in this space, as Sartre wrote, that 'I have to realize the meaning of the world and of my own essence'. In this space my facticity awakes and is moved to decide how close I want to be to what I really am and I am becoming.[2] Hence, I consider intimacy the space from which my passive facticity and my active meaning-bestowing decisions stem in the definition of my being in the world as a sexual creature. As Koestenbaum wrote: 'This transcendental closeness is more intimate than if it were sexual' (1974, 25). The transcendental closeness in which we constitute the meaning of our passive and active sexual existence is what I call intimacy.

As Sartre wrote: 'My existence in the midst of the world becomes the exact correlate of my transcendence-for-myself since my independence is absolutely safeguarded ... Thus I am reassured ... My facticity is saved. It is no longer this unthinkable and insurmountable given which I am fleeing; it is that for which the Other freely makes himself exist; it is as an end which he has given to himself ... My existence is because it is given a name. I am because I give myself away' (1956, 258). I am because I can choose how close I want to be to myself; in doing that I disclose myself to the Other or – in Sartre's terms – 'I give myself away'. My facticity is saved because the passive layers that constitute it can finally acquire a meaning from my choice and the regard of the Other. My transcendental freedom[3] is then used to inform an existential sexuality that is meaningful for me. The social construction that defines my sexual orientation ceases to be an empty category because it becomes a teleological recursive structure whose infinite unfolding of meanings changes while the essential given expressed in its facticity remains the same. Figuratively speaking, intimacy invites the exploration of this eternal maze in which the self is what we are chasing and a dynamic labyrinth is the way in which the self gives itself to us.

Transcendental intimacy

This section will describe the essential features that characterize transcendental intimacy and how they directly influence a person's sexual life. Poetry perhaps can capture the essence of this fluid and fleeting state of mind better than philosophy and explain how we can access intimacy.

Three contemporary Spanish poets agree that transcendental intimacy cannot be achieved spontaneously. While *intimacy is spontaneous, any reflection on intimacy detracts from spontaneity.* For García Montero, time is the synthetic medium that allows us to experience intimacy reflectively. According to García Montero, since poetry is a linguistic invention, a poet can never write about true intimacy; however, he or she can artificially trace its steps back to true intimacy through the reconstruction of a fictional time in which words contribute to the constitution of the intricate tangle of time and feelings from which intimacy stems. Similarly, in *Paraíso Manuscrito* (1982), Benítez Reyes considers intimacy a dialogue between words and memory. In this case intimacy does not refer to an abstract sense of time but to the precise act of recollection of past events in which we recover the feeling of being intimate. Finally, in *La Noche Junto al Álbum* (2001) Alvaro García points to the distant and intellectual sight as a practical device to get closer to the spontaneous feeling of intimacy. According to the poet, it is through this hybrid vision that one can re-create the intimate atmosphere in one's own poetry.

Hence, according to these poets, the transcendental dimension of intimacy can be re-evoked and explored through a use of reflective and transcendental time. This poetic reading of transcendental intimacy is consonant with Gendlin's philosophical and psychological description. In *Focusing* (1982), Gendlin reports a story told by a woman concerning her choice of remaining intimate to herself and her husband. In the story the woman was having dinner with her husband when he dropped some food on the tablecloth; the clumsiness of that small event was sufficient to trigger her rage. First she gives in to her rage, and then she decides to leave the table and go upstairs to her bedroom to practise focusing. This technique, influenced as well by Husserl's phenomenology, consists in letting the body speak its mind without forcing any meaning from it; through a free flow of words and ideas that prompt one's mind, the body is allowed to free some of its passive layers without committing to any active decision of interpretation. Thus, alone in her bedroom the wife let her mind run free while she was attending to the unfolding of her thoughts as a witness. Through this act of intellectual distancing in which she put herself in a modality of active dialogue with what she was feeling, she suddenly discovered the real reason for her anger. A new sense of deeper intimacy was restored. She was mad at her husband because during dinner he was celebrating his promotion, whereas her career was at a dead end because of her maternity.

Poetry, philosophy and psychology seem to converge on the idea that the realm of transcendental or reflective intimacy can be explored and then enacted by a person's existential choices through recollection and distancing. In this short story, intimacy seems to be a two-layered dimension: the spontaneous passive one and the existential, active and transcendental one. In the story, the passive layer of intimacy is represented by the argument between the spouses. Intimacy between the partners was broken because their factual lives were conflicting although they were not actively aware of that. The existential and active layer of intimacy is represented by the decision that the wife made to distance herself from the previous spontaneous intimacy and to be in dialogue with her reaction without imposing any moral judgement on her feeling. Her decision gave the couple a real opportunity to be truly close. The latter layer, the reflective one, allowed them to acquire a more meaningful and intimate relationship, open to new choices concerning their future together. That provided an opportunity for them to constitute a new meaning for their conjugal relationship. On the first passive lower layer intimacy spontaneously erupts as a space that transcends time and space; on the higher active layer it becomes an absolutely free space in which we can constitute meanings that will define our existence. On this second layer, we hold a decisional power. In this story the wife might have not been happy to discover her jealousy towards her husband's career, yet she used that realization to be close to herself and her husband's feelings.

Our passive life can easily become a space of distance that escapes our sight and from which we cannot come back. It is very common, in fact, to decide passively to negate closeness and choose a pregiven social construction that does not feel true to us but is socially accepted. In the story, being angry about clumsiness with the dishes is more socially acceptable than being envious and jealous of one's partner's professional success. Traditionally, women's goal has been to raise children whereas men have focused on their careers. It is difficult to participate in the teleological structure of a social construction in a way that we feel as truly teleological – that is, infinitely unfolding meanings for us – and recursive – that is, participative and actually changing our existence. The essence of our facticity always tries to connect spontaneously with us; whether we want to entertain a dialogue with it is a matter of transcendental and existential intimacy. The next section will go through the two layers of intimacy, the transcendental and the spontaneous one, in relation to cases of forced intimacy.

Forced intimacy

The interplay between spontaneous and transcendental layers of intimacy raises a relevant issue pertaining to consent and ownership of our intimate space. As a matter of fact intimacy does not stem from a willing choice, but from a forceful event[4] that opens a space of which we are called to be part even if we are not capable of fully seeing it. Intimacy opens up to us before we are able to give our consent to it; this is the reason why I characterize the layer of spontaneous intimacy as a forced one. Cases of forced intimacy can be numerous and not necessarily negative for the individual's psychological well-being. Witnessing an accident on the street, being moved by a scene of a movie in the theatre, listening to a touching concert are all cases in which we become intimate with other people, mostly strangers, despite our consent;

we enter in an intersubjective space of intimacy in which a wave of feelings and emotions is spontaneously shared even if we are not ready to assign any meaning to it. In that case, spontaneous intimacy discloses a new intimate space in front of us without our consent; this space might be recollected and cognitively transformed into a place of intelligible meanings to which we can give our consent through transcendental intimacy. For example, after a concert one might decide to talk to the person sitting next to her and share a few words of appreciation about the music or after a car accident the witnesses might decide to cool down together the stress generated by the event. Any space of intimacy is originally disclosed by spontaneous syntheses of egoless matter, more simply by life as it flows in a number of affectant-affected fusions; this opening awakes our volitional body and then our ego which is called to take a position (the noetic yes/no, *Analyses*, 94/54) in relation to the passive matter (this is another way to describe the interconnection of passive, practical and active intention). That yes or no is the primordial root of any consent; yet, it cannot be equated to a cognitive consent in which we decide calmly and in full awareness about what to do. Using a metaphor, the yes or no can be compared to the reaction that our body 'decided'[5] to have if it saw an avalanche falling upon it; there is not so much time to decide, and yet our lower and higher spirit, that is our bodily drives, impulses and instincts and our personal habitual coping mechanisms and basic cognitions are all focused in making a decision. That is the range of freedom at disposal whenever we give our consent under the pressure of passive syntheses; the hyletic flow is so wide and powerful that it can in fact be compared to an avalanche. Even if we are only watching a movie, our senses are so busy in retrieving information that we are continuously called to decide what to own and what to leave to the process of sedimentations on passive layers.

For example, in watching a movie a meaningful memory of mine might be awoken and I might decide to own all the feelings that that memory stirs up in me as mine; at the same time it might happen that my body feels uncomfortable because of that wave of feelings and starts having reactions, like muscular contractions that I might not be ready to own or to fully recognize because my ego is awake elsewhere; maybe the contractions will reveal themselves later on in the form of headaches, although their meaning might not be completely understood.

These examples shed light on a positive form of forced intimacy in which spontaneous intimacy reveals something meaningful and positive for our life. Things become far more complex when the space of intimacy is forced open because of actual violence. While in the positive form of spontaneous intimacy the forced event elicits a recollection that is in a certain way peaceful and comforting, in the case of abrupt violence the interplay between transcendental and spontaneous intimacy is less fluid.

For example, cases of acquaintance and assailed rape represent the condition for a deep conflict between spontaneous and transcendental intimacy, as the forceful event, in this case rape, discloses a spontaneous space of intimacy that the victim cannot be ready to properly name and recollect. Indeed, the common places concerning rape suggest that women are typically assaulted in dark alleys by strangers, the truth is that the existence of an already intimate space between victim and assailant raises the chances of assault and the difficulty of properly naming the event.[6] When acquaintance rapes take place the familiarity of the intimate world already shared with the assailant makes the victim incapable to assign a fitting name for the irruption of the new layer of intimacy; the continuity with the habitual space of intimacy is such that the victim wants to preserve the integrity of that space by renewing its habitual qualities. In that sense, even language does not encourage a proper recognition; for example, according to a jurisdictional language the concept of 'marital rape' did not exist legally.[7] By legal definition, 'a woman cannot be raped by her husband, since the "crime" of rape is ordinarily and legally defined as forcing sexual intercourse on someone other than the wife of the person accused'[8] When acquaintance rape happens it is very difficult for the victim to assign a meaning to the act that would feel true and respondent to the reality. Reading some interviews on the topic, it is very surprising to see that victims are often open to accept marriage proposal by their assailants or to consider the rape as premarital sex. This happens because the acceptance would renew the continuity of the victim's previous intimate and social life; in this way the spontaneous violence of the intimate act is recollected in a transcendental activity that does not recognize the change and therefore does not adhere to the space disclosed by the spontaneous activity. Thus, in this dynamic the actual intimacy with the spontaneous syntheses is precluded since the layer of transcendental intimacy is not anymore capable of grasping the boundaries of the actual event, assigning a proper meaning to it, and being the condition for the possibility of its actual existence. It is as if the brutal event never happened and never left a trace, although we know that on the level of passive spontaneous syntheses it did leave a profound trace.

To use another example, in a study on female victims in Hawaii, Ruch and Chandler (1983) and Luo (2000) remarked that the victims struggled to bring meaning to the rape experience in order to overcome the sense of helplessness, shame, embarrassment and concern about family and/or others' reactions opened up by the spontaneous irruption of the intimate space within their lives. As reported by Tsun-Yin Luo (2000), one woman (DR15) raped by her boyfriend initially felt resentment at the rape incident. She indicated that she perceived the incident as premarital sex and she realized later that her perception arose because she meant to preserve the integrity of her intimate lifeworld; in this way the rape experience never took the meaning of actual violence and even the title 'rape' came to be replaced with marital sex. One college woman (DR15) raped by her boyfriend has chosen to continue the relationship because she felt that continuing to see him would 'make it [the forced sex] less like rape', and she could stop blaming herself as well as stop feeling sorry for herself. Unfortunately, her psychological defence mechanism failed in its mission; the passive syntheses of her spontaneous life were calling for a meaning that was not fully satisfied by the one assigned by her active intention.

When it is difficult to connect with our own space of intimacy that is forcefully opened by spontaneous passive syntheses, we might witness a low rate of reporting the crime because victims are not willing to recognize the violation of the right to consent as they are not still ready to name that space of consent, even on the transcendental and reflective layer. Additionally, that difficulty shows a lowered level of intimacy of the victim with her/his own self; battered wives and rape victims are often accused of 'asking for', 'deserving' or 'enjoying' their victimization.

The women who are raped by boyfriends, dates, lovers, ex-lovers, husbands, relatives and other men that they know might represent the tip of an iceberg which reveals a more extensive pattern relating intimacy with forced sexual relations.[9]

From what emerged it seems to be confirmed that because of its spontaneous layer intimacy is a space disclosed independently of our consent. By consent I mean the act of taking responsibility for the passive matter of our lived experiences and own it. If our consent arrives, it can mature only later through the transcendental layer of intimacy and its active work of meaning-giving activity (*Sinngebung*). Indeed, on its spontaneous layer when the space of intimacy is forcefully opened the victim is not always immediately capable to recognize the violence because of the already persisting space of intersubjective intimacy and because of the habitual tension to keep that space intact and safe by attributing to it an habitual meaning (which unfortunately reveals itself to not be fully fitting to the new space). In fact, the former intersubjective space would not accept an immediate change of meanings, and the latter habitual one would resist the destruction brought forth by the sudden change of events. Yet, it can happen that the transcendental layer of intimacy can be newly triggered by another spontaneous act of intimacy, which would encourage the victim to repossess her space by giving to it a proper meaning and a more truthful interpretation; this event is what we might call epiphany. We can see this dynamic proved in the following story:

> Almost 14 years ago, my first husband attempted to rape me. At the time, we were very close to being separated, and I think he wanted to attempt to bring us closer, back together through a sexual act – he always maintained

that that was his prime means of communication, how he felt the closest. At first I fought and when he attempted to smother me with a pillow, I panicked and became only concerned with how to get him to stop – I was afraid he was going to kill me. So I became totally unresponsive to him – wouldn't talk or anything and he eventually stopped tearing my clothes and pulling me and there was no intercourse. Because it happened in the context of a whole lot of bad things in our marriage (he had been violent to me once or twice before, but not sexually so), I didn't have any particular feelings at the time except relief that it was over. Very shortly thereafter, I left him. I never thought of the incident as attempted rape until almost 10 years later when I was walking away from a session of a women's group I was in wherein we had been talking about specific rape incidents that had occurred to some of the members. Until that time, I think I felt rape was of the stereotypic type of the stranger leaping out of the bushes and never thought of an incident like that occurring between people who knew each other – especially husband and wife, as rape. I think this is true of many married women-they have accepted society's dictum that a man has sexual access to his wife whenever he wants, whether she does or not. Thus, it never occurs to them that this could be a crime, a felonious assault, that this is, indeed, rape. (Source: *Family: Critical Concepts in Sociology*, ed. David Cheal)

As this interesting interview reveals the transcendental dimension of the intimate space can be recovered through unexpected awakenings triggered by the interplay of spontaneous passive syntheses and transcendental activity; the new passive syntheses can irritate the lower layers of the spirit and awaken it to a new now from which it can direct its meaning activity in a new and more meaningful way. That trigger marks out the beginning point of a process of healing that otherwise would be at best incomplete; in fact in order to recover from an experience of forced negative intimacy one should be able to establish a connection with the basic layers of the new intimacy. In cases of violence this reconnection is rarely established because the victim tends to deny the event at worse or at best to assign a meaning to it that is not fully respondent to the event. The next section will consider the moral freedom that is required to explore the contents of transcendental intimacy.

Morality and sexual plasticity

Plastic sexuality is a term used by Giddens (1992) to describe a heightened self-awareness of the fluidity of one's sexual life. Today sexuality has almost completely lost its primary reproductive function; we have sex because we seek pleasure, and the sense of pleasure generally is heightened by self-realization and intimacy. As Giddens remarks, 'When the new connections between sexuality and intimacy were formed sexuality became much more completely separated from procreation than before. Sexuality became doubly constituted as a medium of self-realisation and as a prime means, as well as an expression, of intimacy' (1992, 164). Sexuality is our space of realization because, as Sartre wrote, in that space our facticity is saved by means of the other's regard. In the intimate space of a sexual relationship, whether it is a deep or a shallow relationship, a meaning is given to our facticity, in this case merely to our body, through which we can actually safeguard the meaning of our sexual identity.

The strength of this recognition is proportional to our moral freedom; morality, in fact, limits the space of absolute freedom from which intimacy is generated spontaneously. It is because of moral judgements that victims of rape encounter enormous difficulties in recollecting the actual meaning of their experience. Sexuality needs to be free from morality, for it has a plastic structure that stems from the lower passive layer that is in spontaneous dialogue with our factual existence; in Gendlin's story the moral issue would be represented by the sense of jealousy felt by the wife, and in Zapien's study by the uneasiness experienced by the partners in acknowledging the existing affair. If we allow the first layer to fully exist before our eyes without any moral judgement, we have more chances for closeness and recognition. As Moore (1998) wrote, morality is a matter of imagination and courage. If women had never tried to explore new archetypes, the sexual relationship between men and women would have remained in the Victorian era. The sexual revolution allowed the exploration of new territories that now are morally accepted but were inconceivable at that time. Women gained more intimacy with themselves by acknowledging their moral freedom; the sexual revolution opened the doors to a true participative, recursive and teleological social construction. Although the meanings this construction can bear are potentially infinite, I think that today women are closer than ever before to what they feel is right for themselves.

I partially agree with Giddens when he says, 'Intimacy implies a wholesale democratising of the interpersonal domain, in a manner fully compatible with democracy in the public sphere. There are further implications as well. The transformation of intimacy might be a subversive influence upon modern institutions as a whole. For a social world in which emotional fulfillment replaced the maximising of economic growth would be very different from that which we know at present' (1992, 3).

I agree with the idea that intimacy stems from a subversive influence on modern institutions; however, it does not represent a democratic institution but rather a state of nature. The teleological and recursive structure of what we are originates from a passive spontaneous layer that rubs against us and calls us to make decisions about the meanings we want to attribute to the former spontaneous experience; at this level we can actively decide whether we want to be intimate with ourselves and choose authentic meanings that define our existence. Hence, more than a democracy, this subversive state reminds me of a state of nature in which we are called to decide if we want to enter a space of co-independence, the so-called civil society. In the space of spontaneous intimacy there is no democratic rule yet; it is on its second layer, that of active recollection and distanced dialogue with our feelings, that we can consider case by case whether the moral laws shared in that democratic co-independence can be more or less meaningful for our sexual existence.

Even the imperative of intimacy – 'You have to be intimate! You have to disclose yourself more, not shut people out of your life' – is not a moral rule that can be held in mind in the layer of transcendental intimacy.[10] Similar to what is acknowledged by Lasch (1977) and Bauman (1990), in matters of intimacy and sexual identity any dependency on experts for self-direction, self-creativity and unmediated social interaction can constitute a negative influence. Bauman (1991, 205) refers to Sennett's (1977) concept of destructive *Gemeinschaft* in asserting that damage to social cohesion results from the psychological burdens of incitements to mutual disclosure. Intimacy cannot be a moral imperative.

Intimacy is a transcendental space over which we have no control because it opens spontaneously from the depths of our passive life; it represents our facticity talking to us through its teleological and recursive unfolding. The existential exploration that we can undertake of our intimate life is morally free because it is meaning-oriented. It represents an active choice to cope with our identity in relation to ourselves and others.

To understand and explore intimacy we need to have a critical distance, be available to break any pregiven moral construction and participate in the unfolding of its telos. Intimacy is the voice of our essence talking to us and prompting us to make authentic choices; intimacy is not a narrative obligation but a sort of dance with a passive alterity.

Summary

In this chapter I showed how sexuality defines our existence when it involves an active choice. This choice, though, being involved in a recursive teleological structure, cannot always be conscious because our factual being is usually a mystery to us, a truth whose essence speaks to us from a transcendental space. Metaphorically speaking, I named this voice intimacy. From the depth of our passive life the meanings that define us and constitute the condition of possibility for our existence come from intimacy, whose structure can be broken down into two main layers: a spontaneous and transcendental one. In our lives we are constantly called on to choose whether we want to pay attention to the constitution of meanings that are going to shape the social category through which we will be recognized – in particular when we encounter cases of forced intimacy that has a negative impact on our psychological balance. If this transcendental voice remains on the layer of passivity, it is likely that our sexual existence will be foreign and meaningless to us; if we manage to attend to this voice on an active and transcendental layer and participate in the constitution of meaning, our sexual identity will be an existential one: the fruit of a choice. Our sexual identity needs to be plastic in the sense that its telos cannot be placed in one category once and for all. To fit in an existential sexuality that is meaningful for us, we need to be free from moral and social constraints and be available to entertain an honest dialogue with our facticity.

PART TWO

II.1

Phenomenological research and ethical experience

Background

The differences between theoretical and empirical methods of phenomenological research were discussed briefly in Chapter I.2. Before delving into several original empirical research examples, we will summarize and extend some of what has been discussed in Chapter I.2 regarding phenomenological research so that the empirical methods used in the remaining chapters can be understood as distinct from the philosophical theoretical method utilized thus far and from other types of research methods. It is also the intention within the next chapters to provide several examples of empirical phenomenological research inquiries into ethical dilemmas that arise in different contexts. These illustrations provide the contextual details that relate to the philosophical ideas gleaned from the metaphoric 'top of the building' views discussed in the introduction. These examples are included so that we might 'walk through the building' more concretely as we consider the relationship between theory and practice, but also to consider, the findings from each inquiry in dialogue with Husserl's ethics, notions of identity, intimacy and the Trinitarian layers of time which comprised the findings of the theoretical investigations discussed in previous chapters. It is our sincere hope that the relationship between the theoretical and the empirical is intriguing and helps to deepen our understandings of the relationship between theory and practice and the experiences we have chosen to investigate. Before approaching each of the following three inquiries and their respective findings, a more detailed discussion of the particular empirical phenomenological method used in the examples is offered and its selection justified. Thereafter three chapters follow, each of which considers a different empirical study of the experience of a particular dilemma.

Selecting phenomenological research methods for empirical use

Of the four major phenomenological methodologists, Giorgi, van Manen, Moustakas and Colaizzi, discussed in Chapter I.2,[1] there are a great number of areas of agreement between them. All of them are derived from Husserl's phenomenology and all of them use the application of the epoché and reduction, in order to allow the researcher to encounter the phenomenon in question in a manner that is conducive to phenomenological inquiry and that in some fashion addresses the issue of the consciousness of the researcher and the participants' experiences in this process. In entering the epoché, phenomenologists are urged to make conscious to oneself all of the relevant experiences, presuppositions, beliefs, judgements, ideas and theories, that the researcher holds about the phenomenon in question and to place them in metaphoric brackets – suspended for the periods of the phenomenological inquiry and analysis. We do not forget about them, notes Giorgi (2009); we simply allow them to play in the background while we encounter the phenomenon as it is presented to us in a more naïve manner unencumbered by the usual ways we might consider the phenomenon from what is within and what is termed the natural attitude. This very important part of the inquiry process is done in order to make space for an encounter with the phenomenon as separate and distinct from any particular body of knowledge, ideas or values that we might apply to the phenomenon in question.

The process of entering and maintaining the epoché is for Giorgi (2009), for example, not impossible, but one of *split consciousness*. "[Q]uite often one is very aware of the past as one tries not to let it influence an ongoing experience' (p. 92). There will be then, both an attending to that which is bracketed, in order to maintain it in brackets, and a mindful focus on a naïve encounter with the phenomenon in question – at the same time. This particular mode of split consciousness including the mindful focus on the phenomenon itself is the ethical nature of seeing and describing that phenomenological research demands in order to assure that the phenomenon is addressed descriptively so that we might 'come back to the things themselves', as the phenomenologist's slogan, taken from Husserl, urges us to do.

All of the phenomenological methodologists named above, in embracing Husserl's phenomenology, understand the task of theoretical or empirical research – or consciousness of anything for that matter – to include a relationship between the self or, in this case the researcher, and the object of inquiry (which can also be a subject who is experiencing and has a consciousness) that is understood to be both constitutive of and constituted by consciousness. We are not interested in an absolute Truth, but rather, 'realities are treated as pure "phenomena" and the only absolute data from where to begin' (Groenwald, 2004). For Husserl, the phenomenologist, seeks to be rigorously descriptive of the various layers of consciousness that arise through a phenomenological inquiry in order to do justice to the endeavour in an ethical, understood as purely (or as purely as possible) descriptive, manner.

How each of these theorists understands and describes the method of applying Husserl's ideas in the form of a research method, by addressing the relationship between researcher and the phenomenon and what is bracketed or included in the epoché, differs slightly. And these differences can amount to fairly important nuances of meaning in the findings of a phenomenological research endeavour. Van Manen (1990), for example, allows for interpretative or hermeneutic activity concurrent to descriptive activity within the epoché, as he sees no clear distinction between the act of describing and the act of meaning-making for the phenomenologist. While this seems sensible and consistent with the idea that realities are treated as phenomena, that which was to be bracketed and that which is to enter the epoché and therefore is available to be used to make meaning or interpretation is left unclear in van Manen's (1990) method. Rigorous attention to this distinction is important in the use of van Manen's approach, lest under the guise of hermeneutic meaning-making all that was to be bracketed is merely included and the entire point of the phenomenological inquiry, as a phenomenological one, is lost. His suggestion to researchers is that we guard against this by "actively mak[ing] explicit our understandings, beliefs, biases, assumptions, presuppositions and theories so that we might hold them deliberately at bay and even to turn this knowledge against itself, thereby exposing its shallow or concealing character' (van Manen, 1990, 47). In many studies using van Manen's method, then, it is customary for the researcher to consider and explicitly state up front, almost like a confession, the relevant positions that she holds so that they can be made conscious and used to consider if, in fact, they have bled into the descriptions without the researcher intending so. This then requires that one make all (or as many as one can muster) understandings, beliefs and assumptions clear at the outset. Phenomenologists' critique of this approach includes that the focus is now on the researcher's presuppositions and contents of her consciousness rather than the disciplined description of the phenomenon (Finlay, 2009). For this reason, for these inquiries, van Manen's method was not used.

The other three methodologists generally suggest researchers apply the epoché and reduction faithfully and aim to be as loyal as possible to a description of the phenomenon in question rather than provide an interpretation thereof. Moustakas (1994), however, in addition to the application of the epoché and reduction and a goal of pure description, also considers the researcher's intuitive self-discoveries as a source of coming to an understanding of the descriptive essence of a phenomenon (Friesen, Henrickson & Saevi, 2012).[2] What we call *intuition* is perhaps best understood as part of the consciousness of the researcher and may or may not be relevant to the description of the phenomenon in an essential manner. Moustakas is not entirely clear in his description of what exactly constitutes intuition and how one might distinguish intuition from other aspects of consciousness (e.g. projection, fantasies, ideas, interpretations, sensory information), making this allowance somewhat problematic.

While phenomenological methods all subscribe to the idea that the essential description of a phenomenon of inquiry appears to the consciousness of the researcher and is constituted by the consciousness of the researcher, Moustakas, in suggesting the inclusion of intuition, allows for *more* of the researcher's consciousness to be included in the description than do others. Because these inquiries include an interest in investigating specifically the issues of identity, intimacy and time and will use references to the psychological ego, the intentional ego and the transcendental ego, there is a desire to rely on a method that is not dependent on what the researcher may call *intuition* in the analysis as distinct from that which is bracketed or that which is described and that which may have relevance to particular parts of the identity of the researcher. For this reason, Moustakas's approach has also not been used in this inquiry.

Colaizzi, another methodologist who offers a phenomenological research method, allows, in addition to what remains when applying the epoché, dialogic aspects of the inquiry between participants and researchers (Friesen, Henrickson, & Saevi, 2012). While this dialogic or relational inclusion in the analysis can be interesting and illustrative, and for some phenomena that are inherently relational (e.g. a confession, a performance), perhaps very important to include, it is easy to imagine that each researcher and participant pairing would evoke different relational material and potentially unrelated relational material to the phenomenon at hand that should remain instead in brackets, but with Colaizzi's method would instead be invited into consideration. Most psychotherapists and psychoanalysts would consider this type of material to be related to early relationships, attachment style, personality and psychological development and to be only useful if the researcher has spent significant time developing the self so that she can make this material conscious and take responsibility for it when making meaning of an encounter with another. The process, psychologically by which this occurs, has historically been addressed in psychoanalysis or psychodynamic psychotherapy and often requires many years of therapeutic work in order to be able to enter into relationships without reactivity, projections or other unconscious processes taking over.[3] While, for some researchers, such an approach may be entirely feasible, there is significant burden then on the researcher for having to address the multiple layers of meaning of the dialogical aspects. As a result Colaizzi's method is also not featured in the examples that follow in the next chapters.

Giorgi's method (2009), in contrast, is rigorously described, is faithful to the demands of striving to bracket all presupposed material as one enters and remains in the epoché and takes as the goal of phenomenological inquiries to describe the essence of the phenomenon from this perspective rather than to focus on particularities. This is important because the method itself demands rigour and clarity for the researcher in terms of how to guard against falling into the natural attitude, falling prey to interpretations that may be a collapse of the natural attitude and the phenomenological one, allowing ideas previously bracketed to creep in, or failing to orient sufficiently to the phenomenon or critically consider imaginative variations of the description. Of the four, Giorgi (2009) offers the clearest descriptive method and the strictest understanding of the process. For this reason, Giorgi's method will be used in the subsequent empirical investigations of three different ethical dilemmas experienced by several research participants: An unexpected leadership dilemma, a parenting dilemma and the experience of beginning an extramarital affair against the backdrop of the promise of monogamy. Each will be explored in turn in the subsequent chapters.

The benefits of van Manen, Moustakas and Colaizzi's approaches in considering hermeneutics, intuitive self-discoveries, and the relational intersubjective dimensions could be introduced *after the fact* once an inquiry has been completed through Giorgi's method, and if any of these seems relevant and worthwhile. In particular, in these cases, we will be applying a hermeneutic analysis after the findings are gleaned through Giorgi's descriptive method, so as to invite an interpretation of the findings using Husserl's ideas of identity, intimacy and time. As such, once the analysis is complete, we plan to bring to bear the interpretations noted above to the findings gleaned from the descriptive analysis. We assume that this dialogue will be fruitful, yet it is entirely possible that other ideas or frameworks may be more relevant or may also need to be brought to bear on the findings, depending on what arises in the data and we will remain open to this idea as well. For this reason even the premise of this book will be held in brackets until after the descriptive essence of the phenomena is reached in order to consider how these dilemmas may or may not comport with the theoretical understandings discussed in previous chapters. It is possible, as with all empirical phenomenological investigations, that either a cohesive structure is not reached or that the findings do not comport with the interpretations that we may intuitively consider at the outset. In using Giorgi's methods we remain open to these options and will be able to adjust by adding additional hermeneutic layers after the fact if they are useful in the inquiry. What follows are the methodological details associated with each of the investigations.

Determination of the scope of the three inquiries

In the previous section of the text, the focus was on theoretical phenomenological inquiries into identity, intimacy and time. These chapters used Husserl and Nishida and wove an argument about the importance of identity, intimacy and time in several contexts. The arguments were philosophical ones. In what follows we have selected three types of dilemmas and have collected narrative descriptions of several people's experiences of each. These descriptions are available for empirical study and we now take as our task to consider if and how these descriptions of what we have defined a priori to be ethical dilemmas, demonstrate the shifts in identity, intimacy and time that we explored in the previous section.

In so doing, we do not presuppose that empirical study is somehow the validation of the philosophical theoretical inquiry, in fact the process could have been undertaken in the reverse, where we begin with an empirical study and use those findings to inspire a theoretical study – often this is the case. We chose to offer these examples as a way to rigorously consider how these two approaches might relate to one another and how they might address the issues from different vantage points. You will find footnotes within the chapters in the first part of the book, which is the theoretical portion, that link to the empirical chapters that are relevant and vice versa. This was our attempt to demonstrate the relationships between the two.

The three areas of empirical investigation of ethical experiences presented in the next chapters include the experience of an unexpected leadership challenge within an organization of some kind, a parent's experience of an ethical dilemma while raising a child, and the beginning of an extramarital affair against the backdrop of the promise of monogamy. These inquiries were designed with the idea that such contexts and experiences would be rich and evocative of ethical considerations and would be available for recall and broadly experienced. These general areas for exploration were left relatively open-ended in the form of an interview prompt for participants to respond to and describe as they were lived in whatever ways the participants would come to understand the prompt. The inquiries were designed this way in order to allow the data to reflect the general lived experience of the essence of dilemmas in each context and to allow for a variety of notions of each. Other areas of inquiry could have been chosen, of course, and may be relevant for the same aim, however, the desire was to showcase a few examples of the use of empirical phenomenological analyses in both personal and professional contexts in order to reflect upon and expand upon the theoretical inquiry into Husserl's ethics, discussed in previous chapters. Both approaches are in fact deeply related in phenomenology due to the attention in both on the consciousness of the researcher, the use of the epoché. Yet, because empirical methods begin with descriptions from others there is a possibility to be surprised and inspired in response to the contents from outside of the researcher's consciousness. In addition, the empirical method provides a few starting points to the imaginative variation process, rooted in the material provided by research participants. The researcher does not have the full burden of coming up with all considerations and may have a head start in the thinking inspired by the diversity and specifics of the descriptions. In theoretical methods the researcher is deeply responsible for the unfolding of all the possibilities through principles of logic and the structure of the method and this process, while it may arrive at the same result, demands a great deal of the researcher. Again, in this book we aim to consider both approaches in dialogue and to value and appreciate both as different but equally valid ways to approach ethical experiences and phenomenological research.

Method

The method that has been used for all three of the following empirical inquiries is Giorgi's descriptive method for psychology (2009), for all the reasons discussed above. Institutional Review Board (IRB) approval was garnered to conduct the inquiries with human subjects at two different junctures – Fall of 2015 and Spring of 2017, as the data were collected in two different project periods. Thereafter, several participants were recruited who had experienced at least one of the phenomena under inquiry, for a total of 16 participants – four who described a leadership dilemma, six who had had affairs and six who described parenting quandaries.

In the case of the leadership dilemmas and the parenting dilemmas, all potential participants were recruited via professionally-oriented, highly-trafficked, social networking websites, flyers in the San Francisco Bay Area and referrals from colleagues and friends. The goal was a purposive sample, considered by Welman and Kruger (1999) to be the most appropriate kind of non-probability sampling for this type of project. Potential participants were directed to contact the researcher via email to discuss the project, respond to a few screening questions, consider the consent form and participation process and sign up. They were also asked to forward the call for participants to others who might meet the criteria for participation or wish to participate. Each participant received a $50 gift card to amazon.com in exchange for participation upon completion. This particular incentive was deemed necessary early on because in the initial recruiting process it became apparent that leaders and parents, in particular, are very busy and otherwise less motivated, albeit interested, to devote the necessary time to the research project without such an incentive. This particular incentive, however, did not seem to unduly influence participants who were not otherwise interested and further the addition of the incentive was only instituted after consultation with the IRB through an addendum application to the board, which was approved.

In the case of those who experienced an extramarital affair, these data had been previously collected (also with IRB approval and through purposive sampling via the same avenues) as part of three different studies. The results of these studies have been published previously and analysed as applied to clinical treatment directions for those experiencing some aspect of infidelity (Zapien, 2015; Zapien, 2016; Zapien, in press). These data had also been collected using Giorgi's method (2009) and will be presented here and analysed anew this time in dialogue with the themes of identity, intimacy and time, as noted earlier. The previous analyses of these data focused largely on the psychological understanding and clinical implications and on decision science perspectives.

The screening criteria for each of the inquiries was as follows. For the parenting dilemma, all participants were screened to assure they had at least one child living at home who was 18 or under at the time of the dilemma. The parent could be a biological parent, an adoptive parent, a step-parent or the guardian of that child to qualify. For the leadership dilemma, the participant had to be a self-defined leader at the Director level or above at a for-profit, non-profit, or consulting firm at the time of the dilemma. For the cases presented on infidelity, all participants were screened to assure that at the time of the instance of the infidelity, they had been married for five years or more, did not have an open marriage or identify as polyamorous at the time, and had to have experienced what they would define as an extramarital affair. In order to participate, participants were required to speak English.

This resulted in samples of four leaders, six parents and six cases of infidelity the findings of which are discussed in the following chapters. A small sample such as this is not viewed by phenomenological researchers as problematic or insufficient. The aims of phenomenological research is not to *represent* the universe of possible participants or even variations of the phenomenon through sampling, nor is it to achieve *saturation* (the point at which each subsequent interview does not offer any new insight or contribute new material), through sampling, a frequent goal of qualitative research (Seidman, 1998). Instead, a description of the essential structure of the phenomenon is the goal of phenomenological empirical research and this is gleaned through rigorous methodical analysis of the reduction of the particular details within the narratives collected, which are then viewed through the process of phenomenological abstraction and imaginative variation (Englander, 2012). Imaginative variation is the means through which the researcher moves from what is presented to the consciousness of the researcher from within the epoché to the next level of abstraction through transformation of the narratives to the essential structure of the phenomenon. The burden in this process rests with the researcher to faithfully apply the epoché and reduction and to rigorously consider imaginative variations. Small samples are also often used in phenomenological methods because the transcripts gathered from these types of interviews are often lengthy and rich with detail making for very large data sets in terms of details and considerations. Phenomenological researchers are urged to gather such detailed descriptions from which to begin this process and to utilize the principles of phenomenological analysis to support their case for the description of, and constituents of, the structure of the phenomenon.

Data were collected through two options offered to each participant. In all cases respondents were provided with a prompt to which to respond. They were offered the option either to type their response and send it to a confidential email, or to set up a mutually convenient time for an audio recorded interview with the researcher. While these two options are slightly different and tend to result in slightly different transcripts (e.g. the audio transcripts have more pauses and colloquial language, for example, than the written responses), both forms of phenomenological research are valid and demand the same rigorous application of the method as both are considered evidence of a description of the phenomenon. These different options were offered so as to maximize participation and to offer a means to participation that was in alignment with the preferences of the participants. Interestingly, the parents seemed to prefer to send a typed response, presumably typed when their children were otherwise occupied. The leaders preferred an audio recording, often garnered while they were commuting. In the case of infidelity there appeared to be no clear preference. Regardless of the medium, the same prompt was used. Interviews, when they took place, generally lasted between 15 and 45 minutes. Written responses vary in length but generally can be described to be between 1 and 5 pages of typed text. All audio files were transcribed by the researcher completely, and any identifying details within any of the transcripts were modified to protect anonymity prior to analysis. Every attempt was made however, in these modifications, to avoid altering any important meanings.

The following prompts were used to begin each interview regardless of medium:

> Please describe as fully as possible a parenting dilemma/the beginning of an affair/a leadership dilemma, you have experienced in whatever way you understand the question. Please focus on the description of your experience as if you were experiencing it again including detailed information (e.g. how it was for you) in addition to any ideas and analysis about the experience (e.g. how you thought about the dilemma and attempted or succeeded with its resolution).

In some cases there was a need to follow up with additional prompts to encourage more detail or to clarify aspects of the participant's description. In these cases every attempt was made to avoid leading language and to help the participant to remain in a descriptive frame of mind. For example, additional prompts often included statements or questions such as: 'Please say more about that', or 'Is there anything more you would like to add?'

Analysis

The following steps are those taken with each sample, from within the phenomenological attitude, and result in the findings discussed in the next chapters. As outlined earlier, in entering the necessary attitude, the researcher is urged to bracket personal feelings, ideas and judgements, as well as past knowledge, or non-presented presuppositions, as in psychological theories, about the given description(s), also known as the process of entering the epoché. Phenomenological researchers bracket these aspects of consciousness so that '... critical attention can be brought to bear on the present experience ... without any additional valuing or judging or categorizing that normally occurs from within the natural attitude (Giorgi, 2009, 91). Phenomenological researchers do this in order to come back to the things themselves, or to strive to approximate this aim as an ethics of seeing and taking responsibility for our perceptions.

In approaching a phenomenological inquiry, Ashworth suggests that we are to strive to set aside '(1) scientific theories, knowledge and explanation; (2) truth or falsity of claims being made by the participant(s); and (3) personal views and experiences of the researcher which would cloud descriptions of the phenomenon itself' (as cited by Finlay, 2009). Importantly, this 'setting aside' is carried out throughout the research process and is not just a first step. Thereafter from within the attitude described above, the following steps occurred.

1 Read transcribed descriptions for a sense of the whole.

2 Determination of meaning units. The texts of each transcript were parsed at particular points, to form a discrete meaning unit if, at this particular break, there was a shift in the psychological meaning of the content. This was done to facilitate the transformation of the data, which considers only one meaning unit at a time at this stage.

3 Transformation of each participant's natural attitude expressions into phenomenologically, psychologically, sensitive expressions. Each meaning unit was carefully considered as a description of a lived experience that was then restated in a more psychologically essential manner.

4 Second transformation eidetically with the help of imaginative variation adapted from Husserl (Giorgi, 2009). ' ... an eidos, or a generalization that sets boundaries for possible instances of occurrences because possibilities are considered' (Giorgi, 2009, 197). In this step, the process included a reconsideration of the first transformation and the empirical details of the specific experience were varied and abstracted in the effort to discover a more fundamental psychologically meaningful experience across participants.

5 Identifying the structure of the experience including its constituent parts. Those items which were similar across participant descriptions (now transformed eidetically) were considered as elements or constituents of an underlying more essential structure of the experience in question. According to Giorgi (2009), 'An important criterion ... is whether the structure would collapse if a potential constituent were removed. If it does, the constituent is essential' (p. 199).

6 In this case, considering the commonalities between the structures of all three inquiries and applying the themes discussed previously (e.g. identity, intimacy, time), and any other interpretive frameworks, most notably psychological ones, has been done after each inquiry is concluded.

Summary

In this chapter, a discussion of the relationship between theoretical and empirical phenomenological investigations is presented. In particular, several of the key phenomenological methods are explored and contrasted in order to justify the selection of Giorgi's phenomenological research method for psychology (2009) for the subsequent empirical investigations. This chapter discusses the step-by-step process that results in the findings presented in the subsequent three chapters of three primary research investigations into ethical dilemmas in various contexts. The dilemmas chosen for investigation are those that are surmised to offer an exploration of both the theoretical and empirical phenomenological methods but also Husserl's ethics.

II.2

A leadership challenge

Background

In this chapter we will explore the results of an original empirical phenomenological inquiry into the experience of an unexpected leadership challenge. We selected this particular area to investigate so that we might consider the relevance of ethics in business in addition to personal situations, explored in subsequent chapters. This was of interest because we were curious if dilemmas that occur in what we surmise to be a less intimate context – a professional one – would also have a similar structure to dilemmas that occur in personal more inherently intimate contexts. Our focus is on an *unexpected* challenge because expected challenges in professional life, we surmised, may perhaps be already solved in the mind of the leader as part of business strategy and therefore may not be sufficiently fraught for ethical considerations.

Leadership is often filled with unexpected challenges driven by circumstances, some of which are outside of leaders' control, such as changes in the external market or limitations on behalf of the team, among other issues and experiences. Because leaders are simultaneously responsible for the people who report to them, the customers or end users of the services or products they provide, and the duties of their role, all of which may be in conflict with one another, leadership dilemmas are thought to likely evoke ethics. We also surmised that time (what was being lived, unanticipated and later experienced) and the identity of the leader, the company or Non-profit, employees and customers or society may be highlighted and may change throughout the narratives. While leadership and work environments are not generally thought of as intimate (and, in fact, intimacy is discouraged in work environments in some ways), a great number of the relationships at work can nevertheless be considered intimate in a humanistic sense. For all these reasons this particular scenario was of interest to explore.

To that aim, a phenomenological psychological research study, using Giorgi's method (2009), was conducted among four leaders, understood as Director level or above in for profit, non-profit or other structures. What was interesting about this particular study as compared to the others was that the leaders seemed to be not only less available, presumably due to their heavy work responsibilities, but also seemed to prefer to schedule a convenient time to report their experiences via phone while in transit or while waiting to board an airplane or while otherwise occupied. Because this is unique compared to the other two studies we conducted (e.g. parenting and infidelity), it seems important to mention that the notion of time, as it was lived moment-to-moment and anticipated even within the process of recruiting and data collection, let alone the analysis of the narratives themselves, is seemingly felt as a compressed and pressured experience, among these busy leaders. They clearly were relating to time as a resource and were aiming to save it or use it in particular way.[1] For this reason, the interviews were gathered via phone at the convenience of the participants but with less privacy than the other two groups of participants (e.g. on commutes in trains, while walking the dog on public streets, at the airport). They seemed to want to double-dip – accomplishing two tasks at once – one of which was the interview.

It was also interesting that it was more difficult to find willing participants even with an incentive to participate of a $50 amazon.com gift certificate. The meaning of money relative to time in capitalist economies and as experienced by Director level and above was palpable and made recruiting more challenging. Those who did participate seemed to be somewhat different from those we can imagine to be the superset of all leaders in that they were either leaders of smaller businesses or working in independent ways (self-employed remotely but connected to a larger business). It is possible that those employed in larger companies with more complex environments and responsibilities would have a different view of themselves and time than will not be captured here. While phenomenological research does not concern itself with representing the population or set of experiences to be studied, it is still interesting to note that in this case a leadership dilemma is perhaps better described as a leadership dilemma as experienced by small or independent businesses, even though this was not the original intent.

Among the four participants there was one who was an owner of a food production business, another who was a founder of a small start-up involved in solutions at the intersection of climate change and technology, one who was a Director of a large package delivery firm and the fourth was a founder of a small consultancy. The diversity of types of businesses was interesting. All were at the head of the company with the exception of one Director who was a mid-level manager of a large company operation. The heads of companies were not without limits to their power, however, as there was significant power instilled in their Board of Directors or through responsibilities to shareholders or funders. While these were not mentioned directly, in most cases responsibilities to these groups in addition to employees, subordinates, colleagues and end-users or customers were also among the considerations for ethical action, even if only tangentially.

Examples

In order to provide a sense of the types of descriptions that were collected, in context, we offer a few examples for the reader. The analysis of the descriptions follows shortly thereafter.

> Um so um, We provide uh various environmental foot printing services to large corporations. So it's basically a spend analysis and we take what they have spent their money on and run it through a model to assess all the indirect impacts that the companies aren't in control of. I am a co-founder. Um I design conceptually how we apply um the available models to uh the situations and companies. There's a long story about how people argue over how these things should or shouldn't be calculated. Part of what we do is try to have a simplified approach. I do other things in my life. I am an artist and philosopher of climate art and I do database software applications. So I cofounded it with a uh another gentleman that we were working together on another start up that imploded and we took an idea form that start up and that's how we founded this one. We went through a whole phase of bringing other people on, hiring people for sweat equity and eventually paying people and then scaling back and now it's just my partner and myself. I've stepped away from the day to day. I needed to get paid.
>
> The leadership dilemmas are sort of in retrospect, and less about specific instances and instead a more general thing. But uh I guess I can give one illustration which is um early on in the company when we were sort of staffing up with people um I think I perhaps let go of a certain amount of authority and direction around how we should be developing any of the tools and processes we were using and deferring to people I thought should know better than myself about how to code certain things or how to you know what was necessary. And clearly in retrospect that was a huge mistake because it meant a number of things. One, I let go or just first I let go of realizing I could do the work (laughs). But also it meant the directions of what we design went off in directions that didn't serve us. Had I insisted on keeping more authority around directing the process making decisions

around it, you know I feel like it seems like we would have been better off and avoided problems and kept me more involved.

So around the software kind of thing uh you know so I we felt we needed to build some enterprise scale industrial scale tools if you will, and I felt like the software stuff I was doing was kind of at a lower level, not as bullet-proof in terms of the languages I knew or used or even some of the protocols that's not the right word um or standards I'd used. But the fact of the matter is that in retrospect, you know all this stuff evolves so quickly anyway, you can kind of jump in anytime anyway, so in retrospect, I could have picked up what I needed to know very quickly and built things that worked but I stopped myself before I even started thinking that you know, um uh, um, you know maybe I needed to bring in people who knew better but I realize in retrospect I knew as much as I needed to. But in retrospect, like I let my cofounder sort of just hire people when he found them so for example we hired someone to build us a software application to theoretically manage our process, but you know the decision that he would be hired and be given this task, actually I wasn't even fully in the loop with my partner about the decision it was sort of like hire this guy and then he'll do it. And it's like then he didn't understand my role in the company and wasn't looking at me with any authority about what we were doing or how to do it in fact I had a situation where he felt like I had you know hijacked some leading that he thought was for one purpose and I knew was for another and it came to a point where I wasn't even respected for knowing what we were doing and the fact that I designed it in the first place. And I didn't fix that. I didn't confront it early on. I verified my suspicions about what was going on in his head later. So. I guess that's one. It's all clear in retrospect.

I probably anticipated it a little bit but you know I um think I was going through various other crises because the work we do is not necessarily the work I want to do in the long run. The work we do is helpful but I don't have a lot of hopes that it will impact climate change or what companies actually do. It's a way to do something that is more purposeful than other things that are even more silly to do in terms of ways of calculating carbon but it doesn't like solve something that I am excited to solve uh and so you know I had a little bit of enthusiasm gap there and another gap with my stressing about money.

But the longer narrative frame of all of it is that, you know, in general um uh, how do I put it, I mean I … one of the things that caused me to reflect on um in the long run is a shift; you know when I was in high school and in college when I was basically in structured environments. I rose to the leadership position in almost anything I took on. I became publisher of the magazine in college and and ran the freshperson conference, and was captain of the soccer team and all those sort of things and then after college I started being self-employed so I never got back into a structured environment. But then I got sort of addicted to being free working for myself. Not only am I a little frustrated with myself by letting decades go by not exercising my natural talent. But I now no longer have as much confidence about my natural talent. But also because I took myself out of that. I also told myself stories about whether or not I am presentable enough to clients? Have I got the corporate acumen enough to not, you know, to not seem like a hippie in the room? Or are my attitudes about what's worth doing or not antithetical to what the company might want to present itself as. So some of my ideas about climate change and what we can or cannot do about it might not fit in the room when we are trying to sell a solution – it's about gauging your impact.

So there is a little bit about I self-assess myself out of even being in any real client interfacing even leading the company's vision and where I would be the public face of the company, like an intellect. Uh um we early on brought on a PhD student who sort of became our client facing scientist sort of person. Still it could have been me, anyway, but I was happy to sort of let that go for the interest in the company sort of not try to put my ego in the game. Like I have anything to prove. But in retrospect I think I sold ourselves short there.

Another example follows below.

So um, About 9 to 10 years ago I started a business. I guess I am the Founder, CEO president, CFO, jack-of-all-trades. Over time, I parceled out the job I did to individuals but the role of founder remained mine the whole time.

So, what is most palpable and memorable right now is that I sold my business on at the beginning of this year. I stayed in control and uh stayed in the leadership role for the first 2 months as we transitioned and then I stepped away because the new leadership needed to step in and really learn the business. And right now we are still in transition because … What's happened is that I created a business. I created systems around the business; I hired people and I trained them and 9 to 10 years later is when this new leadership steps on board and honestly I didn't have that much wherewithal about how much of this was created around me and who I am and how I lead. As a result on the other side of the new leadership, my role was replaced by 3 individuals. They have a different style. They just have a different way of doing things. They are different people. And so um a lot of challenges have arisen around that.

Around the 'You don't do it like we used to do it'. Kind of. And I honestly did not know how much of this business was revolving around me until new people stepped in and illuminated from every angle that they were experiencing challenges. And of course my employees were experiencing challenges. And the challenge I am facing right now is how to extract myself culturally from the mechanics of the business and create a successful platform for the new ownership to move forward in the right direction. So a lot of this is just extracting my personality and how I tended to do things. And it's incredibly challenging. You know you move one chess piece another chess piece ... something else happens that you did or didn't anticipate. And when I remained in that position by myself it was far more efficient in many ways because I didn't have to check in with anybody, frankly. I checked in with my employees but I didn't have to check in with my peers. So um that's the dilemma right now – how do I extract my own leadership persona from the business right now and prepare for the new owners.

You know, I didn't know the answer myself because it's hard to be objective about who you are. But everyone else who I was in contact with including the new ownership, has said to me, this business was you. And you know, the new ownership said to me, Why didn't we just say that you were still part of the leadership. Why did we have to say you sold to us? Kind of not because they wanted to lie about it but because they were concerned so many people were so upset about the changes. Although I warned them. I gave everyone, the 6 core staff members, notice that this might happen and I gave them 6–9 months when I knew that this was happening. I wanted to give them a heads up. I had no idea what to anticipate just like they had no idea what to anticipate. I was clear. I didn't have any assurance that this would go through. I was happy to answer candidly any questions along the way, that I didn't have a crystal ball and I couldn't say how this would shake out but that I would try to usher in this new leadership and make a smooth transition.

What has happened is that I didn't come from a ... I started a food business. I didn't' come from a food angle. What I did was along the way I created this new business, with new systems and a new way of doing things, new metrics and new benchmarks of success that didn't necessarily pertain to industry averages and when I came to sell the business, within a week of listing it, two very interested parties materialized and one of them turned out to be my buyer. And they both said, we haven't seen numbers like these in the food business before. And I hadn't ever ascribed to industry standards I just ascribed to my own personal standards and then I created a team of people who had a clear vision of where I wanted to go at least financially and they were on board and they were happy to do it and for years we were very successful which is why I was able to sell my business to this individual. Now he doesn't come from a food background either and he assumed that um he assumed and I assumed to some extent that I wasn't that integral to the running of the business. Both of us have been astounded at the impact that my personality has had or that I was so integral to the running of the business.

He and I are very different. He's a software guy. He will often say to me, 'you have feelings and I don't'. I Find it quite comical because I will say to him you are in the business of people, you have to have feelings because feelings are what matters. He thinks a business is far better off sanitized without feelings. And I said, you can try and run it that way but then you are going to have to be in the business of robots not in the business of people. So, um I think he's been softening to the things we have been talking about and none of it is related to the mechanics of running the business. A lot of it is just related to coaching him how to speak with people and how to express your concern for them. And it's quite fascinating because I didn't think I was doing anything different than anyone else on this planet but as I come to find out it directly impacts the bottom line when you are not kind and not understanding and not interested in other people's welfare. And I got to a point about 9 to 10 years into the business where I thought I cannot possibly be concerned for more people, I had topped off at the number of concerns I could have and for the benefit of my company and my employees I thought I need to step away and other people who are far more interested in driving the business forward and scaling this business need to be running the business. And I felt like managing 45 to 50 people was plenty enough for me and I couldn't take on anymore. He on the other hand, was very different than myself and he feels like he could be a leader of an operation that has 800 employees, 1,000, 12,000, he just doesn't want to be the guy on the hook for all of these people. So it's a very different way of looking at the business.

Some of my employees have said things to me like 'You know the reason I worked for you is because you are not *the man*!' I have worked for larger corporations or worked for 'the man' so I understand what that means. But I think that you know the majority of the reason that people stayed. We had zero turnover. Usually it's anywhere from 50 to 90 percent turnover a year. So we had zero turnover and I was incredibly proud that people wanted to stay and work for the company and they found it a good and safe place to be and they worked so incredibly hard. I was constantly shocked at how hard they worked and now it's the same staff and they all of a sudden want double their income and they want all of these perks and I don't think I had one employee ever coming to me with their hand out saying I deserve this. It was kind of unheard of. And now the individuals who used to work for me and now work for the new ownership have demanded, I mean demanded increases in pay, health insurance. Some of them have health insurance and some of them opted out. They have become very demanding. The new ownership will come to me and say why are these people such jerks. You portrayed them this way and now they are this other way. And I don't have any way of explaining. You know because I try not to be involved in between people but I do get involved in mediation. So if somebody comes to me with a complaint, I'll say I don't want to talk to you about it unless the other person is in the room with us is that ok with you. Most people aren't willing to do it. I feel responsible for their welfare and for the new ownership's welfare as well.

I actually want them to be successful too.

They have actually been doing financially better. They have been doing 15% over revenue we did last year. The most lucrative year yet. They have been doing 15% better. I told them, listen you are going to break the machine. And people are gonna get mad. You didn't take the time to understand how you are driving the machine and how fast you can drive the machine. And everything – the resources, the people, the vendors, the clients even. And their focus was the machine is running like a well-oiled machine. But the difference is the leadership is different. And you are not as agile as I am because you don't know what you don't know and you don't know the people and you don't know the business. So the first 2 months was me running it for them and I thought it was a training situation but nobody was really interested in learning from me and I found that really disconcerting and as of March 6th I immediately took a step back and stated contractually speaking I am now taking a step back and got in the passenger seat or the back seat and now I'm not doing the work anymore because now you are responsible for the work. And that's kind of when the wheels started to fall off and now it's been nearly 3 months that they have been truly the leadership over there and 2 of the 6 people have quit and 2 others have threatened to quit and they have hired 6 new people on. So, it's changing. It's changing rapidly.

I have big concerns about the new people they have hired but didn't take the time to vet. I pointed out my concerns because they asked me to point out my concerns and they are moving forward and I think they are kind of relieved that the old staff are leaving because now they are less likely to be, 'well, she did it this way and the other way was wrong.' The institutional knowledge and who I was as a personality in the business will fade and a new reality will emerge. And what that reality looks like ... The old guard is concerned and they reach out to me on a regular basis. Again, My method is always mediation not ... I don't want to listen to someone venting for an hour when the person who needs to hear it are the people who can make a difference. So, . . .

I don't have a dilemma over whether I should have sold the business. But the dilemma remains how involved should I remain as they move forward with the business. Do I respond to the emails, who do I push these emails to is easy but the biggest dilemma that weighs on me is other people's happiness at the expense of my own. There is only ... I mean I look at it this way. There are you know ... every morning I wake up and I have 100 energy points. And this is a dilemma that many women face even if they aren't in a leadership role. It's a constant push and pull of where does that energy go. I'm 45 now and I am pretty energetic you know I started the business when I was in my early 30s and I had 2 million energy points and I thought I was inexhaustible and I thought I could do anything and I have aged because I have put myself through the ringer. For the first 6 to 8 years of the business I essentially worked 12–18 hours a day, 7 days a week. And I built the business up and I was so energized and so positive and had every idea. It was like a think tank for me. Every idea I had I could execute because I didn't have to check with anyone and I was incredibly scared but I was also incredibly brave at that time. I had millions of energy points and as time has gone on I identified what I am good at and what I have to hire for and what I have to hire for I always sat down and interviewed somebody and said how are you better at it than I am. I can be competent at it but you need to be significantly better than me and I would immediately communicate that to the individual. I would say, wow, you have 6 more years in a kitchen than I do and I would tell them how they were better suited for the job than I was or somebody else was. And so the dilemma over time solved itself. I hired the right people, we were successful and then my energy points started to diminish. By the time I got to 100 energy points I found myself wondering how do I get my life back? How do I work out, continue my personal relationships, and over time especially the last 2 years I started to allocate more energy points to my life and started to withdraw little by little to the business. Now my staff responded most positively because I had spent so much time building them up the moment I said, 'listen I need to take 4 days off. I need to take a week off'. They would rally around me and say absolutely, please do it. Now, it's a big difference between saying I need 4 days off and I am going to take the rest of my life off. SO, that was a very jarring experience for everybody to go through. Essentially 100 energy points would go to the business. Then 90 then 75, then 50 and now by the time I sold the business I was probably at a 40 and now I am at a 10 or 15 and I think my withdrawing myself was very abrupt. And I didn't see at the time any other way to do it other than to force everyone to get used to it as quickly as possible. I did let them know, I said, I'm ripping off the band-aid. March 6th is coming and then you guys are gonna have to deal with that. I am happy to coach you through but

I no longer am in this leadership role and I can say those words and really behave in that manner but I cannot extract my concern. I cannot extract my concern because I am still emotionally tethered to everybody involved.

Findings

While these two examples are only two from four, they demonstrate the breadth of types of descriptions that were received and are examples of the raw data provided for the analysis. While the dilemmas themselves in terms of content and particular details were widely different, all of them considered employees or direct reports or customers or end-users of the product or services of the business – those who have less power or influence compared to the business leader – in their response to the dilemma. These relationships were critical in the formation of the ethical considerations within the descriptions. Through the phenomenological analysis, a coherent essential structure was found. It is described below.

The experience of an unexpected leadership dilemma is preceded by a period of confidence and a clarity of purpose. The leader begins the description of the unexpected dilemma by stating how she understood her role and the company goals and how confident she is in being able to deliver in a meaningful and purposeful positive way against what she understands to be the charge. This understanding guides how she lives the leadership role moment to moment and precedes the awareness that there is an unexpected dilemma at all. In fact, while there may be dilemmas and challenges occurring all along, the expected types of these challenges are lived in a way that are simply consonant with the understanding that the leader has of his or her role and of the goals of the company and her relationship to these goals. They are met with a felt sense that they can be addressed and are simply part of the natural unfolding of leadership and the work.[2]

In the beginning of the descriptions of the unexpected leadership challenges, the leaders seem to be both personally adequately prepared to meet what they perceive to be the challenges that they expect in their role and they believe the organizational structure is supportive of their success. There is nothing to suggest at this juncture that there is an organizational development or human resource issue that should be attended to. What occurs next is an awareness that things are not going as planned and that the business objectives are not being met or relationships internally are strained and this is unanticipated. This new awareness of a conflict is brought to the forefront in the form of discomfort, conflicts between people and/or other unanticipated negative events in the work. Because these experiences were unanticipated, the leader shifts into a reflective process feeling the desire to feel again like a competent leader and enters a new state of consciousness. From within this reflective perspective, the leader considers the role of the self as leader and further, including other possible leader selves for the future that can be or that could have been in this instance. At this moment, many possible parallel versions of the self and outcomes are possible, affording the leader access to an enriched set of possibilities and an expanded understanding of the role and the organization or goals. She is also aware that she could have anticipated the dilemma, if she had had access to this particular reflective view previously, but she is also aware that the discomfort or failure of anticipating the dilemma is what gave rise to the reflective perspective and as such would not have been available earlier by definition.

Thereafter, as the dilemma is lived further and considered reflectively, a new sense of self occurs. There is an awareness that the self could change and because the leader has power over others, in fact, should change to address the dilemma. This is because the identity of leadership, as an ethical and moral duty, is taken up and therefore responsibility for leading is taken up. In particular, the view is that the self should or could change to address the multiple issues and persons' needs, who have less power or control, that have arisen and been brought to the awareness of the leader, through the epoché. A more general transcendental view of what is leadership and, in particular, what is ethical leadership, generalized to include the needs of others who have less responsibility or power, is present. In some cases this awareness makes available a satisfactory change that brings the leader back to the original moment-to-moment sense that all is in order. In other cases, the awareness makes possible the idea that the role or the organizational structure or business objectives need to shift for the leader to be in alignment with her ethics. There is also the possibility of failure or choosing to opt out available through the epoché. In essence this reflective process avails the leader of a new perspective or view of the possibilities and therefore responsibilities that were not accessible to the leader before.

This particular set of findings comports with the change management and transformational leadership literature, one of many theoretical orientations to leadership and organizational psychology. It suggests that ethics and relationships between leaders and subordinates as well as organizational structure are related to the dialogues and reciprocal relationships of the people within the organization. In short, leadership that is transformative is bi-directional, relational and ethical because of the mutually reinforcing qualities that transformative systems have (Price, 2003; Turner, Barling, Epitropaki, Butcher, & Milner, 2002; Carlson & Perrewe, 1995; Burns, 1978). In fact, these bodies of literature discuss specifically how the relationships between leaders and subordinates provides access to reflexive processes and ethical obligations, not unlike the findings described here.

Explication of constituents

There are four essential constituents that support the essence of the experience of a leadership dilemma arising from this analysis. According to Giorgi (2009), a constituent is essential if without it the entire structure would collapse and would not support the description of the experience. Constituents can be thought to be mutually reinforcing of the entire structure.

The constituents of the structure of a leadership dilemma can be described as follows:

1. The leader lives the role of leader moment-to-moment and with confidence and perceived skillfulness relative to their understanding of the business objectives and measures of success.

2. An unanticipated challenge occurs in the workplace that implicates the leader or causes her to reflect and consider the need to make changes.

3. The leader considers what could have been and what could still be in response to the challenge and all the possible impacts of these choices.

4. In selecting a new course of action, the leader is confronted with the responsibility she has to act in accordance of the business objectives and all others who will be impacted and feels an ethical duty.

5. A new sense of what leadership is and should be, in general, as an ethical relational process, is developed.

Some examples taken from the descriptions for each constituent follow:

1. The leader lives the role of leader moment-to-moment and with confidence and perceived skillfulness relative to their understanding of the business objectives and measures of success.
   I began working for a major shipping company when I was 19. In the next 10 plus years of my career with this company I received multiple promotions with increasing responsibilities of both size and scope of operations. This company had deep roots of integrity, honesty, trust and leadership woven into its policies and procedures.

The founders demanded that the trust we have established with our customers and employees was paramount. The expectation was that in everything we do, it must be accurate and our customers trust us to treat their merchandise as if it belonged to us. I did not perceive this to be a threat, rather I felt this tapped into my innate feeling of both belonging to something bigger than myself with a purpose and belonging to a group of people that had common values and goals.

I started in a new position and thought I had a clear vision of the expectations and the needs of the staff and the users. I began to work to deliver against that vision and felt confident that I was working hard towards something good.

2 An unanticipated challenge occurs in the workplace that implicates the leader or causes him or her to consider the need to make changes.

As I began to work more closely with each of the business functions and departments, I realized that my assumptions of what we were trying to do were not consistent with the perspectives of others within the company. I was operating towards one objective and others were going in another direction. What was more confusing was that I began to question my perceptions. Was I right or were they right or should it be some combination of both perspectives and goals?
I became preoccupied for a bit about how I failed to anticipate other perspectives. This was particularly painful because I thought I was a fair person and an astute observer. I was disappointed in myself.

In the next example, a Director is made aware, second hand, of a Manager's lies and workarounds to avoid punishment for failures on the job coupled with a racist comment. What is most upsetting for this leader is that he previously trusted this Manager and found this breach very difficult to accept. It caused him to question the business structure and ethical acts within the structure and his role as leader.

Steve then said, 'There is something else'. I responded to him, 'well there is not much more you could tell me that is worse'. Steve said, 'Well Josh told me that when he found the international packages and told his supervisor about them and that they would be considered a failure because of the time of the day was past the guarantee delivery time, Josh was concerned that he would be demoted back to his part-time job. Josh said that the supervisor said that Josh should not worry about it. Josh then said that the supervisor said, "Don't worry about it, Steve is a dumb fucking Mexican and won't find out."' I responded to Steve and said, 'Well that *is* worse!'

Another describes the challenges brought about by a change in leadership that serves to highlight aspects of the work that were not available as they were synonymous with the personality of the leader.

> Around the 'you don't do it like we used to do it'. Kind of. And I honestly did not know how much of this business was revolving around me until new people stepped in and illuminated from every angle that they were experiencing challenges. And of course my employees were experiencing challenges. And the challenge I am facing right now is how to extract myself culturally from the mechanics of the business and create a successful platform for the new ownership to move forward in the right direction. So a lot of this is just extracting my personality and how I tended to do things. And it's incredibly challenging. You know you move one chess piece another chess piece … something else happens that you did or didn't anticipate.

3. The leader considers what could have been and what could still be in response to the challenge.

   > I am aware that what I signed on to do in this role is not necessarily what is needed and that I need to adapt or leave to meet the challenges. Further, I may need to adapt many times. Leadership is always a changing gig in that anytime I deal with responsibilities for others there will be considerations that are unanticipated. I can not just ignore other people's wishes or needs and continue on with executing my vision!

4. In selecting a new course of action, the leader is confronted with the responsibility she has to act in accordance of the business objectives and all others who will be impacted.

   > Josh was concerned about failing his promotion to a driver, Steve was worried that reporting the supervisor's actions would likely have a grave negative impact on that supervisor whom he was very close to and I was not willing to risk my livelihood in order to conceal these events and actions. I would like to believe that I based my recommendations to Steve based on the belief of doing the right thing for the right reason, but was it? Was I more guarded for simple self-preservation, was it the culture I was brought up in, was it the actual comment that forced a visceral response? Reflecting on both of our leadership ideals and norms, why was it so difficult for Steve and easy for me? Did Steve actually perceive the dilemma in his decision choices, or was it simply he did not want his 'buddy' getting into trouble or losing his job?

5   A new sense of what leadership is and should be, in general, is developed.
    I am reminded of a quote from a CEO that I know, 'If we do the right things for the right reasons, we will rarely find ourselves doing things that are immoral or unjust, and our customers will respond'. Steve and I did the right thing that day, and I hope he was able to learn that valuable lesson that leaders are responsible to ensure that employees are not forced to work in an environment of racism and dishonesty.

Another note:

> I realized that true leadership includes caring for and allowing those I have power over (e.g. employees, colleagues, end users, society) to impact me over and over again as I navigate through time the role. I failed to anticipate their feelings and ideas and needs once and it had become clear that I would continue to fail to anticipate any changes even if I got this one situation right. They would change and the system would change and I would miss it and my only saving grace would be to humble myself and my ideas and allow them to bend them with input and feedback loops. My understanding of my role was that it is not fixed but rather is a responsive guiding role instead.

Philosophical commentary[3]

These descriptions offer a concrete situated example of and insight into the experience of opening to the layers of reality as demonstrated in Chapter I.2 of this book. To summarize briefly the contents of that chapter, reality was defined as real (reality as it is given to us), intentional (reality as it is meant) and intersubjective (reality as it is validated by the community of other subjects). From the second layer of reality, the intentional one, we can observe the intersection between reality and a tripartite sense of time (timeless, linear, living present) and subjectivity (psychological, transcendental and moral). In fact, we can gain a scientific access to what is real if we start from what is real for us (reality as it is meant) and how we interpret it.

It is from the awareness that the participants acquired in relation to Being, time and subjectivity that each came into deeper contact with their identity, in this case their identities as leader. As shown in these interviews, the layers of reality became accessible to them through the transcendental dimension of the reflective ego which applied the epoché in response to discomfort experienced in their passive life, allowing access to options and reflective perspectives of what could have been and what could still be. The new space opened up by passive lived experience and the epoché applied by the volitional ego gives the psychological ego of the leader access to the three streams of time and Being. This opening gives rise instantly to many possibilities and therefore underscores the need to choose from among these possibilities. Through this new sense of time the volitional body of the participant which mediates between its passive lived experience and the always new reflective life becomes responsible for the choices which confer new meanings to the lived experience. This act of responsibility to choose the best from among the options including not choosing (which corresponds exactly to Husserl's categorical imperative – Do the best among all that you can do) is lived as an obligation in which the person is confronting an actual ethical dilemma. Therefore, the reflective active ego confronts its identity of leader through this question – What is a good leader to do in all times and all dilemmas? The active intention of the reflective ego is called to consider the transcendental timeless nature of the identity bound together with the role, leader, in this case.

Because it is an unexpected dilemma (and, in fact, all the dilemmas we will explore are in some ways unexpected and therefore call forth a reflective perspective on what is previously lived in a passive manner) in this opening with the multitude of options, it is not a logical menu of options from which there is a selection of one based on subjective preferences as would be the case if it were an expected dilemma. The considerations provide access to a sense of obligation or ethical duty to act in a way that addresses the needs of others and in a way that adjusts the perspective of the leader on what constitutes a good leader in a more general way. It is the unexpected nature of discomfort that begs the ethical question. What is interesting is that the identity of the person as an ethical and responsible person is bound together with the understanding of what leadership is in this moment. This is because the questions that arise from the transcendental ego are deep ones, such as, 'What is leadership in all moments? What is leadership for all leaders?'.

Summary

This chapter provides an example of an original empirical phenomenological research investigation of the unexpected experience of a leadership challenge using Giorgi's (2009) phenomenological research method for psychology. The findings suggest that leadership dilemmas that are unexpected can cause the leader to consider through the epoché many possible courses of action that push leaders to confront the identity and ethics of leadership in a more general transcendental fashion – shaping their understanding of themselves, their businesses and their impact on those they serve/employ. This chapter provides both an articulated essential structure of the phenomenon and a dialogue between the findings, organizational psychological studies and Husserl's ethics including aspects of identity, intimacy (broadly understood in this case in a humanistic manner) and time.

II.3

A parent's ethical dilemma

Background

In this inquiry, parents, including birth parents, adoptive parents, step-parents and guardians of those under 18 who live in the same household, were recruited through social media networks using a snowball sampling technique to respond to a call for participants for a phenomenological psychological study of parenting dilemmas. The dilemmas themselves were left to the participants to define and select and to discuss in an open-ended manner – describing what they understood to be an example of an ethical dilemma they had experienced as a parent. This study used the phenomenological psychological research method put forth by Giorgi (2009) of six participants' responses gathered either via email or via audio recorded telephone call at a mutually convenient time. Each of these interviews lasted approximately 60 minutes.

The range of topics discussed and covered within the descriptions of these parenting dilemmas are many. Some are related to health, broadly understood, or emotional health, specifically. Others are related to concerns about problematic behaviour or the social and emotional consequences of behaviour, or possible future upsets that may come to pass. In all cases the parents share the belief, that is largely upheld in this historical period in many cultures, that children do not have the full ability to choose for themselves and take full responsibilities for their actions and that therefore parents are called to protect them from any potential consequences of their actions or failures to take action. In all cases the dilemma is steeped in anticipation on behalf of the parent, of what might come to pass, usually experienced as anxiety and fear of a negative outcome of some sort in the future for the child and in some ways for the parent as well or by extension. The descriptions also include a decision that must be made in the present that is thought to bring about a particular type of experience in the future that is somehow more optimal for the self, the child and society. In this way, various notions of time and identity of the child and parent are involved. Another theme, that of attunement, prominent in Kohut's initial theories (1971) and continued in contemporary models of intersubjectivity (Baranger, 2012; Stolorow, Brandchaft, & Atwood, 1987), will be explored in conjunction with these descriptions as they offer a parallel psychological interpretation to the philosophical focus of this text.

It is important to note that these stories are necessarily embedded within the cultural norms of child-rearing and parenting and it is possible that the dilemmas would result in different meanings in different contexts or time periods. Before discussing the findings and the structure of the findings in particular, it is perhaps useful to read some of the raw descriptions to get a sense of the types of scenarios that were offered at the beginning of the analysis so as to make clear the nature of the dilemmas as the starting points for the analysis.

Example verbatim responses

One participant offers a description of a dilemma with food and parenting and anticipated meanings that her son may associate with eating meat, in particular, in the future.

> My husband and I think of ourselves as fairly liberal parents in many ways. We think germs are good for babies and that it's OK for them to eat dirt. We were not strict about a schedule until it became clear that a schedule was in the baby's best interests. When the baby comes home from daycare with a scratch or a bump or we learn that his daycare broke one of his glass bottles or food jars, we are easygoing in response. Overall we are fairly relaxed about parenting. With one exception: food.
>
> Early on we read *Bringing Up Bebe* and were intent on following many French parenting principles around food. We wanted a baby who would eat blue cheese, rather than one who would only eat pizza, macaroni and cheese, and chicken nuggets. We try to be systematic with our approach to meal times, not allowing the baby to snack whenever and wherever he wants. He eats as much whole, organic food as we can muster. We might not care if his daycare breaks a bottle or jar, but we were not happy when we learned that one day when he refused the food we had sent, they fed him a Nutrigrain bar. This is all to say that food is a deal breaker parenting item for us, and so it was a question of food that caused one of our bigger parenting dilemmas.

My husband is a pork-abstaining omnivore and I am a lacto-ovo vegetarian. Before the baby was born and when he first started eating solid foods, my husband and I planned on his eating as my husband does, as a pork-abstaining omnivore. But as our son grew and the date of introducing meat into his diet approached, I began to have reservations about his eating meat. I shared them with my husband, who listened and made his case for why he wanted our son to eat meat. Honestly, I cannot remember what the case was that he made, which goes to show that I was only hearing my own reservations and not my husband's argument in favour of the idea.

Whenever I thought about my son eating meat, I felt anxious. I could not put my finger on why I felt I needed to protect him from eating meat, but I did. I kept thinking of a viral video I had seen of a young boy, eating octopus. The video captured the moment when the young boy discovered that the food he was eating and the animal he had seen in the aquarium were one and the same. When the boy discovered that an animal had died so that he could have his dinner, he was appalled, and he declared that from that day forth he would no longer eat meat.

This was my fear for my son. Not that meat was bad for him or even that his eating meat was bad for animals or the environment. Not that my son ought to be similar to me or that my rationale for being a vegetarian should restrict my son's diet. I knew that there will come a day when my son will understand that meat is not merely food, but an animal that died to become his food. And when that day comes, when my son can comprehend the situation, if he chooses to eat meat I will support him in that choice. But I felt very strongly that it was better for my son to make an informed decision that it is OK for an animal to die for his dinner and *become* a meat-eater than it would be for him to unwittingly eat dead animals before he possessed the comprehension necessary to make such a choice.

My husband was respectful and did not press the issue. Knowing that I felt strongly that our son should remain a vegetarian until he can make the choice for himself, my husband supported my decision. We agreed that, when the time comes, we will teach our son about sustainability, factory farming, and the environment. We will take him to a farm. We will let him know how his dad eats and why, how his mom eats and why, and that he has a choice.

Neither of us wants to force our son to be 'like us'. Both of us want the best for him when it comes to his health and well-being. We very much want to raise an independent child who is capable of critical thinking and makes informed decisions. But until he is capable of doing so, we have to make decisions for him, and for this decision we decided it's better for him to be free from culpability until he can make the choice for himself than to one day feel, like the boy in the viral video, that we thrust something upon him that he feels is wrong.

Another participant offered an ethical dilemma relating to blended families, genetics and family dynamics.

> As a Gay man who wanted to have children, I spent an inordinate amount of time weighing my options and considering what would be the best journal for me and any children that I may bring into my life. The considerations included social, financial, psychological, familial and emotional factors. I tried to balance a path forward that would allow me to have 2 children, leave me enough financial resources to raise them in a lifestyle that I thought was appropriate and not introduce any known challenges that I thought would be impossible to parent through. I believed I had created that family when I adopted my son internationally from an orphanage in 2003 and had my daughter through gestational surrogacy in 2006.
>
> I chose the different methods of bringing children into my life based on the options that were most available to me at the time. It was not critically important to me to be a biological father; however, sharing biology with my daughter has been a joy that I could not have predicted. In no way does the biological link with my daughter diminish the connection I have with my son or raise my daughter in any fashion in my heart of mind. That being said biology has become a tremendous dilemma in our family that we continue to struggle with.
>
> Because my son grew up in an orphanage that he was placed in on his first day of life, I know nothing about his family of origin. There is no information available on his birth parents, potential siblings or extended family. This has been an emotional loss that my son has been quite open about for a great deal of his life. While he has been able to attach beautifully to this family, there is a sense of deep disconnect because of the lack of biological information. My daughter knows her birth mother and has a close and connected relationship with her family. We vacation together, spend holidays together and talk regularly even though she lives on the opposite coast. She knows who her biological mother is by name, photo and location but has no current connection to her. The agreement made at the time of the oocyte donation was that additional information would be shared and contact could be made if any medical emergency warranted sharing of such information. At the age of 18, my daughter would retain the right to make contact if it was important to her.
>
> I know that the egg donor had donated once prior to her donation to me. The first donation resulted in at least one live birth. I have also since learned that she donated once after me, which also resulted in at least one

live birth. Simply put, my daughter has at least two biological half-siblings. There may be additional births from this donor.

The dilemma begins with how I manage this understanding. Both of my children are deeply interested in biology. My son is saddened not to have any information about his biological connections. My daughter has some information available to her which she has not accessed yet. Do I tell my children that I know that my daughter has biological half-siblings or do I simply state that the agreement was focused on the donor's oocyte donation to me only? If I share that knowledge that I have with my daughter and she cannot connect to her two bio half-siblings does it do her more harm and loss, which she is currently not experiencing? Does sharing the information with my daughter disregard any other family's decision to keep that information private or is that the risk you take when you use a donor? What if the other family doesn't know about other connections and doesn't want to know? What if the other families haven't told their children that a donor was involved in their conception(s)? What would it mean to my son that his sister has the ability to continue developing biological connections? Should I wait to see if they try to connect on a 23 & Me type website and let them self-disclose? What does it say to my daughter and son if they find out I knew this information and didn't share it? There are so many questions that I am having to think through with nuances and ramifications. At this time I have opted to not say anything until my daughter asks a direct question. At that time, I will have to assess how old she is and how I think the information will affect her. In regard to my son, all I can do is honour and respect his unique journey with its inherent challenges and remind him that he can't compare his experience to his sister's.

Another participant shares a description of events that required her to make decisions that resulted in what she believes saved her son's life. These were difficult decisions to make in the moment and with hindsight seemed correct and intuitive her. They were also contrasted with another parent who did not make the same decision and came to regret his mistake.

Okay, where to begin? I think it is necessary for you to know the type of relationship my son and I have. It has just been the two of us since he was just six months old. When he was three years old, we moved to Puerto Rico for a teaching job I had acquired. During this time in our lives, we travelled to several different countries. When we returned to the States, we moved back to our hometown in the Midwest. After five years, I grew tired of teaching and we moved to a remote fishing town in the Northwest where I had acquired a job at a hunting lodge in the middle of the mountains. The only way in was by bush plane. We spent two seasons there and it was a wonderful experience for both of us.

Thinking I needed to get my son back into the real world, we moved to a larger city in the Northwest. This is where the trouble began. My son was now eleven. During our first year there, I substitute taught in a larger school district. I left the house each morning at 6:30am and returned each evening at about 5:30pm. I had a friend in the apartment building who would make sure my son got off to school in the morning. After school, he spent time with his friends until I returned home. We spent the evenings together for dinner, homework and TV.

That summer and for the next year, I worked as a temp with the Forest Service. Because money was tight, I also took on a part-time job as a barista a couple of nights a week and often also on Saturdays. My son was virtually on his own for the end of his twelfth year and beginning of his thirteenth year of life and that is when trouble began. I knew most of his friends, some of whom I liked better than others. But, they, like him, were also latch-key children and were virtually free roaming around in the town and wilderness areas nearby. Although my son hated school, he attended class each day. Well, he 'attended', but he wasn't really 'there'. He did just enough to pass. The following summer, they really were free. I called it his Huck Finn summer. They would sleep in the woods or down by the river or at one of their homes ... mine, too. Sometimes he would be gone for a few days at a time. I really wasn't worried about him because he would check in with me often.

However, when school began that next fall, my son decided he wanted to be home schooled. I told him that was impossible at that point in time, so he continued with public school. He was in the seventh grade now and really hated it. Looking back on it all, I sometimes wonder if he would have done better had I allowed him to home school. I don't know. All I know is that he was becoming a very angry child and our relationship had slipped badly. He was not doing any schoolwork at all and skipping many school days. I knew that he had begun smoking pot that previous summer. This continued into the school year. I was so distraught that I began calling around the state to find treatment programmes for him. Unfortunately, all the beds were filled. However, one Wednesday in late September, I received a call from a facility a few hours away where a bed was opening up that Friday. They said that there was such demand that I had to have my son there that Friday or it would go to another boy. I told them we would be there.

When I got home after work on Thursday night, I went to my son's room where the door was locked. I heard some whispering inside and the window opening. I said, 'Son, you have thirty seconds to unlock this door or I will go to the manager and have this door removed and you will never have another door on your room again!' The door opened and there were four very guilty-looking young boys sitting around the room filled with marijuana smoke. As I pointed at each boy individually, I said, 'You, you, and you get the hell out of my house. And, you, get into the living room. We have to talk.' As they left the room, none of them would look me in the eye.

As we sat in the living room, I told my son that because I felt I was failing him as a parent and because he had become so out-of-control over the past year, I had been in contact with a rehab facility and that the next morning, Friday, he and I were going for a 'tour' so he could see where his life was headed. I did not tell him I was checking him into the facility ... it was just an informational tour. He pleaded with me, 'Mom, I'll do better. I'll go back to school. I'll do what you want.' I said, 'Son, I don't even trust you anymore. You don't even look me in the eyes ever. How can I trust you when you can't even look me in the eyes?'

The next morning, as I passed through the kitchen on my way to my son's bedroom, I noticed that a bottle of wine I had left on the counter was gone. When I went into his room to wake him for the trip, I saw the empty bottle on the floor near his bed. When I tried to awaken him, he barely stirred, grumbling, 'I'm not going.' I said, 'Son, I am going out to start the car and you have ten minutes to be there or I'll come in and drag you out.' Ten minutes later, we were driving out of the parking lot for the two-hour drive to the facility. As we rounded the curve from our town onto the highway, he opened the car door and I sped up. He then stuck one foot out the door and I went even faster. When he stuck his second foot out the door, I went even faster still, and said, 'Son, you jump now, it will kill you. Your choice.' He pulled his feet back in, closed the door, and said, 'When we pass through the next town, I'll jump out at the first stop light.' I responded with, 'Go ahead. And I will go to the nearest police station and report you as a run-away and when they catch you, they'll put you in baby-jail.' I did not know whether this was true or not. I just wanted to scare him and show him I meant business. It was all for naught though because he was so loaded from pot and wine he had consumed the previous night that within five minutes, he had passed out.

When we arrived at the facility, I went in to introduce myself. They asked where he was and I told them he was passed out in the car. One of the men went with me. I opened his door and said, 'Come on, Son. We're here.' He kind of stirred, but didn't move. Then the man said in a loud, gruff voice, 'Wake up. Now!' And, he did.

When inside, we gathered in one of the offices with three of the facility clinicians where they explained what their facility was all about. Then they separated us telling my son that they wanted to introduce him to the other boys. I was taken to another office where I signed the paperwork. A few minutes later, we were back in the original office when I was asked, 'Well, what do you think, Mom?' I said, 'You have one bed left? Well, not anymore. My son's sleeping in it tonight.' He turned his head towards me and his mouth dropped open. 'You mean you're leaving me?' And, I said, 'Son, you've left me no choice. This is bigger than me. I can't do it anymore.'

They took him down the hall into the front room where the other boys were and as I left the office, I looked down the hall. The last thing I saw was him looking at me through the glass door with this look of total shock on his face. All I did was turn, leave the building, and climb in my car. As I reached the end of the road, I turned left, stopped on the side of the road, and just cried. I felt like such a failure. All the memories of our wonderful life together appeared in my head and I just cried. It was horrible.

I drove up to the facility each Sunday to see him. We also had family counselling. It was weeks before he even looked at me or spoke without a surly undertone in his voice. There was so much anger there. After our counselling, we would go sit in the front room with the rest of the boys to watch TV and talk a little bit. Let me rephrase that. He never said anything, but I was able to engage some of the other boys into conversation. They began to trust me enough eventually that when I arrived at the facility each Sunday, I was welcomed with a series of hellos and when I left, they all said goodbye. Nothing from my son.

One Sunday, a couple of months in, my son walked me to the door as I was leaving. As I said goodbye, he said, 'Mom, I don't understand it. I'm not scheduled here.' I said confusedly, 'You're not scheduled here? You have to get up each morning. You have school, meals? You have a schedule.' He said, 'No. I mean I'm not scheduled to get out of here!' And, I said, 'No, you're not. And I'm not like the other parents who when you have a break down or cry, that I will pull you out of here. Your schedule is on you. When you buy into this system and graduate from the program, then you will get out. It is all on you, son.' And, I walked out.

Well, he did buy into the system and after a total of nine months, he graduated the program at fourteen years of age. I did not want to bring him back to the same town. It would be like taking a recovering alcoholic to the same old bar and expecting him to maintain his sobriety. So, we moved again, and it was good.

A few years later, as we were passing our old town on our way back from a trip, we stopped by some friends' home down near the highway to say hi. My son asked to borrow the car to go visit some friends and I said yes. One of my friends was working in her garden and I was sitting on the picnic table, when twenty minutes later, my son drove up. He got out of the car and walked towards me with an ashen face. I asked him what was wrong. He sat down next to me on the table and said, 'Mom, if you hadn't put me away, I'd be dead now.' It turned out that of the six kids who were his friends, two were homeless and living under bridges; one of the girls was now a single mother; one of the boys was dead from an overdose; and my son and one of the other girls were the only 'survivors'.

The most unfortunate part about any of this story is that while I was a barista and my son was in the facility, one of the fathers came in and asked me what I had done to get my son into the facility. I gave him the phone numbers of all the facilities telling him to call them and put his child into the first facility in which a bed opens. He never did. His son is the one who died from the overdose. My heart is broken for him. I cannot imagine. This was the hardest thing I have ever done in my life and it is also the most significant.

Findings

These examples, combined with the others, analysed through Giorgi's (2009) phenomenological research method for psychology, result in a cohesive structure of the experience of an ethical dilemma in raising a child. While each dilemma and the description of its resolution is different, including that the dilemma remains still unresolved, the structure of the experience is consistent and can be described as follows. The ethical dilemmas in raising children are encountered against the backdrop of ongoing moment-to-moment lived experience of parenting.[1] This organically-lived experience of parenting is understood in the beginning by participants to be what can be described as the experience of the *good enough mother* (Winnicott, 1953), which was later generalized to good enough parent. While it is not clear from this short excerpt if in fact the totality of the relationship is indeed Winnicottian good enough parenting, at least there is no evidence of problematic parenting or reflections on the quality of parenting in the descriptions. In addition, the descriptions of the children in these stories are positive in the beginning. The dilemma is not yet present in the descriptions at this point nor is it foreshadowed. The parents in these descriptions are not considering what the elements of good parenting are in this part of the description, for example, nor are they considering how well they are doing to measure up in the future to what it means to be a good parent. Because the children are doing fine in the stories in the beginning there is no real impetus to reflect on the role of a parent – it simply is being lived organically at this point. For example, while we may be a friend or a sister or a divorcee or a churchgoer or a citizen, we are not always thinking about[2] what these roles mean and how they relate to other parts of ourselves or how they may shift over time or even how well we are doing in any of the roles relative to what we might expect of ourselves or others might expect of us in each role. There may be moments that bring these roles and facets of our identity into sharp relief, when being a parent, for example, is the object of our intentional thoughts – as in reflection. Parenting, however, as a lived experience in these stories in the beginning, is lived somewhat pre-egoically and organically through time, without reflective moments on the identity of parenting as an object of active intentionality.

The act of reflection on parenting arises as a result of the participant noticing, within the moment-to-moment experience, that there is a dilemma unfolding that is significant because it is anticipated to have a significant future negative impact on the child. In these parts of the descriptions, such a dilemma includes a mounting understanding that there is an issue arising for the child that may become a problem in the future if action is not taken by the parent. This is rooted in the belief that the child cannot act with full awareness and responsibility and further that the parent is aware and therefore responsible due to their relationship with one another. This is not thought to be a singular act to be taken in a moment, like catching the child as he falls off a bench, for example (although that would be a responsible and ethical act to take if one were to notice one's child falling), but the issues in the descriptions are more substantial and longer term – ones that require a more significant adjustment in the relationship between parent and child and understanding of the identity of parent, that has a more lasting potential impact. It is an act that requires of the parent a shift in his or her understanding of the relationship between the two and further the definition of *good enough parent*, so as to make possible a new future for the child.

The dilemma itself is lived as a choice to continue doing what has been done or to change something for the sake of the child and in particular for the sake of what is anticipated, somewhat anxiously, for the child's future, and therefore the parent's future, which is yet unknown.[3] The dilemma is lived with a fair amount of struggle, often considering and projecting forward possible scenarios or meanings that the decision may have for the child in the future and is sometimes met decidedly in an instant and at other times is delayed or postponed or met in stages as in a series of mini-decisions that inform the next set of options or decisions. At the same time there is a considerable struggle with the meaning that various courses of action may have for the child and the parent in the present and in the future. This struggle is considered sometimes through many angles and there is recognition in this consideration that there is power that the parent has over the child to determine his or her fate to a certain extent, and that there is also a powerlessness because the child has some agency, but perhaps not full capacity for clear decision-making, and diminished power and agency compared to the parent. This power is not held lightly throughout the experience of the dilemma but instead this power is what fuels the reflection and therefore the felt sense of obligation to honour what is perceived to be best for the child even if it is not what is preferred for the adult parent self. There is a selflessness coupled with a decided alignment with the role of parent in a larger transcendental manner – not the particular identity of this particular parent but what the role of parent is altogether for children altogether, for all situations, albeit still limited through the lens of accessible cultural meanings. The shift that occurs in recognizing the dilemma, the power of the parent, and then the generalizable ethical role of parenting, is a shift that makes possible a course of action that brings a resolution. It is not a resolution of the dilemma through taking action A or action B, or even in postponing action altogether, per se, although these may also be parts of the resolution. It is a resolution of the dilemma through a reflective perspective on possibilities and identities coupled with an obligation to take action in a relationship where there is power and responsibility for both subjects. In realizing the power of parent over child and therefore responsibility for the future, the parent meets the dilemma with an understanding of the self as a particular parent with particular preferences. This needs to expand to the generalizable *good enough parent* that cares for the particular child now and in the future and further for all children, metaphorically, in general in the future, in mind. The child in the future is not only a particular child in the future but includes a great number of possible outcomes both positive and negative that are not concrete but are projected forward in protentional time as an infinite set of opportunities brought about by the reflective stance for not only this particular child but also for children in general, including all the possibilities for this particular child through development. It is through this shift in perspective, activated by the epoché, that the resolution of the dilemma becomes available to the parent to choose. It is also this view that is wide enough in space and time across identities and circumstances – in fact transcendental – that obliges action in an ethical sense.

In this structure there are all three notions of time discussed in previous chapters. First, the dilemma is described as being lived in the flow of moment-to-moment time – psychological time. When the dilemma is recognized and named a 'dilemma' through a recognition of the need to consider and reflect upon how the role of parent has been lived, it becomes the intentional object of the psychological ego. We are then in the practical ego, which is borne out of an epoché that gives access to the multilayered possibilities of identity and time.[4] The self and the child are considered in this moment and in all future possible moments from this position with some of these options seeming more compelling than others. Within these many crossroads of possible meanings and the obligation to choose one which is rooted in the reflection on identity – What is a good enough parent to do in situations like this? – there is access to the transcendental ego that has access to a timeless position, and the obligation to choose not what is particular to the self and this particular child but that which is unifying for all dilemmas of this type for all intersubjective identities in this relationship to one another. The answer is in taking this perspective and in deciding to hold a space for the future through action or inaction in this moment. Both time and the understanding of the self and other are shifted in this process.

These constituents could also be understood psychologically as an example of various degrees of empathic and attuned parenting (Kohut, 1985; Stolorow, Brandchaft, & Atwood, 1987; Isaac & Rowe, 2000). Attunement, first articulated by Kohut to be a felt sense of the intersubjective – the capacity of a person to feel and think into the inner world of another – is what allows the parent to notice the existence of the dilemma in its fullness. It is through attunement that parents could come into contact with the fullness of the dilemma through anticipation of future possibilities and consideration of one that is optimal for the child, a process well understood and articulated by self and relational psychology (Kohut, 1971; Stolorow, Brandchaft, & Atwood, 1987; Issac & Rowe, 2000). This understanding that the self and the other, in this case the child, are two identities living through time in parallel and the realization on the part of the parent that they are living towards a possible future that is problematic, (at least from the perspective of the parent), gives rise through attunement to a consideration for both identities and the relationship between them in the dilemma. The degree of attunement is the degree of understanding of the meaning of the dilemma now and in the future. It also provides access to possible resolutions to the dilemma that transcend particular preferences the parent may have as a self. The dilemma is in this way an intersubjective one.

In each of these descriptions it could have also been the case that the parent was not particularly attuned to the child and that the child instead was attuned to the parent, for example. In cases like this there is a different unfolding of the dilemma. For example, the child may have a realization that a substance-using parent is living towards a problematic future (and therefore the child too). In this case, the child, if attuned to her drunk driving parent, for example, may be aware that there is a dilemma that requires an ethical decision and/or action to avert a possible negative future, bytaking the wheel or telling someone outside the family about the issues. In the examples within the study, however, the parents can be described to be attuned to their children and this can be interpreted as the mechanism through which the practical ego and a new sense of time are accessed. From the attuned parent perspective, there is a sense of empathy for the other that allows for a consideration of the obligation one has in an ethical sense to protect both the self and the other – in essence to do the right thing on behalf of the other who has less power and who also has a subjectivity that is equally important. What is understood as the right thing, psychologically, from the parenting perspective, is to protect the child from what is anticipated to be negative even if it is difficult for the parent at the time in a self-sacrificing manner due to the power dynamic inherent in parenting.

Explication of constituents

In order to ground this discussion in the data, the five constituents, which were uncovered in this analysis will be discussed below and examples taken from the participant's descriptions will be provided. The constituents are those elements which as Giorgi (2009) describes are essential to the description of the phenomenon in question which neither add anything that cannot be supported by the data nor take away anything that is present in the transformed data. For a set of constituents to be considered essential, each must support the other and they must all not describe a different phenomenon, or one with a different level of specificity or focus than the one in question. For the phenomenon of a parent's lived experience of an ethical dilemma in raising a child the following five constituents were found:

1 The parent lives parenting in a natural moment-to-moment organic manner.
2 The parent notices that what he or she has been living as parent and the child has been living includes anticipated negative possible outcomes for his or her child in the future.
3 This give rise to a consideration of the meaning of several possible courses of action for both the self as parent and the child, who has less power in this relationship.
4 The possible courses of action or even delaying action is considered through the lens of the ethical obligation one has as a parent and this gives rise to new view of the meaning of the dilemma.
5 The new view is that there is a generalizable more transcendental framework through which all parenting dilemmas can be understood – that parenting dilemmas involve navigating towards the best possible future parent self through supporting the best possible future child self.

What follows are some examples for each of the constituents, which further illustrate how each is lived.

1   The parent lives parenting in a natural organic manner.

> Okay, where to begin? I think it is necessary for you to know the type of relationship my son and I have. It has just been the two of us since he was just six months old. When he was three years old, we moved to Puerto Rico for a teaching job I had acquired. During this time in our lives, we travelled to several different countries. When we returned to the States, we moved back to our hometown in the Midwest. After five years, I grew tired of teaching and we moved to a remote fishing town in the Northwest where I had acquired a job at a hunting lodge in the middle of the mountains. The only way in was by bush plane. We spent two seasons there and it was a wonderful experience for both of us.

Or another example as a parent describes the usual ways they have addressed homework:

> Last school year, we discovered our youngest child who was a 6th grader at the time was doing her homework. She would say she was working on it and she did appear to be working on it – as she'd always worked on homework before at the kitchen counter.

Or another describes her son in general and sets the stage for the dilemma:

> My son, Mark, used to go to sleep without any objection, two books and a song, just me and him. But recently he started to get upset at bedtime. He's a really happy kid and doesn't cry a lot not even when you think he should – like if he falls or skins his knees, nothing.

2   The parent notices that what he or she has been living as parent and the child has been living includes anticipated negative possible outcomes for his or her child in the future.

It is interesting the moment in each description when the parent becomes aware of not only discomfort or a conflict but potentially the beginnings of a dilemma because both the parent and child are both experiencing changes and disruptions or issues in a responsive attuned manner.

One parent becomes aware of a significant change in her son's behaviour:

> All I know is that he was becoming a very angry child and our relationship slipped badly. He was not doing any schoolwork at all and skipping many school days. I knew that he had begun smoking pot that previous summer. This continued into the school year. I was so distraught . . . ..

A PARENT'S ETHICAL DILEMMA

Another parent characterizes the dilemma as a struggle:

> That being said, biology has become a tremendous dilemma in our family that we continue to struggle with.

One parent discusses a concern with failing grades and lying:

> Well she got all As so we signed her up for the activity, on Tuesday and Saturdays.
> But in March, we got an email from her teachers saying she was getting Ds due to many missing homeworks. We had been asking her 'What homework do you have tonight? Do you need any help' and the answer had always been 'No'. And later in the evening we would ask 'Did you finish?' and if not, 'You need to finish the last of it up before bedtime.' But we hadn't asked her to show it to us.

Another describes a new upsetting behaviuor and therefore a dilemma on how to parent through this compared to previous approaches and in relationship to a stance that she and her husband had previously taken with regard to sleep:

> Once when he was about 12 months old and just starting to share a room with his sister she woke him up when she was going to bed about an hour after he had been asleep. Nothing could soothe him.

3. This give rise to a consideration of the meaning of several possible courses of action for both the self as parent and the child, who has less power in this relationship.
> My husband is a pork-abstaining omnivore and I am a lacto-ovo vegetarian. Before the baby was born and when he first started eating solid foods, my husband and I planned on his eating as my husband does, as a pork-abstaining omnivore. But as our son grew and the date of introducing meat into his diet approached, I began to have reservations about his eating meat. I shared them with my husband, who listened and made his case for why he wanted our son to eat meat. Honestly, I cannot remember what the case was that he made, which goes to show that I was only hearing my own reservations and not my husband's argument in favour of the idea.

Another notes questioning her parenting style:

> So when we discovered the missing homework situation, we were upset! I felt like a bad parent, that I had let this happen again. Then again, I hadn't

wanted to constantly be looking over her shoulder. We are not helicopter parents unless it is called for – and in this case it was, so we again began methodically checking her homework each night.

One parent begins to articulate the possible courses of action and possible outcomes quite directly:

Do I tell my children that I know that my daughter has biological half-siblings or do I simply state that the agreement was focused on the donor's oocyte donation to me only? If I share that knowledge that I have with my daughter and she cannot connect to her two bio half-siblings does it do her more harm and loss, which she is currently not experiencing?

Another notes a conflict between feeling for her son and her previous stance on sleep hygiene:

I felt like I should be letting him soothe himself, but my gut told me that he was really emotionally hurting and I just felt it was so unfair that he had be woken up like that.

4. The possible courses of action or even delaying action is considered through the lens of the ethical obligation one has as a parent and this gives rise to new view of the meaning of the dilemma and a course of action.

In the case of this parent, additional outside sources are sought to help facilitate an ethical view or new perspective:

Last week, I sought medical help. I spoke to a counsellor and she has her first appointment with the counsellor in May.

Because this participant cannot discern the right course of action, he chooses to delay action and takes a particular new view of the meaning of inaction:

At this time, I have opted to not say anything until my daughter asks a direct question.
    At that time, I will have to assess how old she is and how I think the information will affect
    her. In regard to my son, all I think I can do is honour and respect his unique journey with its inherent challenges and remind him that he can't compare his experience to his sister's.

5   The new view is that there is a generalizable more transcendental framework through which all parenting dilemmas can be understood – that parenting dilemmas involve both navigating towards the best possible future parent self and supporting the best possible future child self.

One parent reflects upon how her decisions in addressing her dilemma were met or not met by other parents in the same situation and the meaning of this more generally through her empathic reaction to this child's fate:

The most unfortunate part about any of this story is that while I was a barista and my son was in the facility, one of the fathers came in and asked me what I had done to get my son into the facility. I gave him the phone numbers of all the facilities telling him to call them and put his child into the first facility in which a bed opens. He never did. His son is the one who died from the overdose. My heart is broken for him. I cannot imagine. This was the hardest thing I have ever done in my life. And it is also the most significant.

Another parent reflects directly on morality and choice or ethical obligations to choose for those who cannot choose for themselves:

Neither of us wants to force our son to be 'like us'. Both of us want the best for him when it comes to his health and well-being. We very much want to raise an independent child who is capable of critical thinking and makes informed decisions. But until he is capable of doing so, we have to make decisions for him, and for this decision we decided it's better for him to be free from culpability until he can make the choice for himself than to one day feel, like the boy in the viral video, that we thrust something upon him that he feels is wrong.

Areas for further exploration

Because the analysis produced an essential structure of parenting dilemmas that demonstrates the three notions of time discussed in earlier chapters and through the participant's reflection on identity and ethics, it would be interesting to consider a parenting dilemma of a parent who had been diagnosed with Narcissistic Personality Disorder – as an example of one of many possible disturbances that can occur in a parents' identity and therefore the capacity to empathically or ethically fully consider others, such as children.

It is possible to imagine dilemmas arising in these relationships and a series of different findings depending on how attuned the children are to the parents in these cases. For example, these cases might result in a partial empathic response that does not crack open the full reflection of possibilities for the other. In this case, it may be that the shift to a transcendental view is impossible due to the incomplete access to the epoché that one might have.

It is also interesting to consider the idea of consent further and to imagine older children or teenagers who voice agency and independence often and therefore begin to challenge the idea of parental control and responsibility. There are some developmental expressions through time that lead parents to realize that teens can in fact consent[5] to their own experiences, or even if we do not share their views and see weaknesses in their decision-making, we relinquish control in order to provide them autonomy – another ethical obligation in these kinds of intersubjective experiences. Parenting dilemmas with teens as a subset of parenting dilemmas, represent a sub-structure of intersubjective ethics and may be slightly different than the structure presented here and is certainly interesting to consider further.

Philosophical commentary on an ethical dilemma within an intersubjective system[6]

In this chapter the ethical dilemma stems from the decisions that the volitional body – in this case only parents' volitional bodies – has to make on behalf of the volitional body of their children. Within the intersubjective system they are living, the parents feel called to make a decision that involves an actual organic, ethical and cognitive reshaping of their children's life. In this case children are not capable of giving their consent (or we do not imagine they are and in many cases we have evidence, cultural norms and a felt sense to support this perspective), the actual decision arises passively from the psychological ego. It is then confirmed by the transcendental ego that actively reflects on the passive experience and objectifies the meanings of that lived experience. The transcendental framework is the space within which the life of the child is redesigned – despite their will – and in this framework it is not linear time, but the living present of the now that allows the parent to make their ethical choice. Despite the fact that they are losing the felt intimacy with their children, because they are deleting that space by overriding the volitional bodies of their child and all the meanings of their passive experience, they decide to act in a specific way because at that time they feel that there would be no future for their children – or it would be a bleak one – and therefore one that contradicts their own identity of *good enough parent*, if they act otherwise.

If they accepted what is available to them through a felt sense of linear time, no decision would be made (as occurred in the case of the parent who decided not to put his child in the rehab centre) because no objectification of meanings would take place in that space. It is within reflective time that the opening through the awakening of the practical ego makes possible the capability to observe the now through multiple options, to meditate upon these possibilities and their possible meanings, and make decisions that would alter the direction of linear time and the meanings it brings forth.

Summary

In this chapter the results of an original and empirical investigation of the experience of a parent's dilemma in raising a child are presented. Giorgi's (2009) phenomenological research method for psychology is used to explore six descriptions of dilemmas in whatever way the participant understands a parenting dilemma. These descriptions include different types of dilemmas and at the same time, all of the dilemmas share some constitutive structural elements. These include the following: The parent first lives parenting in an organic pre-reflective manner until confronted with anticipated negative possible outcomes for the child in the future. This then gives rise to a consideration of the meaning of several possible courses of action for both the self and the child, who has less power or free choice in the dynamic. The ethical obligation the parent has to either select a course of action or to delay action gives rise to a new more generalizable meaning of parenting through which all such dilemmas can be viewed. These findings are considered in dialogue with Husserl's notions of time and ethics and can also be understood psychologically in dialogue with the Self psychology perspectives of Kohut and theories of intersubjectivity most prominently discussed by Atwood and Stolorow (1984). Further directions for additional consideration include investigations of parenting teens and toddlers specifically which may be uniquely interesting as these developmental periods are interesting in terms of identity and agency. In addition, investigations of Narcissism and parenting or other relational or self-object disturbances that may prevent the participant from accessing all layers of time and identity towards an ethical and reciprocally beneficial decision are warranted.

II.4

The beginning of an affair

Background

What follows is an original empirical investigation of six participants' descriptions of the beginning of an extramarital affair, in whatever way the participants understand both the original promise of monogamy and what constitutes an extramarital affair. The experience of beginning an affair is lived in a manner that cannot be said to have clearly understood boundaries with a univocal meaning and the descriptions are very different in terms of the acts that take place. When asked to describe the experience of beginning an affair, each discussed, either via email or via telephone interview, an unfolding of the experience of an act or several acts lived through some amount of time[1] and noted particular turning points or important specific moments within the experience.[2] Each turning point in time represents a particular meaning, subjectively understood, and has a particular sense of ethical obligation relative to the sense that the participants have of their identities and those of the identities of others impacted by the experience.[3] For the participants there is a sense of absolute time or absolute ethics derived from the synthesis of these turning points, which are a result of their reflections of the meaning of the experience. At each turning point, however, there are different views available to the participant, each with its own motivations and therefore obligations. This particular phenomenon, compared to the previous two studies, is unique. The participants and their partners are not necessarily related to one another in a hierarchical manner the way parents and children are or leader and employee are, for example. This particular issue and how it plays out intersubjectively will provide an interesting new view and a slightly different structure because the ethical nature of the dilemma is not present due to power dynamics and therefore responsibilities but is present instead due to the promise of monogamy and the meaning that this promise holds for two (ostensibly) equals.

Which acts occur or do not occur is largely subordinate to the meaning that is layered over the events. It is not the facticity of intercourse, or love, or passion, for example, that is emphasized as meaningful in the experience of an affair or even that an affair occurred but instead a series of moments that have a unified structure and which unveil to the participant the moments in which he or she betrayed what is believed to be the promise of monogamy, which itself is also lived as an experience through time with many varied notions of meaning from the perspective of the self, the lover and the spouse.

In order to understand these layers and their meaning, first we present several narratives anonymized to protect the research participants but also to give a flavour of the stories they provided. Then we offer the structure of the experience of beginning an affair, which was arrived at through the research and analysis process illustrated above. What is notable is that a unified structure was apparent, which is not always the case in empirical phenomenological investigations, and that this structure was coherent in the ways that Giorgi (2009) required. For example, each constituent (in this case there are eight) contributes to the whole of the structure of the phenomenon in that, if it were not present, the phenomenon would be described and lived as something slightly or fundamentally different than the beginning of an affair. Further, each constituent supports and makes possible the others in a reifying manner, magnifying and supporting structurally, the totality of the experience. In fact, in order to intervene in such a structure, if one, for example, wishes to impact the beginning of an affair that is already in motion, but not fully lived, one has only to intervene on each of the constituents as any of them changing has the capacity to impact the whole (Zapien, in press).

Examples

For one participant, the experience is described as follows:

> I am fifty-four years old and have been married to my wife for twenty years. It's my first marriage. We have a teenage daughter. I had my first affair about five years ago. Up until that point I had been entirely monogamous. Before I met my wife, I had been a serial monogamist. It has been a strong and meaningful structure for me.
>
> What led to this affair was a long period of sexual frustration. To put it quite simply: I enjoy sex; my wife doesn't. We had a great sexual connection in the beginning. She was very open-minded, seductive and sexy. After a couple of months, however, I felt like an abrupt change occurred. The excitement was gone and I couldn't discern the reason. The frequency of our sexual encounters decreased and I remember concluding that she

didn't love me anymore. Sex has been frustrating since those first few months essentially.

Over the years I have tried many things to address the issue. We talked a lot. I made it clear what I want. I asked about what she wanted. We read books, worked hard at creating opportunities for eroticism, tried various suggestions. Eventually I gave up. Every once in awhile she would say, 'I know you aren't happy. I'm not either.' But then nothing changed. At some point I came to the conclusion that I can't seduce my wife. We ended up only having sex when she wanted it (very infrequently) and how she wanted it (very rigidly scripted). When I demonstrated any desire or creativity, she would refuse. Eventually, I didn't try anymore. I found her attractive and I yet felt so deeply rejected by her.

For many years I told myself to be patient, and thought that it would get better. I figured we would rediscover our original connection perhaps when our daughter got older or some time had passed or as she progressed through menopause and I told myself it would be better then. Slowly my hopes faded. I didn't believe anymore that anything would change. It had simply been too long and I felt too badly about myself and deeply deprived and I didn't see a path towards change as these events came to pass. I felt stuck in a sexless marriage and felt confined. This was combined with a feeling of life being too short to not have pleasure. I began to feel that I wanted to not waste the next ten years of my life before I am too old to enjoy anything anymore.

The woman I had my first affair with (of a total of two) was somebody I had known for more than ten years. She was attractive but not somebody I would want a serious relationship with. Before we had the affair she had been flirting with me for about two years. First I felt like she wasn't serious or somehow didn't mean to address me (My self confidence was at a zero!). But she continued and made it very clear what she wanted: Sex with me. There was no particular incident I remember, that made me cross the line, I just did. At the very beginning I felt very guilty and suffered from a bad conscience. I almost couldn't do it on my first date with her. But then I had a great time. She fulfilled so many wishes and yearnings I had had for so many years. She loved to seduce, to dress up, to play, and to be seduced. She complimented my body and gave me the feeling I was really attractive, worthy and sexy. What a treat after so many years of frustration! This affair went on for almost two years (with some breaks in between) and it was a wonderful time for me. In addition, she wasn't really looking for a serious relationship with me and I wasn't more deeply interested in her. So in a way the affair stabilized my marriage and took some pressure off it.

Having the affair made me question my value system over and over again, however. At the beginning I suffered from feeling guilty. Then there was some aggression; my wife didn't deserve any better, because she rejected me so, I reasoned. Then I sometimes felt like I sort of wanted her to find out about the affair so that she might understand just how dramatically she had impacted me. Then I just thought, 'Just fuck the values, life is short and I want to enjoy myself'. Then, maybe I thought I should adapt my values. I still think that it is almost impossible to meet all your needs in a monogamous relationship. Now I have two conflicting values: Fidelity to my wife and fidelity to myself. These two are still somewhat at odds. We are in couples counselling working on these issues now.

One participant describes:

So I met her. I met her through a mutual friend who has since actually passed away. She died very young; she died at 41 of an aneurism. They were best friends and we had gotten friendly … My wife and I had gotten friendly with her friend who was also the wife of the town minister of the main church in town, a protestant church, so that was kind of interesting. So they were friends and we were at the minister's house and this lady walked in … and this was in the late Spring or early Summer and … uh … she walked in lightly dressed and barefoot because she had been gardening and she lived around the corner and so I was pretty struck with her immediately … so that's how we actually met and then uh (sigh) … there were various kinds of socializing things and I found myself very attracted to her quickly, uh, um, and I proceeded to be friendly with her and getting her by myself, because that's what you do in these things, and um, we, so we, established a sort of relationship although it was not physical, in fact it wasn't physical or sexual until much later, in fact after, um, my wife at the time and I had split up. So that's the beginning of it. Hmmm. I don't know how to … Well, yeah, it was certainly a love affair at that point, you know, I felt like I was in love with this woman and it was really important to me to be around her. And you know I would essentially do anything I needed to do, which meant upsetting my wife, um, but that bothered me less than needing to be around her. And that would have happened … That was a month or two into the relationship. I don't think I considered it an affair and I know she didn't at the time. My wife knew it was an affair. It was certainly a mess and paradoxical as all get out. (Laughs)

I was smitten, right. I had love affairs but this wasn't really by definition was not a love affair because there was no physical hanky-panky, and that might be legalistic, and that's certainly how my wife saw it and I certainly see her point of view, um, you know, affairs I have had I'm cheating on somebody and I'm having sex with somebody else and seeing them so I mean I was seeing this woman and there were probably a few times when I saw her, you know sub rosa, and I would cover it up somehow, but not much. I mean mostly we ... at that point, mostly we were talking on the phone. And uh, there wasn't a lot of opportunity to see each other. It's pretty pathetic in hindsight (heh heh). I guess I never ... again the affair would have been ... it was from my wife's point of view. 'You're having a love affair!' I mean I could see her point. I was in love with somebody else and you know it was important for me to be in contact with this other person and you know, I would do what I had to maintain that relationship and you know it was to the, uh, to the detriment and ultimately to the abandonment of my relationship with my wife. So, well my relationship with my wife was damaged. This didn't do the ... it was the culminating blow to that relationship but that relationship was already on thin ice in many ways. We had certainly reached an impasse so this, you know, just drove a stake through its heart. I'm really not a very monogamous kind of a person. It's um ... monogamy is not a very natural state for me ... I'm pretty bad at it and it's easy for me to, you know, ... I'm ... it's easy for me to form strong relationships with people and in particular with women and um ... Unfortunately I haven't set up my relationships as open relationships because I would probably, you know, that's relatively rare in my generation, you know in your generation that's somewhat common and there are people who live that way, they are in an open relationship and I'm sure it's hard and there's aggravation back and forth but I would be better off that way or just not getting into exclusive relationships um ... I mean that's paradoxical because I'm also extremely domestic. I mean even though in the long run I am not really. I've thought about this a lot especially in the last twenty-two years, At the end of the day I think I'd rather not cohabitate and I think I'd rather not have exclusive relationships and it's hard to do in our society unless you are a some kind of a ... Or if you like to have real relationships it's hard to not get to a point where people are seeking commitment. I mean for a long time before I started getting married in my twenties I refused to get into relationships and was always breaking up with people and they'd say, 'Hey I want more.' And I'd say, 'No, I don't do that.' And then I foolishly decided to start getting married (laughs), to my considerable detriment and expense. So yeah, I was kind of interested in discussing this because I've thought about this A LOT. I mean, in some respects I'm a classic Don Giovanni type. You know the Don Giovanni story? I love passion and, you know, I love beauty and I love passion and hey, that's the whole incipient ... any incipient affair in the parlance of our time is just full of that stuff in terms of the actual ... you know, I'm a person who's pretty easily bored. I'm easily bored by people. I'm actually not easily bored at all, but you know, I'm very interested in things. I'm a very curious person who experiences a lot but I find that people you know there's a monotony to a relationship with anybody as you may have noticed ... (Laughs) ... I literally don't understand, I mean ... there are lots of people who have been married for decades and they are sincerely not tired of each other you see ... there's little bits and pieces ... My parents, were like that. They were married for forty years and I mean while there were strains and there's bullshit in a relationship like that they thought they were very close. And in many respects he said, 'Black', and she said 'White', and that's very common. But what I find is I don't know how anybody can stand to be together for that long. Classically I'm good for about six or seven weeks and then sayonara, so long. We've done remarkably well. We've been together twenty-two years and it's a tribute to her. I was madly in love with her at first and we're still quite close even though there're definitely severe strains in this relationship. Luckily we work it out and we're still very close and we work it out in most ways. We still have a lot in common. I've been telling her for years, you are the best of the lot. (Laughs) ... You annoy me less than most people. You know, I love intimacy. If you are gonna get intimacy, you are gonna have relationships and if you are gonna have relationships you are gonna have ... you are subject to domesticity and dailyness so ... well, you know, and of course much of this has to do with our institutions. Modern bourgeois marriage has been described by me as a dead love affair latched onto a poorly defined business partnership, which is a very jaundiced view but it's absolutely true. No love affair survives for years and years it's just not in the way we ... I mean marriage is in a lot of respects an economic institution and nobody thinks about that very hard ... well, I guess some people do. Smart people have prenups and all that jazz but you know, ... so you kind of got a love affair gone cold and then this business partnership where the contract wasn't very carefully spelled out and then there's lots of room for disagreement. That's very troubling to me; um I don't know what to do with that. People have been thinking about this for a long time. There's a whole history of marriage reformers and various kinds of proposals. So that's . . .

I think I would be ok with my partners having affairs. I mean I'm not very jealous. I think I mean I would be the kind of person who could thrive in an open marriage. I haven't tried it. I don't know if that's true. It may be an illusion. But ... I might find, oh my god, especially if I wasn't getting any. Often that's the situation; it is bad because one person is off having fun and the other person is dealing with whatever in the nest and domestic relations or just the fact that, hey so-and-so doesn't love me anymore and I feel like crap. You know, you are talking about you don't (sigh) I suppose people do but I wasn't able to get together with anybody that I wasn't in love with at some point. I can't ever have sexual passion separate from love and just the excitement about the other person. And in the case of this particular affair, it got me very excited to see her for the first time. Not sexually ... that's the feeling. It's exhilaration. That's what love is. Just I liked the way she looked. I liked the way she sounded. We are from about fifteen miles away from each other in New Jersey. So we have a very similar culture in a lot of respects so there was this kind of recognition, oh my god, this is this person who is REALLY a lot like me. Um ... I don't think she was really, you know. I think she fell in love with me because I fell in love with her. You know, I turned my full attention on her and that's pretty hard for anybody to resist; I don't mean me in particular, although I am extremely charming. If I give you my full attention you will know you have gotten somebody's full attention. And she was in this sucky marriage and you know knocking nickels together in a small town in the North Eastern US. And you know all of a sudden here is this guy with hmmmm, with significantly more material and social resources than she was used to, so that had to be attractive. (Laughs) ... I don't think she's very materialistic, so it wasn't the lure of wealth or anything, it was more the attention. It was like ... Oh, somebody who gets me! That's a big issue for her. Nobody got her. Nobody saw her. Nobody realized what she was like. And she's pretty special in her way. She's a pretty amazing woman. She's very creative ...

I've been on the verge of packing it in more than once in the last two years and I've backed away from that mostly for practical reasons and then I realize that hey, I still like the sound of her voice and you know I still like the way she looks. I have thought about this a lot. It interests the hell out of me. I am constantly in and out of relationships that are similar to this one to this day. I actually don't have any on the books today. But I was in one last summer and I was supposed to have lunch with someone on Wednesday who I was very close to; we were not having an affair but it was an intense friendship and we were really. I have not had a physical affair since I've been with her but a lot of near misses. And um ... will continue to. And she knows I'm friends with people and she's more or less jealous depending on the person and how much time I'm spending and one thing that's very different is the way I live now ... I'm out and about more now. I do all this public stuff and networking so I'm out a couple nights a week and I'm out having lunch with people and coffee because of the work I do because I'm a consultant. And we do all this community stuff so it's not what it ... when at the beginning of our relationship it was impossible to cover up because all I did was go to work and come home so ... (laughs) ... Yeah, it's a lot more relaxed. That's a bone of contention in our relationship I mean if any week I have to be out ... three times a week is pushing it and any more than that she's pissed. And she feels neglected and alone. That pattern of our relationship was that I went to work and we were together all the time. And I changed my life after our family business closed and so yeah, you know ... I wondered I don't know how people ... It's hard to have an affair unless you are somebody who travels a lot. Or else they are ... Madmen. Don Draper just didn't come home and he didn't explain himself. I go into the City and I work and I come home when I come home and you deal with it. But I have never lived like that. So I don't know how people do it. That's the other thing that baffles me. I don't know how people do that and I don't know how people stay married for many years ... (Laughs) ... I guess when I met her I kind of believed that getting into a relationship would kind of save me or whatever, and I no longer believe that ... When I think about a friend of mine, who I was supposed to have lunch with the other day, I mean I would have jumped into bed with her in a minute if that was a possibility but actually breaking up this relationship and her marriage and saying let's start over again ... I mean lots of guys do that stuff but I'm over that. I know nothing is going to save me. I don't have any romantic ideals about it anymore. It's a peak experience that I don't mistake for having any deep spiritual meaning anymore ... (Laughs) ... I'm too old for that shit. I'm not a boy anymore. But I'm still a lover.

Or another participant notes:

I'm gonna try to not be metacognitive about this or like, totally overly analytical. I guess the first experience that I had, uh, with I guess what would be considered an affair would be ... I guess I had been married a couple of years? Like maybe 2 years? Or so ... And my two upstairs neighbour boys, who were just a few years younger than me at the time, had come down, and you know, we were hanging out and partying a little bit and um, one of the guys ended up just kissing me. And you know I kind of, ... I was really taken aback by it. Right? I didn't think anything of it but I just remember thinking how hot it was! And how turned on I got! And we would have probably gone a little bit further, um his hand was like down my pants and up my shirt just a little bit and his friend interrupted us in the bedroom and we stopped. And, um, a couple of days later he ended up coming downstairs and we ended up having sex. And I think for me, ... the like the beginning of an affair, I guess, I kind of didn't really consider it sort of like an affair? ... until I started seeing this guy on a regular basis. And um so, I think, you know, that was my first experience with, you know stepping outside of, of my marriage with my husband and you know I'd already been really unhappy ... Like our sex life was nonexistent and um I ... so for me it was like that initial ... like when he first kissed me you know, and kind of felt me up, it was that initial like WOW, this was really exciting, but I didn't really consider it cheating, you know? I just kind of, just dude, I because I was like wow, like truly the intention was on his part and not mine and he really surprised me out of the blue by kissing me, right? But when I had him come down those couple of days later and actually intended on having sex with him, and you know, got showered and dressed in lingerie and had condoms, to me that was when a sort of at least an affair in my mind began because the intent in my mind was to connect with someone other than my husband and by connect I mean sexually connect.

This was my first taste at being very agentic in my sexuality and saying, 'I wanted this!' You know? Although he hit on me initially, I wanted this. I ended up . . . .

Let me back up a minute ... my husband at the time and I ... just a very quick background ... My spouse and I were studying abroad. I married him and I'd just turned 21. I'd been with girls before and one guy. And so the whole heterosexual like marriage thing to me was very, um, very different but very exciting and something that I was excited to try but I didn't really have something like a template. I didn't know how to be in that relationship but I have always been such a sexual person and I kind of have a tendency to separate sex and love and so for me those first two years of marriage where things were very rough for a variety of reasons, you know, new marriage, you know, language stuff, you know, we were living in a ... like we were just starting out, you know? And I kind of, like I knew that the sex was so important and I couldn't kind of figure out what was going on but I had to know in my heart that it wasn't me. I was like, dude, because I hadn't had issues before, you know, with the few partners I had in my life. And so he and I struggled those first couple of years, I was like, It's gonna get better, I was in grad school and I thought we just needed to kind of like iron things out and it'll get better and so when the upstairs neighbour hit on me it just kind of validated these feelings that I had that I was desirable and that I was worthy of sexual attention and I was worthy of a man's affection and desire and that's why it took me so off guard, caught me so off guard. But that's why a couple of days afterwards when I started to think about it I was like, you know, I was just like, fuck it man, I am sick of like waiting around for this to happen and this just feels good. Like for once this just feels good. It just felt really, really good. And so that's why I said, you know ... I didn't think about this as being a one-time thing or a multiple time thing I just thought about it being like, come down and let's make this happen. And I think that, now looking back reflecting back all those years ago, I have to admit I was excited. I was excited that somebody showed interest in me like that and he was attractive and um I think that as I continued to sort of see him I realized how much I missed sex and how much I missed intimacy and physical connection and how I wanted that in my life. And of course I wanted it from my husband and I thought in the meantime maybe I should just do my own thing and when we reconnect however we reconnect then that can kind of go by the wayside.

We were married for ten years and separated for two and I think that, you know, really early on, and now that we are divorced he told me that, he said, 'I kind of checked out really early on'. He came to America, things were really rough and he just kind of checked out and I didn't realize that at the time. I was trying to make this marriage work, I mean I'm a committed loyal person, you know, I'm like a Taurus, you know? I'm stubborn, like I'm gonna make this work! What we both kind of, . . . at least now looking back what I now realize is that he wasn't in a place to handle who I was sexually, what I needed sexually, and emotionally and physically, and I kind of wasn't in a place to handle what he needed, especially emotionally. And I think that my sexuality was very threatening to him and I think that he was the one partner of mine who has used sex as a tool and purposefully withheld sex because he knew that was what I wanted. And so from early on . . . I was really frustrated because I was studying human relationships in graduate school and I was like you have got to be kidding me! Right? Really early on I said you know I'm just going to do my thing on the side and so I'll just have this social emotionally monogamous relationship. And I'll just have lovers. It wasn't an ideal situation but it became this sort of like way of being that I couldn't . . . Like sex is too important to me and the times that we would reconnect were . . . um . . . We went to some counselling for a while and then he ended up starting an affair which was really devastating because that was during the time when I really had 100% committed to him and I'd broken up with the people in my life and I was kind of monogamous with him for about a year and that's when I'd found out about a situation that he had started. And I know now looking back, this is maybe TMI, but looking back, I know now that I was much too forgiving of him during those times because I knew what I had done.

There was one other person that I'd become emotionally connected with and that to me was more of an affair because there was that emotional connectedness as well. Before it was just kind of sex but I kind of fell in love with this guy while I was married to my spouse and that in my mind is probably the big affair that I've had in my life. It was the guy who hit on me – the upstairs neighbour – it was his best friend. So, um, in fact we still see each other every once in awhile, we're still really good friends, but you know for me it was kind of this kind of idea that you know I was gonna stay married and there was kind of no chance for us and so it really was this kind of clandestine very like, um, really sexy affair. It reminded me so much of that movie with Richard Gere and Diane Laine called . . . uh, shit I forget the name of it; the one where she cheats on Richard Gere with a hot French lover. I think that particular movie . . . I'm sorry I'm getting totally sidetracked. I'm a bad interviewee ... Sorry, anyways, that particular movie does a very good job of encapsulating the feeling of the affair and starting off and the excitement and the thrill ... I mean to me it wasn't the tabooness of it, that wasn't appealing and I didn't like having to sneak around, but I knew that my husband couldn't handle it if I actually said, 'Dude, I want to see other people'. And I wanted to see other guys but I always kept it very separate and I was always very careful and very intentional to not have him find out. Because it was never vindictive. It was never about me wanting to hurt him; it was all about me wanting to get my needs met. And I felt that this was the way I was gonna handle it because I couldn't compromise my sexuality. That was a deal breaker for me in marriage and I thought this was the best way of handling it. I think it was what I knew how to do at the time. You know, I spent a lot of years compromising too much and now looking back I wish I would have just ended things sooner. He and I were both so unhappy. But I think that some of that emerged in the latter years of our marriage, that we really were just always missing each other and not always on that same page. And I have to believe that there was a reason I stayed. Other than grad school like, I was in the middle of my Ph.D. It was the worst time to get divorced. We had no money. You know, and we had kind of grown up together from twenty to thirty and I kind of feel like it sort of played itself out how it needed to. There is a part of me that feels like I missed out a little bit and there's another part of me that feels like I had some support during grad school when I think a lot of other people didn't. And so I think it's kind of like, I kind of wish that things would have been different and we kind of would have ended things sooner and saved us both quite a bit. Maybe that's what I needed to go through. I think, I guess, I think I've had a couple of experiences since then and I've become much more aware after the work that I've done on fidelity and monogamous and non-monogamous relationships and I think the one thing I struggle most with is how to be this sort of agentic self and how to be yourself and how to be an individual and what that means when you are in relationship, whether they be friendship or lovers or collegial or whatever. And one of the hardest things I really struggle with is that if there's somebody who asks me to be sexually or emotionally exclusive there's a need or desire that person has, just like I would do the same. And one of the things that I have yet to sort of reconcile is that the people that I choose to be with in my lifetime, whether those people are mine ... are, I don't quite know how to say this ... This is sort of my life and my experience and I choose to maybe be with a partner and these satellite partners or experiences or whatever and I mean this is my way of experiencing the world and my sexuality and I think that one of the cool things about an affair is that the new relationship energy, I know the poly people talk about this a lot, and just the excitement of new that awakens the different part of who you are that awakens the parts that are dormant and just that inner connection that occurs when intimacy happens. For me it's usually sexual; I have a tendency not to get wrapped up emotionally in affairs but, you know, to like smell, you know the smells and the tastes and the newness of it is part of the thrill. And I think that the intention is also part of it too and I think that is what we are kind of struggling with in 21st century sexuality. We are much more agentic and much more aware and much more individual and we kind of know more what we want than we ever have before especially as women and so ... which is so exciting. But at the same time we have these very ancient dialogues and very archaic dialogues and scripts about sexuality about sexual pleasure and emotional pleasure and connectedness and even the word affair which I try to not be so cognizant about ... just tell her what you experienced. I don't know I would probably use the word encounter or hook ups or when it was emotional ... I don't know, I think affair is such a hard word for me. I was in love. I was in love with him for many, many years. Um, and um, so I think he was the closest thing to a traditional notion of an affair. It was emotional and sexual and the pining and the longing that comes with that so I would probably under most circumstances say affair um but I would probably call him my situation or I might I dunno ... I wish that I could give you a better word to use because it's ... I don't even really like lover. Like how do I describe this person? You know? It was a connection that was aside from my life. And that's why an affair can be so powerful in the beginning stages. It's like excitement and fear all at once. Is this what I want? Can I want this? Should I want this? Wait. This feels so good. I'm not supposed to want this. What are the ramifications of this? What are the consequences? Can I do this on the side? Should I have this be the main event? You know? What is it like to have both? And my husband had said something to me once; he said he thought he was polyamorous. And I'm like, 'Dude I taught you that word'. And no, you are not, and I'm like, here, in love with two people. And so I think that those beginning stages for me ... those are the things I thought most about and for me I kind of thought about my needs and it sounds so selfish today but back then I was at a point where I needed it and it was worth the consequences!

Findings

The beginning of an affair, or an instance of infidelity, is described as an experience that occurs within an otherwise sexually monogamous relationship that feels unsatisfactory. This relationship is experienced as lacking in important ways and hopeless to improve, from the perspective of the person who begins an affair. There is a parallel account within the description of the experience of the affair that includes how it is that the one who has had the affair came to understand both their desires and how they came to understand how hopeless these desires feel to actualize within their primary relationship. These desires, the dissatisfaction and the hopelessness form the backdrop against which the affair begins. These feelings also precede the affair in time and form a sort of psychological ego that feels rooted in the sensations and feelings that comprise this gestalt and also feels that this experience is unbearable. This particular set of sensations is experienced as an eternal now – a state of suffering and pain that is unfair and intolerable.

The specific areas that are experienced as lacking can be described as intimacy, but understood in a broader way than psychological notions of intimacy tend to put forth.[4] This version of intimacy includes sex and passion but also includes a psychological intimacy that is less easy to describe without psychological jargon. Participants describe a lack of attunement (Kohut, 1986) or a lack of being known or fully seen, or of having their needs misunderstood or neglected – a lack of attachment (Bowlby, 1979; Johnson, 2014). It includes connection in a larger sense, perhaps even transpersonally or spiritually, but also in a sexual sense. It is also understood or experienced as a lack of novelty, creativity, or stimulation, and lack of sexual satisfaction. It is as if those who begin affairs feel that they are not being seen or understood and that there is no room for their needs to be fulfilled. In part this is described by the one who has the affair not as an unwillingness fully on the part of the spouse, but rather as a lack of capacity that the spouse has to see and understand the self, similar to failed attunement (Kohut, 1986; Stolorow, Brandchaft, & Atwood, 1987). While this is understood and reported as a sexual dissatisfaction, it is also related to a lack of excitement, lack of playfulness and a general sense of boredom and disconnection. Because the psychological ego views time as an eternal now and the other is viewed as static at this point in the narrative, monogamy is experienced as an unending march towards a life of stasis – both romantically and sexually.

This is viewed as a problem that has no solution to the person who is experiencing it because he or she has tried everything that he or she thinks is possible and has given up. What is interesting is that there is a general poverty of ideas with respect to possible interventions that marriage and family therapists, for example, or self-help authors might offer. In general, participants seem to note that they have had a few conversations with the spouse about this issue, brought about by a reflection on the circumstances and experiences, which resulted in no substantive change or insight and which reinforced hopelessness. In fact, these conversations are reported to be a small opening in the reflective life of the couple, and are quickly shut down by the spouse, according to the one who begins the affair. It is as if he or she enters the epoché willing to speak about the situation and is told that there is no room for such a reflective life in the relationship and is returned back to the natural life, where there are two psychological egos living in the eternal (hopeless and unsatisfying) now. There is a need for intersubjective acceptance of possibilities and a willingness to reflect together on time and identity in order for possibilities to exist within the relationship.

After these attempts, the one who begins the affair embraces a persistent and unchallenged view that it is hopeless to talk about the issues with the partner or to work on the issues because the partner offers no capacity to reflect upon the needs of the one who begins the affair or on their shared circumstances. It is the partner or spouse who is perceived to be the one who must change to alleviate the problem who is somehow also unable and/or unwilling to do so. The view of the one who begins the affair is that he or she has an appetite and appreciation for novelty, passion, connection and sex that is inherently greater than that of the partner in sexual and romantic relationships. The one who begins the affair views the self as good because he or she is a partner who has what is perceived as an intact sense of desire and has navigated this conflict well (e.g. having tried to improve the situation for a long time and remaining loyal despite the challenges of having what are viewed as appropriate and healthy desires that remain unmet) and the partner is viewed as bad (e.g. withholding, wilful, boring, deficient, or/and lacking sexual vitality and being unresponsive to the attempts that have been put forth) and these are understood as fixed and inherent characteristics of the partner. The perception of the spouse is one of a fixed identity living the eternal unchanging now. With this view of the self as good and the other as bad, and both as fixed and unchangeable, the one who begins an affair experiences the self as deserving of passion, novelty and sexual satisfaction. The sense of deserving is a notable turning point in that it provides a justification of the acts and experiences that follow for the one who begins an affair. It also highlights a particular ethical view – one that includes an obligation to the self to seek satisfaction on the part of the self; the perception is that the other is unwilling/unable to participate and has, from the view of the one who begins the affair, already failed to deliver a relational experience in line with the ethics of the monogamous arrangement. While there may be no cultural or social support for such a rationale, nevertheless the rationale seems to be consistent among the descriptions.

At the same time there is largely a lack of curiosity about the partner in this particular experience – what the partner may want, feel, deserve, or be experiencing in parallel or what the consequences may be for them with this set of constituents. There is a lingering in the perspective of the psychological ego and little reflection or engagement of intentionality towards the other. For this reason, the partner is not fully animated as a subject in the mind of the one who begins an affair. This is in part because he or she is perceived as fixed for now and forevermore and further as bad or damaged and irrevocably so, and in addition, predictably so. With this view, no new novel experiences in the realm of sexuality, eroticism, and/or intimacy are thought to be possible to arise from this other or to be possible with the other and therefore the hopelessness and lack of curiosity seems justified and the other then inspires no further endeavouring through curiosity.

While there is acknowledgement that the situation is stuck and unsatisfying, divorce/breaking up or opening up the relationship to others are interestingly not considered in earnest as possible options for solving the dilemma – as possible structural solutions. These types of options would certainly relieve the stuckness and yet they also each conflict with the fixed view of the self as a good partner who is loyal to the original promise, something that the one who begins the affair is unwilling to consider seemingly. The structure of an affair, as opposed to the structure of divorce or opening up the relationship, necessitates the lack of realistic consideration of a structural solution changing the original commitment. In fact, to make such a structural shift is an intentional act that takes the couple out of the stasis that they find themselves in and requires a reflective stance and a decision or an ethics of seeing the situation in a new way – one unresolvable if they stay together in the monogamous structure and therefore one requiring change and movement towards some new arrangement. Within the reflection that gives rise to a new structure, there would be the possibility of an ethical stance towards the other through taking responsibility for one's interpretations of the situation and through allowing the other his or her subjectivity. Instead, in instances of beginning an affair, the primary relationship continues in an unsatisfying fashion with little motivation or attempt to change it or improve it and no path to resolve structurally what is perceived as hopeless and no openness to shifts and changes within the current monogamous structure, because the reflection of the situation does not include the other as a full subject and therefore does not allow multiple views of the experience. The beginning of an affair, in effect, is an instance of a refusal to enter into the transcendental ego state.

The beginning of an affair then occurs with all of these constituents in place and occurs as the one who begins an affair meets someone outside of the relationship during the flow of daily activities, again as part of natural life and from within the perspective of the psychological ego and experiences the self, compelled by curiosity and interest towards another, who is also reciprocally curious and interested about the one who begins an affair. This mutual interest is not necessarily understood as erotic or sexual at the particular moment in time of the first meeting, in part because this requires reflection and intentionality in order to be named as such rather than only experienced as such. It can be also reflected upon and named but usually this is after several contacts with the person with whom the participant later comes to have an affair with. What is interesting is that even if the mutual interest is reflected upon and named as such, often the experience is not registered as an experience of an affair unfolding at the moment that interest is registered. Instead there is a reciprocal reinforcing sense of curiosity and interest for the other and the other for the self that deepens and develops the connection over some measure of time, fuelling each other into further escalating interest, until a point when eroticism or passion is experienced in an act that has sexual significance. What constitutes an act of sexual significance differs for each participant in that each has a different sense of boundaries and embodied sensibilities about what constitutes sexuality and what is potentially 'over the line' distinguishing ordinary friendliness from flirting and from sexual intentions. This recognition of interest, and the recognition of a sexual atmosphere can take moments or years to reflect upon and name for the self and it is not experienced as a choice or a decision that occurs at a particular moment in time, even though there are clearly choices that the one who begins an affair makes to facilitate the possibility of mutual reciprocal interest developing over time. The process is experienced as a particular set of feelings (e.g. passion, novelty, interest, deserving) overriding judgement. The meaning of the choices that are made that influence the creation of the sexual atmosphere is not understood until after these choices are made and in fact because of these choices and the resultant feelings. At the moment the experience is recognized and named as erotic, is the same moment that passion or sexuality come to become conscious or intentional objects of the one experiencing the phenomenon. That eroticism has occurred generally is grasped through reflection with hindsight on a moment of a clear and undeniable active sexual and/or intimate activity where a line is crossed for the one who begins the affair. At the same time of this grasping are also additional feelings of concern or the awareness of the ethical obligation vis-à-vis the monogamous commitment. It is in the moment that the sexual atmosphere is recognized, that the decision or clear choice point and therefore obligation to the spouse and to consider ethics can become available. It is only possible if within this moment the participant also believes that he or she is choosing to act rather than that he or she is tempted to act or otherwise unable to access choices. The self as agent is important in this moment and is only available through reflective life which leads to the possibility to access the transcendental realm of ethics. Here is the absolute understanding of the self as agent, and therefore others as active agents, who can shape experience through space and time towards infinite possibilities. It is with this perspective that one recognizes that one can let the affair unfold or pause and act in any number of infinite possible ways (e.g. jump up and down and scream and run away; pivot and buy a coffee; stab the other and face the consequences; write a book about ethics). For those who have the affair, this moment is not fully embraced until after the affair is begun and only later through reflection and a felt sense of regret is the transcendental realm of choice and ethical obligation reached.

In retrospect, within this realm of transcendental ethical reflection, there is a recognition that there were many small actions in which the one who begins the affair actively wilfully participates that occurred prior to the moment of recognition of the affair, to facilitate the development of the affair, that can be categorized as erotic or flirtatious in hindsight. There is also a reflection after the fact that the primary relationship was headed towards crisis or a break-up all along. The beginning of an affair is lived pre-egoically, in an embodied manner, and similarly the relationship headed towards divorce, is also lived pre-egoically, in an embodied manner, and is the backdrop against which the affair develops. Only once eroticism is noticed with an outside other and therefore the acts that allowed it to build in which participants engaged as active agents is there guilt and concern about the affair in some form and only then do ethical questions arise.

Explication of constituents

In phenomenological research the resulting descriptive structure is provided as a whole, however it is also comprised of constituent parts that reinforce one another. Discussion of how each supports the larger structure as a whole is provided below.

The constituents of the structure are as follows:

1 Dissatisfaction and hopelessness in the relationship.

2 A value of novelty and passion in romantic/sexual relationships.

3 A sense of deserving sexual satisfaction and intimate connection.

4 The partner and self are viewed as fixed characters.

5 Lack of curiosity for the partner as a subject.

6 An experience of desire and passion overriding and overtaking one's judgement.

7 The affair is not recognized as an affair until after it begins.

8 Divorce or opening up the relationship are not considered options for resolving the issues.

These eight constituents are derived from the descriptions collected and each structurally supports the essence of the development of an affair in that if one (or more) is not present, the entire experience would be better described as something other than the experience of beginning an affair. For example, if one is dissatisfied and feels entitled to satisfying sex but is also curious about the partner's experience or he or she seems not to be a fixed character but instead is capable of change, perhaps counselling will be pursued or additional endeavouring for improvement will occur and the infidelity will be less likely. If divorce or opening up are considered in earnest, an affair is not necessary. If one does not experience desire overriding judgement but instead considers the unfolding affair or a theoretical affair more directly and reflectively before it occurs fully, perhaps this pierces the idea that one is a good partner more directly and one is more directly confronted with the dilemma and is less likely to go forward with the act itself – or at the very least is confronted with agency and responsibility for ethical action. It is this mutual structural reinforcing quality of the constituents that makes them essential in phenomenological analyses.

In considering the essential structure in dialogue with Husserl's ethics, identity and time, there are instances within the eight constituents that represent the different layers of time. For example, the beginning of an affair is largely lived in the flow of time with each moment unfolding into the next. There are choices and acts but they are lived as extensions of the inner experience or psychological ego that includes a series of fixed perceptions about the self and others and that are consistent with past views and that are projected into the future as stable and ongoing. The moment that there is mutual interest between the self and another outside of the marriage, there is an opportunity for reflection about both the flow of time and the meaning of time to the self and other. If this occurs before a line is crossed that is sexual and undeniably 'over the line' relative to one's understanding of how monogamy is to be lived, there is an opportunity to act in a way that is ethical – considering the original promise, the lived experience in the moment and the subsequent acts needed to bring these inconsistencies into alignment. If this moment is not met ethically, the mutual reciprocal interest has the potential to develop into a more significant breach of the promise of monogamy – the point that those who began affairs note was the moment of no return. This occurs when a sexual line is crossed and the act itself brings into sharp focus the various layers of experience. There is both what is happening in the flow, there is the reflective process that considers both one's identity (Who am I if I am doing this?), and the transcendental (What is the just or right thing to do in this type of situation? e.g. considering the spouse, right action, and the nature of the conflict, the experience of the others involved). The fundamental constituents cannot remain together if one encounters the transcendental. One of them must change. In fact, the beginning of an affair can only exist if the transcendental perspective is not accessed through reflection. Without these shifts, the affair is made possible, as a parallel split resolution to the dilemma that is lived in the flow of time and rationalized from within this perspective. In fact the ethical choice is not act or not act, it is to take a reflective perspective first and to access the transcendental notion of time from which to consider acting or not.

This particular dilemma can also be understood psychologically as an example of narcissism in that there is a refusal to acknowledge the full subjectivity of the spouse, the potential impact on the spouse or partner, an entitled stance, and there is a valuing of the self over the spouse in this dilemma due to the lack of curiosity. The beginning of an affair occurs as the self and its discomfort becomes important. The ethical obligation is then aligned with the self only – the obligation to bring the self to a state of no more discomfort. It may also be understood less broadly as an instance of sexual narcissism (Hurlbert, Apt, Gasar, Wilson, & Murphy, 2008) in which narcissism is restricted solely to the sexual and romantic realm.

Limitations and directions for future research

While we cannot say that this is the universal essence of an affair, because there are possibilities that we can imagine of infidelities that can fall outside of this description. For example, those who pre-plan affairs and seek them out deliberately (although those might better describe the essence of a hook-up), or those who are not particularly dissatisfied but seek them out in addition to their primary relationship, for example (and I might also call these instances cases of poly-oriented persons needing to come out, because people who can truly love and be satisfied with more than one relationship are more in line with the polyamory position, rather than those who are monogamists engaging in infidelities), or those who initiate an affair as retaliation for a spouse having had an affair previously. Obviously there are many more possibilities than those described above. The burden of drawing the line somewhere on what exactly we are aiming to describe in order to articulate a structure that is essential, hangs together as one structure, and gets to the heart of the issue – infidelity – is important; in these six stories, however, deliberate hook-ups or lack of dissatisfaction was simply not present in the data, therefore we conclude that the more general psychological phenomenon includes dissatisfaction and a pre-egoic recognition of the infidelity. Additional research among these various types of infidelity may provide nuanced views of the phenomenon not accounted for here and certainly would evoke different notions of ethics. This is recommended for future consideration.

Philosophical short commentary[5]

The constituents of this study show a clash of realities between partners and their Mitwelt (shared world) that we decided to observe on an ethical level. The distinction that was introduced in Chapter I.2 between *Real* (reality as meant) and *Reel* (objective reality) is useful here to see how the boundaries of the reality as an intentional content and reality as such conflate in a way that is difficult to recognize and discern for those who are living that experience in a moment-to-moment fashion. Initially the two partners share an intersubjective Mit-welt whose intentional contents are meaningful and produce value for the individuals. In a moment that none of the participants can identify, the passivity of the lived experiences stop being interpreted and bringing meaning to the Mit-welt. Hence, their shared world shrinks and becomes, metaphorically speaking, mute to them – this explains the lack of curiosity that the one partner feels for the other and that we surmise may be occurring bi-directionally. Intimacy, as discussed in Chapter I.5 and I.6, is lost because a new world is being created without the full subjectivity of the partner; also, the volitional body does not want to acknowledge its existence – this lack of recognition is detrimental to the old Mit-welt which cannot regenerate itself without intersubjective input. The individuals involved in the beginning of the affair do not allow access (actively) to their passive intentions and for this reason the activation of meanings that could create a sense of intimacy is not possible. Nevertheless they experience intimacy with the new partner because a new world of active meanings is being created there, but it cannot sustain itself for too long because it is too thin since it does not allow the access to the full range of passivity that the person is experiencing. The life of the partners (self included) is seen as fixed because that realm of intimacy is precluded in order to safeguard the axiological worth of the new world. The need for nurturing is fulfilled by the sexual desire and passion experienced towards the new person. The ethics of this lived experience resides exactly in the will to not allow access to the intimacy of the Mit-welt which for some reason stopped growing before the beginning of the affair. The volitional body of the partner that initiates the affair makes the decision to negate that access in order to maintain a view on reality that is ethically acceptable to the self.

Time plays an important role in this decision. The partners who start an affair apply their active intentionality – that is the giving meaning activity whose intentional content is the passive syntheses – within linear time; yet, they make their decisions in the now which intersects the passive syntheses in which they live at the beginning of the affair. They do not have full access to the world of passive syntheses because of the ethical decision of their volitional body. Yet for all of them reality starts taking a new shape with the awakening of that now through dialectic time (in Nishida's vocabulary) or phenomenological time (Husserl's vocabulary). The partners realize that something has actually changed in their life when from the depth of passivity a new meaning needs to arise and that would change their view of reality; if accepted, this change would bring back meanings and intimacy into their lives. A new linear time at that point can start flowing which is more aligned with the timeless time of their psychological egos. It is in that alignment that all those involved in the beginning of the affair can make actual ethical choices because they are aware of the three layers of reality (passive, active and transcendental) and they can actually own the corpus of their lived experiences by giving them a meaning that is corresponding to their ever changing world. Reality (Reel) remained the same, but everything changed. The reality in which the wider circle of friends, co-workers, family live did not change, but the reality (Real) of their intimate Mit-welt is hopefully renewed and had a chance to acquire a more aligned and flowing meaning.

Summary

In this chapter an original empirical investigation of six accounts of the beginning of an extramarital affair are explored using Giorgi's (2009) phenomenological research method for psychology. These accounts do not necessarily include any similarities in the acts that transpire but through the analysis, evidence is found for a unique essential structure for the phenomenon. This structure includes the following self-reinforcing constituents: The marriage or monogamous relationship is experienced as hopeless and dissatisfying. The one who has the affair feels dissatisfaction with the shared experience of passion, novelty and sexual intimacy in particular. These aspects are viewed as irreparable because the persistent view is that the partner of the one who has the affair is unable or unwilling to participate in intimacy or novel sexually passionate experiences. The one who has the affair begins to feel that there is no reason to be curious about this fixed and stuck other or the relationship and further begins to feel entitled to sexual satisfaction and intimacy. He or she reasons that he or she is a good spouse having tried to fix things but also having an intact sexual, sensuousness and creative sensibility. There is no real consideration of divorce, breaking up or opening up the relationship. This unsatisfying relationship then careens towards death and boredom. The one who has an affair eventually meets someone in the course of everyday events in whom there is mutual curiosity. This is only passively lived rather than named the beginning of an affair, even though the curiosity fuels mutual self-reinforcing acts and experiences lived through time that build the intimacy that is lacking in the primary relationship. The affair is recognized only when it is actively grasped after a clear sexual line is crossed that cannot be passively lived anymore. In this chapter the many pivotal moments and shifts in the perspective and perceptions of the identities of the self, other and spouse as well as experiences of the different layers of time are explored and linked to ethical decision-making.

Conclusion

This book was organized into two sections. The first part was theoretical and attempted to elaborate a theoretical phenomenological method that is designed to reactivate meanings while keeping an empathetic contact with life through the analysis of the lived experience. Each theme (e.g. reality, time and intimacy) was analysed in two chapters, a static one, focused on the eidos of the phenomenon, and a genetic one revolving around the 'life' of the phenomenon. The new meanings emerging from this methodological application were considered the main points of entry into the process individuals use to access the layers of reality. For an individual to dwell in one of the layers of reality (*Real*, *Reel* and intersubjective) involves shifts in the experience of identity, intimacy and time that determines each time a different direction in the decision-making process.

Each main theme was analysed according to a *construens* and *destruens pars* (hence the six chapters of Part I) that drawing upon Husserl's genetic and static approach, aimed at unveiling the presuppositionlessness and interconnectedness of science and reactivating old layers of meanings. The first two chapters within Part I were dedicated to the description of reality and the way in which individuals approach it. Through these chapters we discovered how, from a phenomenological Husserlian point of view, reality and ethics are structured in a tripartite manner. This is because Husserl distinguishes between reality as an intersubjective reality, reality as intentional content (Real) and reality as an objective essence (Reel). The study of reality as intentional content gives us access not only to the intentional web with which the individual engages reality and defines its layers but also to the way in which the individual itself is constituted as a passive atom of reality. This process of active and passive constitution occurs through three forms of intentions, hence the tripartite structure. These three forms of intentionality include: Passive, active and practical intentionality. Each of these three forms of intentionality expresses three positions of the subject that shift in time and space. Passive intentionality is egoless and does not involve any personal subjective responsibility or any sense of time. Active intentionality is a space or location where there is a subject and her ego makes a decision to give meanings to what was passively lived and given to it; this position involves mostly a linear sense of time. The decision the subject makes in this position passes through an act of practical intentionality. Practical intentionality is mainly expressed by a volitional body that is driven by an ego who decides in the now (or living present) to own and take responsibility both for the passive synthesis of its life and the active meanings it attributes to the process.

These three positions taken by an ego and the non-ego, in the case of passivity, can be co-present and coexisting because of the tripartite structure of time. In fact, the nature of timeless time is such that the linear sense of time blurs with the living present. This means that there can be at once a passively lived timeless time (no time), an active linear time and the living present – this particular moment. This tripartite structure, emerging from Ferrarello's interpretation of Husserl's ethics (2015), was conducive to understand and interpret the context in which ethical decisions are made. We further suggested that in order for a decision to be fully ethical, the subject must align with all three positions within all three notions of time. The experience of the ethical decision-making process discussed both in the theoretical analyses and the empirical studies we put forth is first lived in a passive manner. From the realm of passivity the volitional body of the subject is called to make decisions about its passive life in an active and meaningful way (transcendental level). This means that in each given moment the subject has to decide whether to own its region of being by an act of responsibility and assign it a meaning or to refute to undergo this process.

In general, the chapters in the first part of the book are mirrored in the form of explorations of actual examples in the second half of the book in a practical way through the three studies conducted by Nicolle Zapien, a psychologist and phenomenologist, using empirical phenomenological research methods. The theoretical phenomenological method applied in the first half of the book becomes an empirical phenomenological method using Giorgi's method of analysis of descriptions of actual lived experiences in order to illustrate the application of Husserl's phenomenology of ethics. As Husserl wrote, psychology is an ontological region which finds its foundation in the psychological layer of the individual, which, in turn, corresponds to active and passive intentionality, while ethics is the ontological region of the volitional body, which corresponds to practical intentionality.

In particular, the study of leadership dilemmas in Part II of the book parallels the first few chapters in Part I of the book. In this study we saw how the essence emerging from the data suggests that leaders exert an act of active intention in making decisions (practical and active intentionality) in relation to a passive world that demands a change. This change is lived passively until discomfort is sufficient enough to marshal an active view of the situation, which gives rise to the decision (the volitional body) to take a stance. This is fuelled by a sense of power the leader ostensibly has over his or her direct reports and the implied responsibility for righting the course of events.

Chapters I.3 and I.4 were specifically dedicated to a theoretical examination of the issue of time, since time is a decidedly important component of how we understand individuals constitute reality. In Chapters I.3 and I.4, Susi Ferrarello focused on a theoretical view of time using the *destruens* and *construens* application of the theoretical method. The goal of the *destruens* part in Chapter I.3 was to question the meaning that two representants of Eastern (Nishida) and Western (Husserl) tradition assigned to time in order to see if a common ground in relation to time was possible. Next, in the *construens pars* (Chapter I.4), Ferrarello reassembled the data gathered from the previous chapter and saw how they would have interacted with the meaning of time as experienced in cases of mysticism and schizophrenia. As shown from the study, what changed was the ability to access an active ego, mainly the transcendental one, but also the ability to return to the passive ego, specifically the egoless one that must move from day-to-day in a linear manner. Differently from mystics, schizophrenics cannot move within the three layers of reality and time with the same easiness as mystics and this affects the decisions they make and the meaning they assign to their meant reality (Real). Understanding this form of inability allows us to reactivate the meaning of time according to at least its three layers (linear time, timeless time and living present). and explains how disruptive it can be for individuals to lose one of these layers, as in the case of schizophrenia. In fact in this case, we demonstrated that there was no possibility for them to return from the timeless to linear time.[1]

Chapters I.3 and I.4 are mirrored in Part II of the book and taken up in an empirical study of parenting and the way in which parents deal with time and ethical decisions. This study is an interesting example because, as we noted, parents are obliged to make decision for the future of their children without letting the volitional body of their children to interfere with the decision-making process. Parents' volitional bodies arise from an egoless passive layer of time and emerge in a temporal space in which the boundaries between their volitional bodies and that of their children is blurred in a living present that is decisive for the future existence of their children. In the decision-making process the parents are almost obliged to override the decision-making process of their children and lose the boundaries with the volitional bodies of their children in order to act according to their ethical call which consists in protecting the survival of their children.[2] Consequently, the parents move within the layers of time and reality in such a way that they make their ethical decisions in the now (the eternal living present) so that they can preserve the linear time and the egoless time of their children. This is particularly interesting because while many dilemmas might include a need to make a decision on behalf of another in order to ward off an anticipated future that is bleak, rarely do we feel so deeply responsible for the choices we make than those we make as parents on behalf of our children. This study included exploration of situations that were filled with a sense of obligation and therefore pressure to decide ethically.

The empirical study of parenting dilemmas revealed that parents live parenting in a passive manner that feels sufficient because their children are seen as living towards a future that is bright and the parents believe themselves to be good enough parents until something shifts and they come to see a more dismal potential outcome for their child. This causes a reflective stance (from the active and transcendental ego which acts in the linear time upon what lived in the timeless time by the psychological and egoless ego). The parent then begins to consider possible changes (it is the practical and moral ego that makes decisions in the living now) and the obligation to make a change in order to protect their child in the future that is unknown. The choosing of a direction is done from a transcendental mindset, including a sense of what good enough parents do for their children in all times and situations and therefore what should be done in this case.

Chapters I.5 and I.6 were aimed at reactivating the meaning of intimacy and consent. The choice fell upon these concepts because it was necessary to analyse what happens when the entrance to one or more of the different layers of time, reality and subjectivity are unavailable or closed off. We believe, in fact, that if the awakening transition from the passive world to the active one through practical intentionality is prevented or cut short a loss of intimacy is the result. In Chapter I.6, Ferrarello described what happens when the access to intimacy is forcibly lost or spontaneously opened through non-consensual acts. We discover that consent seems to be a grey area between the wakefulness of the volitional body that stems from passive synthesis and the meaning-making activity that the ego exerts on those volitions. It might be that intimacy opens up without any active consent, for example with strangers watching a movie in the theatre. Or it might happen that intimacy is broken by a force-like violence and not because of the facticity of the acts but because the subject also does not want to fully acknowledge the change that occurred in her passive life. This implies that all the drives, instincts and motivations that animate the vital force of passive synthesis are lost and they cannot feed anymore the intimate connection between the active ego and its practical intentions. This dynamic is discussed with the following examples: Rape, violence and crime. In the case of marital rape, one example that is put forth includes the idea that frequently the event is not acknowledged and named rape because to do so is to change the meaning of the marriage as well – a meaning that is also not wanted. To acknowledge the meaning of the act that was rape within marriage is to acknowledge perhaps a larger issue with the identities of the marital partners (what once was a 'good marriage' is called into question), and therefore a sense of the past and future.

These theoretical findings in relation to intimacy and consent were empirically validated in what emerged in Part II in the study of affairs put forth by Nicolle Zapien. What was discovered here was that the passive egoless life of the partner made possible the developing interest for another person. This spontaneous intimacy was often rejected by the volitional body of the individual (and the responsibility for this volition is also rejected), and therefore the meaning of the active ego for the situation. This involves a loss of intimacy and curiosity both for the partner who was left behind and for the partner who experiences an intimacy instead with another. The two intimate worlds were kept apart and so they could not feed a shared vital intimate world. This leads one partner to see the other as a fixed character who could not or would not change.

It is our hope that the thematization of the link between the theoretical discussions in Part I of the volume and the empirical examples in Part II can encourage other studies in which this theoretical and empirical analysis is made possible. With this book we also saw a possibility and perhaps even a need to facilitate a greater ability to access all three layers of time, reality, subjectivity and intentions. We thought that understanding this structure might enlarge a space for what can be intersubjectively validated and might enhance human empathy, sympathy and compassion. For example, if we were to design empathic trainings, we would insist on the capacity of the student to access the tripartite sense of reality in all its facets and her ability to suspend any judgement about what is discovered in these layers. Being able to simply see what is in there might help to expand the embodied understanding of what is ethical for different ways of conceiving reality and might foster a sense of reality that does not lose its facticity and does not fall into nihilism. An expansion in this direction of seeing can be conducive to meet in a common time-space where there are more possibilities and creative meanings that are humanizing and could potentially solve some of the most prescient problems we as humans face. We want to avoid both relativist and nihilistic solutions that abdicate responsibility for practical action, or positions that are inherently not intimate or empathically engaged with others; the goal is neither to choose moralizing and stigmatizing problematic fixed structures, nor to espouse nihilistic positions in relation to reality. Simply, we want to be humble and accept the fact that the intricacy of reality requires a never-ending effort of observation and reflection. To use Husserl's example, the North Star exists whether we see it or not; yet our ability to see its facticity requires a continuous effort of unfolding its sense and the meaning that that image holds for us. We think that being able to validate and access the tripartite structure of reality and time can facilitate this effort because it would give us an opportunity to act from a creative, transcendent and perhaps spiritual space of possibilities while at the same time still remaining partially tethered to the realities of space, the body and time.

Ferrarello, Zapien

Notes

Introduction

1 F. Thilly, 'Psychology, Natural Science, and Philosophy', *The Philosophical Review*, 15, no. 2 (1906): 130–144; P. Cushman, *Constructing the Self, Constructing America* (Reading, MA: Addison-Wesley, 1995); T. Potts, 'Metaphilosophy', *New Blackfriars*, 49, no. 576 (1968): 417–428; Mary Calkins, 'Psychology: What Is It About?' *The Journal of Philosophy, Psychology and Scientific Methods*, 4, no. 25 (1907): 673–683.

2 As it concerns Stumps, even though it seems that I (there's this I here) his intention was not to separate philosophy from psychology, in his empirical works (Stumpf, C., 2015, 'Vorlesungen über Metaphysik', in D. Fisette and R. Martinelli (eds.), *Philosophy from an Empirical Standpoint. Essays on Carl Stumpf*, pp. 445–474) Stumpf initiated a distinction between physiological psychology and descriptive psychology – the former focusing on natural phenomena and the latter on what we might call today philosophy of mind. As he writes: 'Thus the time in Würzburg marks for me the beginning of a new line of work to which I have remained faithful to the present day, which, however, has made me an outsider to the great majority of my colleagues. My work of observation and experimentation has absorbed my time and strength even more than is the case with most experimental psychologists. Although I fully appreciate the saying of Aristotle that theory is the sweetest of all, I must confess that it was always a joy and a comfort to pass from theory to observation, from meditation to facts, from my writing-desk to the laboratory; and, thus, in the end, my writing-desk was neglected and has not produced a single textbook or compendium, which indeed ought to have been its first duty, even at the time when I was an instructor. However, I never intended to spend so much of my lifetime on acoustics and musical psychological studies as I did later on. I had counted on a few years. But it was, after all, not musical science but philosophy that always remained mistress of the house, who, it is true, granted most generously great privileges to her helpmate' (Stumpf, 1924, 396–397).

I.1 The phenomenological method, a theoretical 'application'

1 For Kant, phenomenology indicates the 'science' that studies the aspects from universal to human experience: 'The most universal laws of sensibility play an unjustifiably large role in metaphysics, where, after all, it is merely

concepts and principles of pure reason that are at issue. It seems to me a quite particular, although merely negative science, general phenomenology (*phaenomenologia generalis*), must precede metaphysics. In it the principles of sensibility, their validity and their limitations, would be determined, so that these principles could not be confusedly applied to objects of pure reason' (Kant, 1986, 59, translation slightly modified; compare Heidegger, 2007, 3).

2 By phenomenology of the spirit Hegel meant to refer to the study of the experience of consciousness. According to Joseph Kockelmans, 'it was only with Hegel that a well-defined technical meaning became attached' to the term phenomenology. For Hegel, 'phenomenology was not knowledge of the Absolute-in-and-for-itself, in the spirit of Fichte or Schelling, but in his *Phenomenology of Spirit* (*Phänomenologie des Geistes*) he wanted to solely consider knowledge as it appears to consciousness' (Kockelmans, 1967, 24). Similarly, Peirce used this term to indicate the study of the manifestation of consciousness' object, but in 1905 he changed the word into phaneroscopy in order to be more specific about the kind of study he was conducting.

3 Many seminal phenomenological philosophers have addressed disciplinary issues in psychology and have performed psychological analyses, including Heidegger (1927/1962), Sartre (1948/1939, 1948/1940, 1956/1943), Merleau-Ponty (1943/1962, 1942/1963), Marcel (1965), Schutz (1932/1967), Bachelard (1938/1964, 1958/1964), Levinas (1954/1969), Ricoeur (1974, 1981) and Gadamer (1960/1989). Phenomenology has had particularly extensive application in clinical psychology and psychiatry, for instance in the work of Jaspers (1913/1963), Scheler (1913/1954), Binswanger (1963), Boss (1963), May, Angel, Ellenberger (1958), Straus (1966), van den Berg (1972), Laing (1962, 1963), Barton (1974) and many others.

4 For the chronological evolutions of the phenomenological method, see Wertz (2005): 'Since the late 1960s, there has been an increasing attempt to formally specify workable procedures of psychological science that may be followed and used as a guide for novice researchers and a framework for scientific accountability' (Wertz, 2005). Amedeo Giorgi has led the way in developing, articulating, and justifying phenomenological research methods that have been applied to the full spectrum of psychological subject matter (Cloonan, 1995). In keeping with phenomenology, Giorgi's (1975; Giorgi & Giorgi, 2003) approach to psychological research involves the collection of concrete examples of psychological subject matter and the analytic reflection on their processes, meanings and structures. Giorgi (1985) has delineated the various phases of phenomenological psychological research, including the formulation of the topic and research problem, the constitution of research situations, the various sources of description, the steps of analysis, and the formulation of results'. Also, Finlay (2009) writes, 'Some adhere reasonably closely to Giorgi's framework based on the reduction and imaginative variation while, at the same time, offering their own emphases (e.g. the open lifeworld approach of Dahlberg et al., 2008; van Manen's, lived experience human science inquiry based on University of Utrecht tradition, 1990; the dialogal approach, Halling et al., 2006; the Dallas approach, Garza 2007; Todres' embodied lifeworld approach, 2005, 2007; and Ashworth's, lifeworld approach, 2003, 2006). There also exist a number of phenomenological methods which focus on rich descriptions of lived experience and meanings, but which do not explicitly use Husserlian techniques such as eidetic variation. Smith's Interpretative

Phenomenological Analysis (IPA), which has gained considerable purchase in the qualitative psychology field in the United Kingdom, is one such example. Smith argues that his idiographic and inductive method, which seeks to explore participants' personal lived experiences, is phenomenological in its concern for individuals' perceptions. He also, however, identifies more strongly with hermeneutic traditions which recognize the central role played by the researcher, and does not advocate the use of bracketing (Smith, 2004).' Finally, Churchill reports: 'Amedeo Giorgi (1970, 1975, 1985, 2009), hired by Van Kaam to develop phenomenological psychological research methods, brought the existential phenomenological movement to the forefront in America, along with his colleagues and students. Giorgi, having been trained at Fordham in experimental psychology with a specialization in psychophysics, played the central role of articulating the need for a "human science" foundation for the entire discipline of psychology and in developing a "scientific" phenomenological research method that has been applied for decades to a broad diversity of subject matter (see Wertz & Aanstoos, 1999; Wertz et al., 2011). Duquesne became the center of phenomenological psychology starting in the late 1960s, and in 1973, Misiak and Sexton would write that "through its diverse and substantial contributions ... [Duquesne] has earned the title of the capital of phenomenological psychology in the New World" (p. 62). By the late 1990s, former students and associates of the Duquesne circle were teaching in approximately 50 colleges and universities throughout the United States and Canada (for further elaboration of this history, see Cloonan, 1995; Misiak & Sexton, 1973; Smith, 2002). Two direct offshoots of Duquesne include the current programs at the University of Dallas and Seattle University, each with strong clinical and interdisciplinary interests. The University of Dallas's original undergraduate and doctoral programs in "anthropological phenomenological psychology" started in 1972 under the combined leadership of Robert Romanyshyn and Robert Sardello; its current undergraduate and master's programs in psychology continue to emphasize existential phenomenology, depth psychology, and human science research (Churchill, 2012; Garza, 2007; Kugelmann, 1999, 2011). Seattle University's 2-year program in existential-phenomenological therapeutic psychology started in 1981, with Duquesne graduates George Kunz and Steen Halling playing key roles in envisioning and developing the program (Halling, 2005; Halling, Kunz, & Rowe, 1994). Independent but kindred developments would include the contributions of Howard Pollio in Tennessee, Clark Moustakas in Detroit, and Max van Manen in Canada, all of whom subsequently utilized phenomenology in developing psychological research methods programmatically at their own graduate institutions. Other phenomenologically oriented psychologists like Robert MacLeod (1947) and Ernest Keen (1975) worked individually to promote their applications of phenomenology to the fields of social psychology and clinical psychology. More recently, Wertz et al. (2011) compared phenomenological psychological research methods with four other contemporary qualitative research methods: grounded theory, discourse analysis, narrative research, and intuitive inquiry. (For prototypic and exemplary research from the Duquesne tradition, see Aanstoos, 1984/1993; Churchill, 1984/1993, 1998, 2006b; Colaizzi, 1967, 1969, 1973, 1978, 2001; Fischer, 2006; Fischer, 1974, 1978, 1985; Giorgi, 1970, 1975, 1976, 1983, 1985, 1989, 1992, 2000, 2009; Giorgi, Barton, & Maes, 1983; Giorgi, C. T. Fischer, & Murray, 1975; Giorgi, W. F. Fischer, & von Eckartsberg, 1971, Giorgi & Giorgi, 2003a, 2003b; Giorgi, Smith,

& Knowles, 1979; Mruk, 2013; Rao & Churchill, 2004; Valle, 1998; Valle & Halling, 1989; Van Kaam, 1959, 1966, 1987; von Eckartsberg, 1967/2005,1971, 1986, 1989; Wertz, 1982, 1983, 1985, 1987; see also the independent work of vanManen, 1990; Moustakas, 1994; Pollio, Henley, & Thompson, 1998). Due to limitations of space, we have confined ourselves to an exposition of the early development of phenomenological research methods in America (for a discussion of international developments, see Churchill, in press.'

5. C. Moustakas, *Phenomenological Research Methods* (Thousand Oaks, CA: Sage, 1994); M. Van Manen, *Researching Lived Experience: Human Science for an Action Sensitive Pedagogy* (Albany: State University of New York Press, 1990); but also (Borgatta & Borgatta, 1992; Swingewood, 1991), psychology (Giorgi, 1985; Polkinghorne, 1989), nursing and the health sciences (Nieswiadomy, 1993; Oiler, 1986), and education (Tesch, 1988; van Manen, 1990). J. Smith, *Interpretive Phenomenological Analysis* (Thousand Oaks, CA: Sage, 2009).

6. It is very difficult, if not impossible, to find an agreement on the meaning of the word 'essence' in philosophy. According to Mohanty (1928) essence indicates entities *sui generis* that phenomenology explains as essential truths

   that can be visible to the researcher after applying imaginative variation another technical term that Drummond (2008) explains as follows, In systematically varying the idea of a tree, for example, we recognize that there are features, such as the capacity for self-nutrition, without which we could no longer take something to be a tree. We thereby come to an awareness of the necessary moments of the thing, that is, of its essential features, which in their definite relations form the essence of the independently existing object, an essence that Husserl identifies as a concretum. Similarly, in systematically varying the idea of green, we recognize that there are certain lightenings and darkenings of shade which would prevent us from continuing to call the color "green".

7. Giorgi seems to be the only one of these four who explicitly discussed imaginative variation.

8. Clearly, this use of the word 'transcendental' is not strictly philosophical and in line with Husserl's idea of transcendental.

9. For a critique of Moustakas's understanding of epoche and reduction, you can read Applebaum's article at the following URL http://phenomenologyblog.com/?p=896

10. For a short bibliography of Moustakas's works: C. Moustakas, *Loneliness* (Englewood Cliffs, NJ: Prentice-Hall, 1961); *Individuality and Encounter* (Cambridge, MA: Doyle); *Loneliness and Love* (Englewood Cliffs, NJ: Prentice-Hall); *The Touch of Loneliness* (Englewood Cliffs, NJ: Prentice-Hall); *Who Will Listen?* (New York: Ballantine); *Rhythms, Rituals and Relationships* (Detroit: Center for Humanistic Studies); *Phenomenology, Science, and Psychotherapy* (Sydney, Nova Scotia: Family Life Institute, University College of Cape Breton, 1990); *Heuristic Research: Design, Methodology, and Applications*.

11. J. A. Smith, and V. Eatough, 'Interpretative Phenomenological Analysis', in *Research Methods in Psychology*, ed. G. Breakwell, C. Fife-Schaw, S. Hammond, and J. A. Smith (3rd edn) (London: Sage).

12 P. Colaizzi, 'Psychological Research as the Phenomenologist Views It', in *Existential Phenomenological Alternatives for Psychology*, ed. R. Valle and M. King (New York, NY: Oxford University Press, 1978).
13 On this point, I will write more in the following chapters. By egoic I mean the activity that is guided by the presence of an active and aware ego, which is in contrast with egoless activity where the ego is dormant and passive.
14 A good example of how Husserl's normative ethics would appear to be can come from Hua XXVIII, 442, 90, 93, 108; Hua XXXVII, Beilage XXI in which he mentions the laws for the consequence, the law of fourth excluded, the law for conflicting values, the laws of axiological absorption, the laws for the willing of choice, the law for conventionalization.
15 In the first chapter in the second half of the book, further discussion of the phenomenological method will be offered in order to describe and justify the method used for the empirical studies presented in the last chapters of the book.
16 Drummond (2008) defines static and genetic as follows: static phenomenology, while abstracting from the temporality of experience, identifies the moments and structures that belong to a whole of intentional experience and object; genetic phenomenology considers experiences in their temporal dimension and seeks to disclose the origins of experiences in the temporal flux of consciousness (161).
17 As it pertains to the notion of stability of perception as an optical illusion, see J. Fisher and D. Whitney, 'Serial Dependence in Visual Perception', *Nature Neuroscience*, 17 (2014): 738–743.
18 See, for example, M. Manassi, F. Hermens, G. Francis, M. H. Herzog, 'Release of Crowding by Pattern Completion', *Journal of Vision*, 15, no. 8 (2015): 16, 1–15.
19 I use intuition here in the Husserlian sense to indicate the insight that is referred to the essences that the phenomenological research try to discover and describe. As Drummond (2008) writes, 'In essential insight there is a determined material content in the universal which renders it inapplicable to any object whatsoever but definitive of and applicable to a particular kind of object or to an object having a particular property or attribute. Because of the presence of this materially determinate core, Husserl claims that essential insight (as well as idealization) yields a material a priori or, alternately, a contingent a priori'.
20 I use empirical here as opposed to theoretical in a philosophical sense, as an hypothesis derived from the analysis of facts. See C. Benjamin 'What Is Empirical Philosophy?' *The Journal of Philosophy*, 36, no. 19 (1939): 517–525.
21 The vast majority of research is quantitative, and only a minority is qualitative – they are not at all equal alternatives.
22 The original evidence or necessity (*Notwendigkeit* or 'systematische Einheit der Normgerechtheit') (Hua-Mat IX, 453) is felt from Koerper, which discovers its organ – Leib – as 'Titel fuer solche Evidenz' or 'Evidenz des Koennens' (Husserl, 1966, § 31, Hua-Mat IX, text 32). Classification is guided by feeling, which recognizes facts as they are and assigns to them a sense of relationality based on a sense of their proportion more than on what they really are – since what they are will remain unknown to us.

23 See C. Daly, *An Introduction to Philosophical Method* (Broadview Press, 2010); Donald E. Polkinghorne, 'Incarnate Phenomenological Reflection', *Theoretical & Philosophical Psychology*, 9, no. 1 (1989): 46–51; J. Martin, 'Life Positioning Analysis: An Analytic Framework for the Study of Lives and Life Narratives', *Journal of Theoretical and Philosophical Psychology*, 33, no. 1 (2013): 1–17; T. Toadvine, 'Phenomenological Method in Merleau-Ponty's Critique of Gurwitsch', *Husserl Studies*, 17 (2001): 195–205. According to Smith (2005. Merleau-Ponty and the Phenomenological Reduction, in *Inquiry* 48), in Merleau-Ponty's eyes, the methods of phenomenology and the empirical sciences are similar in great measure.

24 In Husserl's phenomenology 'theoretical' has three meanings: doxic, categorial and act-complex. Any object is always known in a theoretical attitude and recognized as a cognitive object, despite the fact that they are apprehended according to different attitudes whose layers can be synthesized and expressed in a theoretical act-complex.

25 This is not dissimilar to the steps within Phenomenological Research that include imaginative variation; see Englander (2012) for a discussion on this issue.

26 See M. Rein and D. Schon, 'Problem Setting in Policy Research', in *Using Social Policy Research in Public Policy-Making*, ed. C. Weiss (Lexington, MA: D.C. Heath, 1977), 235, 251; M. B. Miles and A. M. Huberman, *Qualitative Data Analysis: An Expanded Sourcebook*, 2nd ed. (Thousand Oaks, CA: Sage, 1994).

27 Through a General Systems Approach we can include not only the dynamics of interactions but also relationships among various elements of the systems, up and down hierarchical/panarchical levels. Features of systems thinking include complexity, circularity and reciprocal influences, learning potential, flexibility, cooperation and their holistic and cross-disciplinary potentials. *Systems thinking* is a broad term that includes various systemic approaches and includes *Systems Theory* and *Systems Perspectives* (Clemson, 2012).

28 The difference between theory and paradigm expresses itself also in Husserl's decision to leave out any strict distinction between subject and object of research in order to acknowledge the presence of the researcher in the investigation as a bearer of a system of beliefs that need to be parenthesized methodically.

29 According to A. Collen, *Systemic Change Through Praxis and Inquiry*, Vol. 11, *Praxiology: The International Annual of Practical Philosophy and Methodology* (New Brunswick, NJ: Transaction Publishers, 2003). 'The theory should have … a capacity to generate testable hypotheses' and should comply to 13 evaluative criteria to evaluate the scholarly quality of a theoretical research:

- Express a problem not yet adequately understood.
- Provide a compelling rationale for finding a solution.
- Conduct a thorough review of relevant theoretical and empirical literature.
- Review critically lines of thought related to the problem.
- Provide a critical analysis of major alternative theories.
- Note the theory's agreement with known facts, or provide a clear rationale for the disparity.

- Clearly define concepts (allowing for the possibility of operational definitions) and the relationships among them.
- Develop a theory with internal consistency, logical coherence, and plausibility, while allowing the possibility of and testing for disconfirmation.
- Note the assumptions of the theory.
- Keep the level of jargon to a minimum.
- Indicate the degree of generalizability.
- Provide an advance in thinking that contributes to the theory in the subject domain.

I.2 Husserl's ethics and psychology

1 'Physical Reality. A Phenomenological Approach' by Jean Ladrière (1989) reconstructs the process of thought by which this concept is constituted.

In this process, reality is transferred from the lived experience of existence, apprehended in the simple consciousness of oneself, to what gives itself, in experience, as an independent source of givenness, and finally to the world, as ultimate condition of the phenomena. In physics, we have an approach of reality in terms of representation, not lived experience. But in contemporary physics, representation (as theoretical construction) is intimately connected with our action or praxis. What is really described is not the manifest as such, but the manifestation (as process). The discourse of representation is not about the phenomena themselves but about the conditions in which the phenomenon constitutes itself as phenomenon. The discourse of physics becomes thus more and more transcendental. But it integrates the transcendental discourse in the representation, giving a concrete appresentation (in a mathematical construction) of the non-representable process of the becoming manifest of reality.

2 For more on the phenomenological analysis of *real* and *reel* see Husserl's *Logical Investigations*, in particular the fifth and sixth Investigations. Note that in the second edition Husserl modifies the distinction of *real* and *reel*. See also Hua XXII, 286 and Hua XXVII, 206. Sometimes the term 'reel' has been translated in English with the adjective 'genuine'; see, on this point, E. Kohak, 'Jan Patocka, Philosophical Readings and Selected Writings', Chicago Press, 1989, 26. Also, R. Bernet, E. Marbach and I. Kern, *An Introduction to Husserlian Phenomenology* (Evanston, IL: Northwestern University Press, 1993), 89–90.

3 As he noted at the time, Fink chose to submit the Sixth Cartesian Meditation (*SCM*), as opposed to newer and more substantial work, largely because it did carry that original endorsement from Husserl. The choice was thus more ceremonial than philosophical. Fink saw its submission as 'an act of piety [Pietät]', a statement of critical allegiance to Husserl and to his project. And as he noted in a letter to Hermann Van Breda, his Habilitation was in fact seen by the University as a case of 'political reparation'.

4 On the closeness between Husserl's and Fink's thought see: R. Bruzina, *Edmund Husserl and Eugen Fink: Beginnings and Ends in Phenomenology, 1928–1938* (New Haven; London: Yale University Press, 2004).

5   Here I use the word 'meaning' as in Frege's 'Sinn' to indicate what a referent expresses.

6   The bridge between the transcendental and natural attitude – which is the everyday attitude or mindset that we have as we move through time, encountering everyday objects, without much consideration of the fact that they are constituted by consciousness – is the psychological ego. We are often in a state of the natural attitude and are moved to encounter the psychological ego through the application of the epoché and the reduction. This change in attitude is what makes possible the ability of consciousness to reflect upon itself – for the phenomenologist to consider the structure of the experience of perception of anything (Zapien's first note to Chapter II.1).

7   In fact, Giorgi, in his articulation of the descriptive phenomenological method for psychological research (*The Descriptive Phenomenological Method in Psychology: A Modified Husserlian Approach* [Pittsburg, PA: Duquesne University Press, 2009]), suggests that we are to remain loyal to the descriptions themselves, neither adding nor subtracting material in the analysis that is not directly linked to the descriptive material, and that only through descriptions of experience are we to find the essence thereof. Before proposing an essential structure, the phenomenological researcher asks herself if all the steps are completed in the analysis and if anything that should have been bracketed could have crept in. In each of the three studies presented in the second half, for example, before presenting the findings, what is critical is the question whether the data support the findings and where in the data there is support for the findings. In the examples in the second half, there will be an explication of constituents section for each study. This helps aid the reader in following the decision-making of the researcher directly (Zapien's note to II.1).

8   As it concerns the use and application of empathy in the phenomenological method, see: M. Englander, 'Empathy Training from a Phenomenological Perspective', *Journal of Phenomenological Psychology*, 45, no. 1 (2014): 5–26; V. Gallese, 'The Roots of Empathy: The Shared Manifold Hypothesis and the Neural Basis of Intersubjectivity', *Psychopathology*, 36 (2003): 171–180.

9   For Fink, world-belief is 'the primal happening [*Urgeschehen*] of our transcendental existence' (Fink, 1988, 187), such that 'existing-within-the-belief-in-the-world and believing oneself to be human are inextricably one and the same' [*Im-Weltglauben-sein und im Selbst-glauben als Mensch sein sind untrennbar eins*] (KS, 115/109, translation modified). Hence, rather than as the 'natural attitude', Fink preferred to denote the mundane predicament of human existence as *Weltbefangenheit* (captivation in/by the world) (see Bruzina, 1995, 57–60; D. Cairns, 'Guide for Translating Husserl', in *Phaenomenologica*, vol. 55 [den Haag, Martinus Nijhoff, 1976], 95). Human beings as such are imprisoned by ontic preoccupations.

10 By spiritual here I imply the reflective layer of human matter (matter indicates, instead, the undifferentiated being within and throughout which we live). According to Husserl human life flows through two main polarities, a natural one, which indicates the unquestioning attitude, and the spiritual,

which refers to the reflective one. For example, my body and the people I interact with are matter and I relate to them in a natural way when I do not question their meanings, in a spiritual way when I assume a reflective point of view in relation to the sense that they have for me.

11 This particular idea is illustrated concretely in subsequent chapters, II.2, II.3 and II.4, where original empirical phenomenological studies are offered. For example, in the case of a leadership dilemma, the leaders experience themselves to be competent leaders from the perspective of the psychological ego, then they question themselves and all past and future acts from the perspective of the reflexive ego, and finally they come to understand themselves in relationship to ethical leadership for all time and circumstances. In these cases the identities and various states of the ego are synonymous with the view that is taken (Zapien's note to II.2, II.3, II.4).

12 The theoretical and practical application of the phenomenological method has precisely the goal to reactivate meanings and their essence through a methodical navigation of these three egological layers of reality and through a rigorous analysis of the outcomes brought forth from each of their egoic shifts. For example, if we are working from a theoretical standpoint our natural ego compares different sources with each other and is led to take the authority of these sources for granted, the same as when we work in an empirical way and collect data from different interviews. Yet, when we decide to apply the phenomenological method, either on theoretical sources or on practical data, our transcendental and practical egos come to play. The natural attitude of the psychological ego is questioned by the psychological ego itself which decides (practical ego) to apply the epoché in order to gauge the sense of the sources (if we apply the theoretical phenomenological method) or the meaning of the data (if we apply the empirical phenomenological method). In this shift the *ego that makes the decision* to perform the epoché, that is the practical ego, helps the other two egoic layers to gain a more rigorous and meaningful understanding of the data which will lead to a consequent reactivation of the sense implied in the analysis of that lived experience (whether it was theoretically or empirically analysed).

13 Nishida, James, Dewey.

14 Giorgi's application of the phenomenological method, which will be used in the second part of this book, takes into consideration only the static side of the Husserlian method.

15 From 1913 on Husserl adds to static and descriptive phenomenology a new kind of phenomenology, a genetic one. In the third footnote of the second edition of *Logical Investigations* and even more in his *Analysen zur passiven Synthesis* (1918–1926) he uses genesis in a new way. Bernet et al. date the beginning of this method to 1917. According to their interpretation, in static phenomenology constitution is the activity of an I that is led by a stable object considered as a pure objective correlate of our consciousness (1993, 196). With the static approach objects are taken as they appear in the present, leaving aside the history of sedimentation and layers that contributed to the constitution of their present being. As it shows, this method does not exclude the kinetic experience of the object. Yet, there is

not a complete meeting of the subject with the static object. We learn in *Formal and Transcendental Logic* (Hua XVII, 316) that static phenomenology consists in disclosing the connections of the intentional reference of the unclear and modified mode of givenness (e.g. entertaining someone's claim that 'The car needs new air filters') to the clear and more original mode of givenness (experiencing in the flesh that, e.g. the air filters are indeed dirty and that is why the car is not starting readily). In contrast, genetic phenomenology consists in explaining the connectedness of the intentional references which belong to the history of the constituting mind. In which case each individual experience of consciousness would be seen to have its own temporal genesis; e.g. that the car is not starting readily and that this has happened before and was due to dirty air filters itself has a genesis of learning something about cars, their functioning, etc. Husserl says (Hua XV, 616), to '"to presuppose" is not "originate" '. In the static analysis one asks about the relation of founded and founding but not about the genesis, the origination, of the phainomena (see Hua, XIV, 40; Lee, 22). Of course one may speak of static phenomenology as having to do with the relationship of what enjoys validity earlier (*geltungsmässig Früheren*) to what has validity later, but the analysis does not have to do with the coming to be of either the founded or the founding.

16 For example, in the second part of the book we will examine the case of an ethical dilemma that parents had to face in relation to rearing a child. In that case the ethical phenomenon cannot focus solely on the static description of the present phenomenon because the parent is living a dilemma in relation to the future of their child and making a decision that applies mostly on the child's future. The dilemma is all about and made of time as it is considered in its static and genetic features.

17 For this reason, differently from J. Donohoe, in his *Husserl on Ethics and Intersubjectivity* (Amherst, NY: Humanity Books, 2004), I will not use the static and genetic methods as a chronological thread to follow and to interpret Husserl's ethics and apply it on psychological cases. While that methodological approach would be absolutely reasonable and respectful of the order of Husserl's discoveries, his static phenomenology illuminates only the theoretical and scientific side of ethical issues and his genetic phenomenology sheds light only on its practical side. From this follows the dichotomizing interpretation and use of Husserl's ethics as a first logical ethics and a second personalistic ethics.

18 According to recent researches, their sense of reality is embedded in organic matter as much as ours is. See, J. Parnas and M. Henriksen, 'Disordered Self in the Schizophrenia Spectrum: A Clinical and Research Perspective', *Harvard Review of Psychiatry* (2014); J. Parnas and M. Henriksen, *Disturbance of the Experience of Self: A Phenomenologically-Based Approach*, 2015, 235–44.

19 It will be possible to see how the ethical decisions made in relation to the experience of a leadership challenge, rearing a child and beginning of an affair involve a triadic structure of reality, time and egoic (or egoless) intentions. All these cases show an effort of stepping back from a natural egoic position and accordingly a view of reality and sense of time is required in order to solve the ethical dilemma the participants are presented with.

20 The translation of the word *Geist* in English is always problematic. The words 'mind', 'wit', 'spirit', 'intellect', 'ghost' capture only partially the sense endowed in this German word.

21 This example is parallel to the findings of one of the phenomenological studies presented in the second section of this text, Chapter II.3. In this case, parents do not decide to act (or not act) on behalf of their children in response to a theoretical dilemma. They only feel moved if the dilemma becomes bothersome enough to register in their conscious awareness as a problem. This awareness and naming of what had until then been passively lived through sufficient discomfort is what gives rise to the impetus for action (or the decision to not act); see Nicolle Zapien's note to Chapter II.3.

22 In Part II of the book Nicolle Zapien will analyse contents only from a static perspective, which means that the volitional body will be understood solely from the outcomes of its decisions of owning its passive lived experience. Passive intentionality and timeless time will be grasped and unfolded only from the point of view of the active intention of meaning-giving activity to what was previously lived.

23 See also: Hua XV, 283: 'Müssen wir nicht sagen: Das Ursein ist das total strömende absolute Leben, in dem notwendig eine korrelative Synthesis waltet, die Synthesis, welche das Ich konstituiert (eine Konstitution, die einen total anderen Sinn hat als die in Stufen <geschehende> Weltkonstitution, die durch Erscheinungen leistet), andererseits eben diese, die ontifizierende Konstitution, bzw'; and Hua XV, 283 'Diese primordiale Welt ist Welt meiner Erfahrung, sie ist in meinem strömenden Erfahren konstituierte, erfahrene Einheit vielfältiger Sondereinheiten – unter ihnen Ich-Mensch selbst, "darin" mein Leibkörper als eine in gewisser Weise zentrale Einheit-, ich leiblich in der Welt, ich leiblich mit dem Vermögen, alle Dinge wahrzunehmen, an sie heranzukommen, mit ihnen praktisch beschäftigt zu sein, die Dingwelt dadurch verändernd und evtl. mich selbst als Menschen durch mein menschliches Tun verändernd'.

24 As a sidenote it is interesting to see how Husserl's position in relation to time summarizes some of the main positions held in the history of philosophy: the idealist, realist and relational ones (as Bardon summarized them in his book, *a Brief History of Time*, OUP, 2013). According to the idealists, such as Parmenides, Augustine and Kant, time is a property of our mind; as for realists, such as Newton, Dainton and Russell, time does exist as an absolute unit that can be perceived either through moments of awareness or as a sui generis entity that contains bodies and events; finally the relational position, defended by Aristotle and Leibniz, considers time relation as a 'legitimate category of scientific and mathematical accounts of the universe' (*A Brief History of Time*, OUP, 2013, 58).

25 See: Hua, VIII, 4: 'Zeiten, Gegenstände, Welten jedes Sinnes haben letztlich ihren Ursprung im Urströmen der lebendigen Gegenwart – oder, besser, im transzendentalen Ur-Ego'; Hua VIII, 53 'Darüber hinaus formuliert er eine sehr einfache These: Das ichliche objektiviert sich durch Reflexion.' Hua VIII, 36.

26 Ricoeur's work on narrativity, because a narrative per se also requires a before and after. In fact Ricoeur writes that through such narratives 'time

becomes human'. The 3-volume *Time and Narrative* is I think the work where this comes up most.

27 I borrow this term from Gebser (*Ursprung und Gegenwart. Zweiter Teil: Die Manifestationen der aperspektivischen Welt* [Flensburg Fjord: Novalis Verlag 2011]) in order to indicate the synthetic ability of time which organizes and synthesizes the information that it provides. See also on time and self, Lohmar, *On Time. New Contributions to the Husserlian Phenomeology of Time* (Dordrecht-Boston-London, Springer, 2010) and Simenov (2015).

28 From this perspective phenomenology and physics are on the same continuum: from a static perspective matter is an association of atoms and the force that keeps them together is their valency bonds. Yet, we cannot observe matter only from the perspective of their bonds in just one moment in time because the observation would be deceiving at best. As Levere writes 'atoms cannot be studied in isolation, but as they react' (2001). As Heisenberg noticed, 'Matter produces the force of gravity and the force of gravity acts on matter'. Matter is a field and a flow (Chang, 2015). The field, as Schroedinger remarks, 'tends to be fixed, but the force it radiates is unpredictable' or as Einstein later explained 'matter radiates waves whose frequency depends on its own structure' (Levere, 2001). Taking away the waves from the matter would make the description of the matter lacking, not seeing the matter and being focused only on the waves would make the description of the waves at best highly mysterious. It is impossible to draw a line of demarcation between the visible and invisible, the material and the becoming, the being and time, real and ideal, given and meaning. There is the elegant equation of the physicist Pauli that proves the interconnection between the two, meaning and reality (Peat, 1987, 56, 14, 16). Consequently, genetic and static eyes are both necessary to understand the elusive nature of time and the concreteness of being that time describes.

I.3 The Trinitarian relationship of the world

1 On the attempt at separating morality from religion, see, for example, the debate between W. W. Bartley, *Morality and Religion* (London: Macmillan and New York: St Martin's Press, 1971) and E. D. Klemke, 'On the Alleged Inseparability of Morality and Religion', *Religious Studies*, 11, no. 1 (1975): 37–48. Also, James Gaffney, 'Newman on the Common Roots of Morality and Religion', *The Journal of Religious Ethics*, 16, no. 1 (1988): 143–159 and Wes Avram, 'On the Priority of "Ethics" in the Work of Levinas', *The Journal of Religious Ethics*, 24, no. 2 (1996): 261–284.

2 See previous chapter on the notion of reality and the distinction between *Real* and *Reel*.

3 Hereafter, I will use logic as a synonym of epistemology and science of knowledge.

4 As K. Nishitani, Nishida's student, reports, in *Nishida Kitarō* (University of California Press, 1991), Nishida lectured extensively on Western philosophers and Husserl's Logical Investigations were certainly part of these lectures. As

B. D. Elwood reported in 'The Problem of the Self in the Later Nishida and in Sartre' (*Philosophy East and West*, 44, no. 2 [1994]: 303–307), 'it was Nishida who first initiated a discussion of Husserl in an article of 1911, shortly after the first French article on Husserl. In 1955, Gino Piovesana observed that Husserlian phenomenology became familiar in Japan after 1921'. Arisaka (1996) writes 'Nishida was also indirectly influenced by the development of the phenomenological movement through his students' visits to Europe. Nishida spent his prolific career producing works of metaphysics, epistemology, aesthetics, ethics, religion, logic, mathematics, and science. He was especially influenced by William James, whose theory of "pure experience" he adapted in his own maiden work, *An Inquiry into the Good*. During the 1920s and 1930s his theories reflected elements of German Idealism, in particular Fichte and Hegel, Neo-Kantians, British Hegelians,

and Marx. During this period Nishida developed his signature theory, Basho no Ronri ('The Logic of Place'), and other influential theories of history and human action. He taught at Kyoto Imperial University from 1910 to 1928 (professor emeritus from 1929) and the Kyoto School formed around him' ('The Nishida Enigma: The Principle of the New World', *Monumenta Nipponica*, 51, no. 1 (1996): 1–21.

5 However Nishida warned Nishitani to keep meditative practice distinct from philosophical practice.

6 See also, the passage, 'My logic of place, as a self-identity of contradictions, is no other than a hypothesis of logic with attempts to understand the world from the standpoint of the self-realization of this historical self' (NKZ, 10, 118).

7 On the debt of the Zen tradition, we are referring here to Buddhism; see, Agnieszka Kozyra, 'Nishida Kitarō's Logic of Absolutely Contradictory Self-Identity and the Problem of Orthodoxy in the Zen Tradition', *Japan Review*, 20 (2008): 69–110.

8 For the mathematization of Nishida's thought see J. Maraldo, 'Translating Nishida', *Philosophy East and West* (1989).

9 On this point it might be interesting to observe that the Greek etymology of the word *kalos*, which means good, beautiful and the like, is derived from *kaleo*, which means to call, name. Hence, what can be grasped and accordingly named is good.

10 'Two things, which both retain their uniqueness, oppose each other, negate each other, are simultaneously linked with each other and are united in one form, or, conversely, they relate to each other, are then linked to each other, and are then united in one form – it is this process that is always necessary for things to become individual and unique as they are, for things to become themselves. It is according to this model that we think of the world of things in interaction, of the material world' (NKZ, 11, 374).

11 'I did not think of various universals simply as a transcendence of universal of judgment. The process of judgment itself is considered from the standpoint of a more concrete process of self-realization' (NKZ, 9, 5). Also, Wallace (1894, 59–66) deals with this point in reference to Hegel's thought. Nishida read and taught Hegel.

12 Here material is meant as a synonym of the Greek hyle, natural matter.
13 Here the closeness to Aristotle's notion of energeia and entelecheia is striking.
14 See G. Kopf, *Temporality and Personal Identity in the Thought of Nishida Kitaro* (Philosophy East and West, 2002), on this point: 'Dialectical time: the eternal now transcends the dichotomy between a symmetric (a. In relation to the progression from created to creating, noema to noesis, when the noetic aspect encompasses the noematic one) and asymmetric conception of time (even subjectivity qua noesis can't envelop the self-determination of the eternal now)'.
15 It is worthwhile mentioning that before Pascal the idea seems to have been present also in Nicolas of Cusa, Giordano Bruno and Alain de Lille.
16 As N. Yûjirô (1983) remarks in the introduction to Nishida's collection of works: 'In the "World of Physics" Nishida uses physics in order to explain this interlacing of worlds (NKZ, vol. 10), the world of physics and the world of rhythm.' According to Nishida the religious sentiment arises spontaneously in human beings living in this world because this world in fact does not exist unless it is supported by the transcendent (NKZ, 11, 361).
17 See, for example, T. McCall, *Which Trinity? Whose Monotheism?* (Cambridge: Eerdmans, 2010).
18 It is relevant here to say that by religion I mean the relationship between the absoluteness and human beings. Similarly, in the 'Essence of Religion' Nishida defines religion as 'the relationship between God and human beings', while by morality I mean the interconnection between goals and means.
19 The world of life (…) biological though it may be, is already contradictorily self-identical (…) and as such it is the world of the self-determination of *topos* [i.e. the field of consciousness] (1945, 4).
20 Within the empirically explored examples in the second half of the book, this is most clearly illustrated in the accounts of the dilemmas of parenting. Through the recognition that action on behalf of the child by the parent may impact the child who has less power and control over her future, the parent comes into contact with the ethical obligation and with multiple streams of time. She is at once required to self-determine – to choose to act or not act – and to live what is unfolding through time. This gives access through self-determination to ethics. How should a parent act? This is a larger question than that of the particular child, or particular circumstances. (Zapien's note to Chapter II.3)
21 This particular issue is so interesting in the essential structure of an affair. In these cases, in Chapter II.4, we see that an affair arises because people are both living their primary relationships in such a way that the deep disappointment and lack of intimacy within these relationships is lived somewhat passively and are also living the eroticism with another person somewhat passively. In both cases, the fullness of what is lived is not actively grasped and named 'marriage careening toward hopelessness and divorce' or 'flirtation sliding into an affair'. In both cases, it is only after some time passes and the situation becomes more significantly defined (e.g. the

marriage has little life left or the affair is consummated in a clear and sexual embodied breach of the original promise) that the participants in the study come to recognize actively that they are living these experiences. After this recognition and active synthesis, participants can recall many choices they made all along that brought about these circumstances and in effect were already present to them but only partially acknowledged (Zapien's note to Chapter II.4).

22 In phenomenology, J. L. Marion (*Givenness and Revelation* [Oxford University Press, 2016]) and I. Kern ('Trinity: Theological Reflections of a Phenomenologist', in *Essays in Phenomenological Theology*, ed. Steven W. Laycock and James G. Hart [New York: SUNY Press, 1986]) wrote about the Trinitarian view of the world. For Marion the Trinity describes a very specific relationship, even a logical one, between Givenness and being in a genuinely religious context. For Kern Trinity indicates the dimensions within which human life is lived, the three 'faces' of the One Nature, Society and Self as a helpful tripartite schema for considering the 'manners' of a deific relatedness. The Trinitarian view of the world I am describing here resonates also with Fink's description of the triadic structure of the ego which emerges with the performance of the reduction' ('Husserl's Philosophy and Contemporary Criticism', in *The Phenomenology of Husserl*, ed. R. O. Elveton, Chicago: Quadrangle 1970): 116.

23 I use dialectic and circular terms interchangeably because Kopf noticed Nishida's notion of circularity is dialectic, just as Nishida had in mind Pascal's idea of circle.

24 Edmund Husserl, *Späte Texte über Zeitkonstitution* (1929–1934). Die C-Manuskripte, Hrsg. von D. Lohmar, 'Husserliana Materialen VIII' (Dordrecht, 2006), 110: 'This primal impressional flowing present of the concrete originally presence has then the following quite universal structure: a) the phenomenological residuum of the proper perceivable side of mundane realities etc., namely the sensation-hyle, the originary hyle in its own temporalization; b) the I with all open and concealed egological components, belonging there: all components of the worldly apprehension, all components of the worldly "reference", of what is essentially according to a horizon [Horizontmäßig], of the worldly representations and so on.'

25 Hua-Mat VIII, p. 84: 'Temporalization of the concrete present as impressional present of persisting unities and pluralities [...] [it] is the first and more original temporalization of the time-mode present, and then of the time-mode past.'

26 I borrow this term from J. Gebser, *Ursprung und Gegenwart. Zweiter Teil: Die Manifestationen der aperspektivischen Welt* (Flensburg Fjord: Novalis Verlag, 2011). See also on time and self D. Lohmar, *On Time. New Contributions to the Husserlian Phenomeology of Time* (Dordrecht-Boston-London, Springer, 2010) and Simenov (2015).

27 As in Sartre's elucidation of the need for the world to appear to me in order is necessary, yet totally unjustifiable (Sartre, 1943, 1992). He states, 'Order is me' and there 'should be this order' (Sartre, 1943, 1992, p. 309)

28 'Here, it is not only what is intentional (*das Intentionale*) that is a temporal object (*zeitlicher Gegenstand*), but also the intending experience (*das*

intendierende Erlebnis), this last one also a "pole" itself, and all these poles lie on coinciding time series (*sich deckende Zeitreihen*), and all these time series in their unity of coincidence make up the whole experiencing (*Erleben*), the stream of experiencing' (Hua XXXIII, 279).

29 I find the argument between Nagel, Engels and Mayr, which has been summarized by E. Mayr in 'Idea of Teleology', *Journal of the History of Ideas*, 53, no. 1 (1992): 122, instructive, in the following passage: 'Nagel and Engels have criticized some of my views. Engels's monograph is the most complete treatment of the teleology problem in the German language. In the following account I have included an answer to their objections. Before doing so I want first to clear up a number of assumptions that have been a confusing element in the recent literature. This will allow me to show that the following assertions are invalid. 1. Teleological statements and explanations imply the endorsement of unverifiable theological or metaphysical doctrines in science. This criticism was indeed valid in former times, particularly in the eighteenth and early nineteenth centuries, as well as for most vitalists right up to modern times, including Bergson and Driesch. It does not apply to any Darwinian who uses teleological language (see below). 2. Any biological explanation that is not equally applicable to inanimate nature constitutes rejection of a physico-chemical explanation. This is an invalid objection, since every modem biologist accepts physico-chemical explanations at the cellular-molecular level, and furthermore, since, as will be shown below, seemingly teleological processes in living organisms can be explained strictly materialistically. 3. Teleological language introduces anthropomorphism into biology. Many philosophers, indeed, have made human intentions and purposive acts the starting point of their analysis of goal-directed activities in other.'

30 As Husserl put it: 'The I ought not properly be called I, indeed, it should not be named at all because then it is already become objective. It is the nameless, beyond all that is graspable and beyond all not as what stands or hovers or exists, but as the "functioning", grasping, valuing. He further notes that it is not an object (*Gegenstand*), but a primal substance (*Ur-stand*). The nameless is not "being", but "functioning". If our names are a result of a display of something which comes to be present and absent, and then we learn to have it before us in a way that is indifferent to its presence and absence, "I" is never present or absent precisely in this way and therefore what the transcendental I refers to is not properly a name' (Husserl cited in J. Hart, *Who One Is. Meontology of the I: A Transcendental Phenomenology* [Springer, 2009], 72, 104–5). This might imply a form of transcendental psychologism that cannot be fully discussed here.

31 For example, in Nicolle Zapien's study that we are going to read in the next chapters, life-changing decisions seem to be taken from the very centre of this circle. The mother who has to decide what to do with her addicted son is reasoning in terms of eternity because her choice is strongly grounded in the now, but at the same time she is betting on a future in which she believes as if it was a reality standing already there in front of herself; and it is her ethical decision that puts in communication those two layers of time with each other. The cyclical or practical time is that stream of time that

connects through a moral goal what is only known as an idea with the now that is ontologically there underneath our feet.

32 To read more on the phenomenological analysis of real and reel see Husserl's *Logical Investigations*, in particular the fifth and sixth volumes. Note that in the second edition Husserl modifies the distinction between 'real' and 'reel'. Also Hua XXII, 286, Hua XXVII, 206. Sometimes the term 'reel' has been made in English with the adjective 'genuine'; see, on this point, E. Kohak, *Jan Patocka: Philosophy and Selected Writings* (Chicago Press, 1989), 26. Also, R. Bernet, I. Kern and E. Marbach, *An Introduction to Husserlian Phenomenology* (Evanston: Northwestern University Press, 1993), 89–90.

33 Cf. Badiou's (reference) critique of philosophy that does not acknowledge its conditions and thus pretends to be outside of dialectic.

34 See Hart (2009): 'This kind of "ontology," since Plotinus, has been called "meontology." Just as in the case of Plotinus' refusal of the property of being to the One, so the analogous *meon* (μη' ον) in Husserl is not simply non-being or nothingness, not a mere *nihil negativum*. (Even though the "myself" is central to this work, "meontology" is not to be confused with a "me" (first-person singular accusative) ontology, where the being referred to becomes an absolute; even though we feature the "myself" and "ownness," the English first-personal accusative pronoun, "me," is to be distinguished from the Greek word for a negation or privation, "not" or "non," *me̅* (μη'). Yet teasing out its peculiar "kind of being" or non-being is a difficult matter. We have already had occasion to mention that the referent of "I" is not a kind; we will show how "I" is not a sortal term and how, when we refer to it, we do so without ascribing properties. It is surely not what is present among what we make present and never simply over against us (*Gegenstand*), but rather is the primal shining and showing by which all that comes to light is brought to light but itself is never among the displayed and articulated beings brought to light'.

35 On this point it woud be useful to refer to Husserl's and Nishida's meontology – or ontology of nothing.

36 More on the confusion of psychologism or logicism, see my *Husserl's Ethics* (2015), Lotze (1885) and D. Willard, 'The Paradox of Logical Psychologism: Husserl's Way Out', *American Philosophical Quarterly*, 9, no. 1 (1972). A dialectic point of view should help to keep these levels of reality as separated from each other. In describing human experience Husserl prefers to avoid the word causality because it is 'laden with prejudices (deriving from naturalism)' (Hua I, §37) and he prefers instead to think of '*motivation* in the transcendental sphere (and in the sphere of "pure" psychology)' (Hua I, §37).

37 A. Feenberg and Y. Ariska ('Experiential Ontology: The Origins of the Nishida Philosophy in the Doctrine of Pure Experience', *International Philosophical Quarterly*, 30, no. 2, [1990]) remark that in Nishida's theory of pure experience, subject and object are not foundational categories but arise from reflection within an original unity, pre-reflective consciousness. He lists 4 concepts of experience: 1. experience as epistemological foundation, 2. Immediacy vs reflection, 3. Experience as

building, 4. Experience as ontological foundation: the phenomenological-existentialist idea of experience as the unsurpassable horizon of being versus objectivity understood as a detached 'view from nowhere'. For J. W. Krueger, 'pure experience for Nishida is both the primordial foundation of consciousness and the ultimate ground of all reality', in *The Varieties of Pure Experience: William James and Kitaro Nishida on Consciousness and Embodiment. William James Studies*, vol. 1 (2006), 12.

38 'The last of the nine chapters deals with teleology and theology in a treatment that is novel and audacious. Based on her view that being for Husserl is revealed through decisions and deeds or, in her own words, that "practical intentionality is the decisional movement or the self determination of being (...)". Her use of the term theology (...) raises a new question (...), if a theological discourse is different from philosophical discourse and, if yes, in what relation with it?'

39 For example, this definition of teleology would not allow to accept Dewey's pragmatic and functional approach to propositional logic as deontologizing (see Suppe, *Science and Inquiry*, 24).

I.4 Pathological and mystical time

1 A. Steinbock, *Phenomenology and Mysticism* (Bloomington: Indiana University Press, 2007).

2 A force perhaps comparable to Bergson's 'élan vital' (1908), Henry's metaphysical notion of 'Life' (*C'est moi la verité*) (2008) or to Levinas's notion of God as a radical alterity, 'beyond Being' (*au de la d'étre*) (1991).

3 There is a wide range of different experiences of schizophrenia which might not match what I am going to describe in this chapter. As my introduction says, what I mean to do here is to describe a way of seeing reality that does not match the validated intersubjective view of it and to show how this version of reality is interlaced with ethical decisions and one's specific positionality in relation to time. There has been a number of psychiatrists and authors who themselves have been diagnosed with schizophrenia and later wrote about it: https://www.madinamerica.com/2012/01/a-psychiatrist-remembers-his-recovery-from-schizophrenia/; https://www.ncbi.nlm.nih.gov/pmc/articles/PMC2659312/ http://people.com/archive/her-own-mental-illness-behind-her-a-young-doctor-reaches-out-to-the-victims-of-schizophrenia-vol-28-no-19/.

Besides, for the sake of our discussion we can organize the literature around psychotic disorders such as schizophrenia into two big groups: (a) those who focus on the distortions of time and argue against the medical model and in particular against its use to pathologize 'psychotic' or 'thought disorders' like schizophrenia, and likewise (b) those who compare 'mental illness' in general and schizophrenia in particular to mystical experience. As it concerns the first group, I might cite the works of: Deana B. Davalos and Jamie Opper, 'Time Processing in Schizophrenia', in *Time Distortions in Mind: Temporal Processing in Clinical Populations*, ed. A. Vatakis and

M. J. Allman (Leiden; Boston: Brill, 2015), 93–114; Yvonne Delevoye-Turrell et al., 'Predictive Timing for Rhythmic Motor Actions in Schizophrenia', in *Time Distortions in Mind*, 136–67; Jeffrey A. Lieberman and Michael B. First, 'Renaming Schizophrenia', *British Medical Journal*, 334, no. 7585 (2007): 108–108; Ryan D. Ward et al., 'Interactions of Timing and Motivational Impairments in Schizophrenia', in *Time Distortions in Mind*, 168–89. As it concerns the second group of studies, I might cite Richard Noll, 'Shamanism and Schizophrenia: A State-Specific Approach to the "Schizophrenia Metaphor" of Shamanic States', *American Ethnologist*, 10, no. 3 (1983): 443–459; Julian Silverman, 'Shamans and Acute Schizophrenia', *American Anthropologist*, 69, no. 1 (1967): 21–31; Kenneth Stifler et al., 'An Empirical Investigation of the Discriminability of Reported Mystical Experiences among Religious Contemplatives, Psychotic Inpatients, and Normal Adults', *Journal for the Scientific Study of Religion*, 32, no. 4 (1993): 366–372; Roger Walsh, 'Phenomenological Mapping and Comparisons of Shamanic, Buddhist, Yogic, and Schizophrenic Experiences', *Journal of the American Academy of Religion*, 61, no. 4 (1993): 739–769; William Earle, 'Phenomenology of Mysticism', *The Monist*, 59, no. 4 (1976): 519–531.

4 The interview continues: 'I feel like I'm not a natural human being or a proper human being or something like that. I have always tried so much to be a real human being, but I have the feeling that I'm not (…) I don't feel like I have a core or a substance … Increasingly, I began to feel that I sort of fused with the surroundings … And I had a hard time recognizing myself from hour to hour, day to day (…) I had this idea that I didn't look human and that everybody was sort of being nice to me and played along. Seriously, when I passed others in the street, they were polite and didn't stare too much, but they would think 'what was that?' That is, I really thought that I wasn't recognizable as a human being (…) I must have been 4 or 5 years old. I was starting dance class and I was looking in the mirror. I was standing next to the other kids and I remember that I looked alien. I felt like I sort of stuck out from that large wall mirror. As if I wasn't a real child. This feeling has been very persistent from very early on' (cited in Henriksen & Nordgaard, 2016).

5 More on the intersubjective world in the next chapter.

6 In the Fusus al-Hikam, Ibn al-Arabi writes, 'we say that knowledge of the Real is outside of time (*qidam*) and knowledge of human being is within time (*muhadath*)' as translated by Aisha Bewley, p. 6.

7 While in Chapter I.3 by comparison with Nishida I termed them as material, lifeworld and creating world.

8 Since these layers cannot be conceived one without the other, the passive, psychological and linear time layer contains elements of activity that are proper to the practical one. On a passive layer the ego awakes in a now and starts synthesizing the passive matter of its experience into an understandable linear time.

9 For those who want to read more on the comparison between Merleau-Ponty's and Nishida's notion of reality, see, for example: J. Y. Park and G. Kopf, *Merleau-Ponty and Buddhism* (London: Lexingthon Books, 2009); Anya Daly. *Merleau-Ponty and the Ethics of Intersubjectivity* (London: Palgrave MacMillian, 2016).

10 Instead, for some schizophrenics there is just the world they inhabit, they are not able to hold another world. It really depends on how the schizophrenia (or other 'psychotic disorders') are manifesting in that particular person.

11 On dissociative disorders: Valerie Gray Hardcastle and Owen Flanagan, 'Multiplex vs. Multiple Selves: Distinguishing Dissociative Disorders', *The Monist*, 82, no. 4 (1999): 645–657; Anne P. DePrince and Jennifer J. Freyd, 'Dissociative Tendencies, Attention, and Memory', *Psychological Science*, 10, no. 5 (1999): 449–452; Daniel B. Wright and Elizabeth F. Loftus, 'Measuring Dissociation: Comparison of Alternative Forms of the Dissociative Experiences Scale', *The American Journal of Psychology*, 112, no. 4 (1999): 497–519; Eric Eich et al., 'Memory, Amnesia, and Dissociative Identity Disorder', *Psychological Science*, 8, no. 6 (1997): 417–422.

12 According to Chittick (2016), by this term Ibn al-Arabi means the origin of the whole.

13 Here it would be useful to expand on the literature around the notion of 'Individuals and Universals' in Husserl. See, for example, F. Kersten, 'Universals', in *Research in Phenomenology*, 4 (1974): 29–33; S. Bertolini and F. Fabbianelli, 'Ontologie fenomenologiche: individualità, essenza, idea', *Discipline Filosofiche*, 2016.

14 There is some literature that points out the similarities between psychedelic drug experience and mystical experience, although the meanings that can be drawn from both experiences do not necessarily equate. See, Walter Houston Clark, 'Religious Aspects of Psychedelic Drugs', *California Law Review*, 56, no. 1 (1968): 86–89; J. Kellenberger, 'Mysticism and Drugs', *Religious Studies*, 14, no. 2 (1978): 175–191; John L. Cheek, 'Paul's Mysticism in the Light of Psychedelic Experience', *Journal of the American Academy of Religion*, 38, no. 4 (1970): 381–389; Bruce Bower, 'Chemical Enlightenment', *Science News*, 170, no. 14 (2006): 216–220.

15 This conclusion of mine can find support in the studies of Blankenburg, 1965; Bovet & Parnas, 1993; Minkowski, 1933.

16 Minimal self is a 'thin' phenomenological notion referring to the first-personal manifestation or givenness of experience (Zahavi, 2005, 2014) – a structure that assures the subjectivity of experience, often designated as 'mineness', 'myness', 'for-me-ness' (Hart, 2009; Henry, 1973; Klawonn, 1991; Zahavi, 2005).

17 It is true that the 'incomplete' minimal self enables normally silent or anonymous regions to emerge with alien prominence within the very intimacy of one's own subjectivity – it is, as Ey puts it, 'a modification within the self' (1973, 417); but if we do not allow any meaning validation of these regions, no sense of self, hence no actual witness can ever emerge. The life of consciousness entails an incessant immanent self-affection, imbuing the first-person perspective with its affective dimension, an experiential feel of self-presence or self-familiarity, and an inchoate sense of singularity.

18 For example, this dynamic can explain the sense of intimacy illustrated in Zapien's study on the beginning of an affair in Chapter II.4 in the second part of the book.

19 Here I am reading the minimal self through the interpretive grid provided in chapters I.1 and I.2, i.e. the interconnection of practical, active and passive intentionality.

20. For a small selection of readings on the topic: E. Minkowski, *Le temps vecu* (Paris, France: d'Arey, 1933); E. Minkowski, *La schizophrénie. Psychopathologie des schizoïdes et des schizophrènes* (Paris, France: Payot, 1927); O. Doerr-Zegers, 'Adicción y temporalidad', *Psicología Médica Argentina*, 5 (1980): 381– 397; L. Fouks, S. Guibert, M. Montot, 'Minkowski's Concept of Lived Time', *Ann Mèd Psychol*, 147, no. 8 (1989): 801–809; T. Fuchs, 'Phenomenology and psychopathology', in *Handbook of Phenomenology and the Cognitive Sciences*, ed. S. Gallagher, D. Schmicking (Dordrecht, Netherlands: Springer, 2010), 547–573; T. Fuchs, 'Temporality and Psychopathology', *Phenomenology and Cognitive Science*, 1 (2013): 75–104; K. Vogeley and C. Kupke, 'Disturbances of Time Consciousness from a Phenomenological and a Neuroscientific Perspective', *Schizophrenic Bulletin*, 33 (2007): 157–165. D. Zahavi, 'Inner Time-Consciousness and Pre-Reflective Self-Awareness', in *The New Husserl: A Critical Reader*, ed. D. Welton (Bloomington: Indiana University Press, 2003), 157–180.

21. A schizophrenia study from the 1970s showed those treated with psychosocial care and limited use of antipsychotics had a lower relapse rate and earlier discharge date than those who received psychiatric treatment-as-usual with a neuroleptic. For example, W. T. Carpenter, 'The Treatment of Acute Schizophrenia without Drugs', *The American Journal of Psychiatry*, 134, no. 1 (1977): 14–20; S. M. Mathews, 'A Non-Neuroleptic Treatment for Schizophrenia', *Schizophrenia Bulletin*, 5 (1979): 322–332; John R. Bola, 'Treatment of Acute Psychosis without Neuroleptics', *The Journal of Nervous and Mental Disease*, 191, no. 4 (2003): 219–229.

22. See, G. Stanghellini, 'At Issue: Vulnerability to Schizophrenia and Lack of Common Sense', *Schizophrenia Bulletin*, 26, no. 4 (2000): 775–786.

23. For example, N. O. Kirillov and E. P. Dmitry, eds, *Nonlinear Physical Systems: Spectral Analysis, Stability and Bifurcations* (Wiley-ISTE, London, 2013); T. A. Mattei, 'The Secret Is at the Crossways: Hodotopic Organization and Nonlinear Dynamics of Brain Neural Networks', *Behavioral and Brain Science*, 36, no. 6 (2013): 623–624; discussion: 634–659; P. Thomas, A. V. Straube, J. Timmer, C. Fleck, R. Grima, 'Signatures of Nonlinearity in Single Cell Noise-induced Oscillations', *Journal of Theoretical Biology*, 335 (2013): 222–234; L. Avilés, 'Cooperation and Non-linear Dynamics: An Ecological Perspective on the Evolution of Sociality', *Evolutionary Ecology Research*, 1 (1999): 459–477; A. Bystritsky, A. A. Nierenberg, J. D. Feusner, M. Rabinovich, 'Computational Non-linear Dynamical Psychiatry: A New Methodological Paradigm for Diagnosis and Course of Illness', *Journal of Psychiatric Research*, 46 (2012): 428–443; W. Lücke and P. Nattermann, 'Nonlinear Quantum Mechanics and Locality', in *Symmetry in Science X*, ed. B. Gruber and M. Ramek (New York: Plenum Press, 1998); W. Lücke, 'Nonlinear Schrödinger Dynamics and Nonlinear Observables', in Doebner et al. [32], 1995, 140–154.

24. As Zapien's study shows in the second part of the book, the space of intimacy is lost whenever one denies him/herself the access to its own passive life; for example, in the case of a beginning of an affair in Chapter II.4, the partner involved in the affair denies him/herself access to the world of his/her passive life in order to avoid facing the actuality of his/her life and accordingly his/her intimate world.

25 On this point, Laing's remark (*The Politics of Experience*, 1967) concerning schizophrenia is interesting. There is no disease but a rational answer to an irrational system. The schizophrenic finds another way to express her meanings, since the conventional ones are revealed to be unsuccessful.

26 Here is the longer quote:
> [T]he one-sided emphasis on space, which has its extreme expression in materialism and naturalism, gives rise to an ever-greater unconscious feeling of guilt about time, the neglected component of our manifest world. As we approach the decline of the perspectival age, it is our anxiety about time that stands out as the dominant characteristic alongside our ever more absurd obsession with space. It manifests itself in various ways, such as in our addiction to time. Everyone is out to 'gain time', although the time gained is usually the wrong kind: time that is transformed into a visible multiplication of spatially fragmented 'activity', or time that one has 'to kill'. Our time anxiety shows up in our hapti-fication of time ... and is expressed in our attempt to arrest time and hold onto it through its materialization. Many are convinced that 'time is money', although again this is almost invariably falsified time, a time that can be turned into money, but not time valid in its own right. A further expression of man's current helplessness in the face of time is his compulsion to 'fill' time; he regards it as something empty and spatial like a bucket or container, devoid of any qualitative character. But time is in itself fulfilled and not something that has to be 'filled up' or 'filled out'. Finally, our contemporary anxiety about time is manifest in our flight from it: in our haste and rush, and by our constant reiteration, 'I have no time'. It is only too evident that we have space but no time; time has us because we are not yet aware of its entire reality. Contemporary man looks for time, albeit mostly in the wrong place, despite, or indeed because of his lack of time: and this is precisely his tragedy, that he spatializes time and seeks to locate it 'somewhere'. This spatial attachment – in its extreme form a spatial fixation – prevents him from finding an escape from spatial captivity ... (22–23)

27 For example, as M. Riemer remarks in 'Anisotropy of Time', *Consciousness and Cognition*, 38 (15 December 2015): 191–197 the anisotropy quality of time shows how we cannot manipulate the direction of the perceived time flow, and consequently, we do not possess complete experimental control over the presentation of temporal stimuli. A thorough consideration of this fact is of great value for future research on time perception and will strengthen the conclusion drawn from psychophysical experiments.

28 Newton wrote, Absolute, true, and mathematical time, of itself, and from its own nature, flows equably without relation to anything external, and by the means of motion, which is commonly used instead of true time; such as an hour, a day, a month, a year, in *Scholium to the Definitions in Philosophiae Naturalis Principia Mathematica*, Bk. 1 (1689); trans. Andrew Motte (1729), rev. Florian Cajori (Berkeley: University of California Press, 1934), 6–12.

29 This distinctive feature of time was alluded to by William James when he wrote that 'to realize a quarter of a mile we need to look out of the window and *feel* its length [...] To realize an hour, we must count

now! – now! – now! – now! – indefinitely. Each *now* is the feeling of a separate *bit* of time, and the exact sum of the bits never makes a very clear impression on our mind' (James, 1890/1950, 611).

30 I am using the term emergent not in a technical sense but as a means to describe Husserl's notion of awakening. The verb that Husserl uses is 'erwachsen' as in Hua XXXI, p. 7: 'Es erwachsen so Gegenstaendlichkeiten wie die objektiven Werte, wie zum Beispiel Kunstwerke, wirtschaftliche

Güter u.dgl., die bewusstseinsmassig gegeben sind als Sachen, die mit objektiven Wertpradikaten behaftet sind. Das Letztere sind Pradikate, die offenbar aus der Gefiihlsintentionalitat entspringen.'

I.5 The ethics of intimacy

1 In this sense Merleau-Ponty's notion of flesh can be useful in dialogue with Husserl's notion of body when he writes, 'The flesh is not matter, is not mind, is not substance. To designate it, we should need the old term element, in the sense it was used to speak of water, air, earth, and fire, that is, in the sense of a general thing, midway between spatio-temporal individual and the idea, a sort of incarnate principle that brings a style of being wherever there is a fragment of being. The flesh is in this sense an "element" of Being' (*The Visible and the Invisible*, IV, 139).

2 I explained the meaning of this expression in Chapter I.2 where I referred to the concreteness of being and its inner interrelation.

3 The terms usually employed by Husserl to express habits are: *Gewohnheit*, *Habitus*, *Habitualität*, *das Habituelle*, or the Greek *hexis*; sometimes he also uses the verbal phrase 'possession' of (*Besitz*), the 'having' (*Habe*) of a skill, or 'habits of thought' (*Denkgewohnheiten*). Husserl uses '*Habitus*' to express the concept of 'demeanor' or 'comportment' as combined with human personal abilities.

4 Incidentally, this thesis is not new, of course. In his *De Anima* Aristotle addresses this same issue using the word *orexis*, desire.

5 More on intentionality of feeling in my *Husserl's Ethics and Practical Intentionality* (Bloomsbury, New York, 2015).

6 See, for example, Hua XXXI, 8: 'These value determinations are not the arbitrarily varying characters of feeling, they are predicates, that is, elements that are identifiable; but the sources from which the objectivation for these predicates are drawn are the feelings and the contents of them accruing to the matters in questions. But in the final analysis, one must distinguish here between the intentionality of feeling itself, and the objectivating – be it passive or, in higher levels, active – the objectivating that objectivates the contents arising in the intentionality of feeling and that makes use of them in order to constitute new predicate layers with respect to matters that are constituted in other ways.'

7 This is particularly clear in the example put forth in the study of affairs in Chapter II.4. In this case, desire, passively intended results in an affair and can

only be integrated through active meaning-making of the experience towards a higher aim (e.g. divorce, opening up the marriage, fully living the new relationship, more awareness and depth in all of these experiences). (Zapien's note to Chapter II.4).

8 See, E. Husserl, *Experience and Judgment: Investigations in a Genealogy of Logic*, trans. J. Churchill and K. Ameriks (London: Routledge & Kegan, 1973), § 16, 75; *Analyses Concerning Active and Passive Syntheses*, § 26.

9 As I was explaining in the previous chapter this is the space that is difficult to be reached by schizophrenics.

10 There is a rich secondary literature on the notion of consent. Here I will not follow this literature because my goal, as stated in my introduction, is to reactivate the meaning of intimacy and see if its sense can be intersubjectively accepted and validated. Nevertheless, here follows a sample of the wide literature on this point: for example, N. Zapien and M. Levand, 'Sexual Consent as Transcendence', *International Journal of Transpersonal Studies*, in press; R. Gillon, 'Consent', *British Medical Journal (Clinical Research Edition)*, 291, no. 6510 (1985): 1700–1701; S. D. Pattinson, 'Consent and Informational Responsibility', *Journal of Medical Ethics*, 35, no. 3 (2009): 176–179; T. Ploug and H. Soren, 'Informed Consent and Routinisation', *Journal of Medical Ethics*, 39, no. 4 (2013): 214–218.

11 Hua, 39, Beilage XVII, 223: 'Treten in der A1-Periode mir fremde Menschen gegenüber, sich als Menschen normal ausweisend, so sind sie Menschen, die ihrerseits Erfahrung von dieser selben A-Welt haben, in Bezug auf sie personale Einheiten sind wie ich; und für mich sind sie als das im Einverständnis gegeben und ich für sie'; Hua 42, 276: 'Und da ich eines und das andere wei., werde ich mich entsprechend bestimmen lassen und nicht ohne Weiteres zustimmen, nicht ohne Weiteres ablehnen.'

12 Hua 42, 192, 'Und in dieser Hin-sicht bin ich dafür interessiert, dass meine Urteile anderen als richtig gelten, dass sie von ihnen anerkannt, in Zustimmung übernommen werden und eventuell auch meine Begründungen dafür. Selbst wo ich schon einsehe, dass sie falsch und die Begründungen untriftig sind, mag ich interessiert sein daran, dies anderen zu verdecken und mir den sozialen Wert des klugen Mannes zu erhalten. Hier ist nicht das Urteil selbst durch einen Wert des Urteils motiviert, sondern Wert ist hier, dass mein Urteil Anderen als richtiges gelte, dass sie mir zustimmen und mich für einen wahr Urteilenden halten, mich als das beurteilen.'

13 For example, in the study of marital affair that Nicolle Zapien did in the second part of the book we can see how consent is an act that takes place before our actual understanding of it occurs. So we can argue that there are at least two levels of consent, a spontaneous embodied one and a cognitive reflective one.

14 See, for example, R. Gelles, 'Power, Sex, and Violence: The Case of Marital Rape', *The Family Coordinator*, 26, no. 4 (1977): 339–347; S. Ghosal and S. Ghosa, 'Socio-political Dimensions of Rape', *The Indian Journal of Political Science*, 70, no. 1 (2009): 107–120.

15 I mean generative as transformative, see A. Steinbock, *Home and Beyond: Generative Phenomenology after Husserl* (Northwestern University Press, 1995).

16 The study of instincts is not only a genetic concern. He touched on this topic in the Fifth of the *Logical Investigations* (see Hua XIX/1, 409; see Lee, 43 ff.).
17 See, for example, on the theme of impulses in Husserl there is this interesting issue of *Alter*, 2001, 9 (R. Barbaras, 'Pulsion et perception') entirely dedicated to it.
18 In the study of parenting and in the study of affairs in chapters II.3 and II.4 respectively, we see an illustration of this. In these descriptions parents and lovers are living a passive intentionality that is not yet actively grasped and named love. In the former case it might be lived only as a stream of passivity or might be actively intended as duty, for example, and in the latter often it is lived passively or named something along the lines of 'harmless flirting' for the subject. This will be explored further (Zapien's note to chapters II.2 and II.3).
19 Dante's verses: 'Love, so swift to grasp a tender heart, /is what made him want my once fair form/wrenched from me with much yet felt offense. / Love, which won't let beloved stay apart/struck me with such strong enjoyment for this man that, as you see, it has not yet abandoned me', (*Divine Comedy*).
20 Although most habits are invisible because they become embedded within a natural attitude and then they become part of a natural life, one can see them through a reflective attitude.
21 Hua XIV, 378: 'I am not only an actual but I am also a habitual ego, and habituality signifies a certain egoic possibility, an "I can" or "I could", or "I would have been able to", and this ability to become actual refers to ego-actualities, to actual ego-experiences, that is, as actualization of ability. In a word, I am (and without this would not be an I, I can not think of myself otherwise), an ego of capacities.'
22 Yet, in the next chapter I will show how the decision to become intimate is located on a lower pre-predicative level of which we cannot fully be in control or aware.

I.6 Forced intimacy

1 And yet as we see in the study of affairs, an experience that is largely judged by many to be problematic ethically and morally, the issue of passivity and choice is important. In these cases, people choose and act and are both responsible for those acts but at the same time the essence of an affair includes that it is lived passively in many cases. To passively live an affair against the backdrop of moral judgement shapes how we choose and therefore how we take responsibilities for these choices. It is only after a clear line is stepped over that those who have affairs actively grasp what has been lived passively up until then and become fully able to accept responsibility for these choices. We can surmise that the judgement may in fact shape the experience – psychoanaysis has much to say about how we hide from ourselves those aspects that we fear would be judged. (Zapien's note to Chapter II.4)

2 *Intimacy* comes from the Latin superlative *intimus* (the most inside possible).

3 While it is not frequent to discuss transcendental freedom as applied to existential sexuality and the same as applied to existential leadership, we can see how transcendental freedom allows leaders in their dilemmas to access the fullness of their dilemmas and largest purposeful responsibilities. Once one has access to the perspective of transcendental time and identity, freedom and responsibility for choosing and acting becomes the ethical imperative (Zapien's note to Chapter II.2).

4 I use the word event here in Badiou's terms.

5 We are in fact always talking about the volitional body, which makes decisions despite the low level of cognitive awareness involved.

6 Amir Menachem's research (1968) on patterns of victimization revealed that 48 per cent of the rape victims knew the offender. Forced intimacy arises spontaneously in a place where an intimate space is already created; this generates the problem of naming the forcefulness of the event because the victim desires to keep the intimate space intact. Pauline Bart's (1979) examination of 1,070 questionnaires filled out by victims of rape found that 5 per cent of the women were raped by relatives, .4 per cent by husbands, 1 per cent by lovers and 3 per cent by ex-lovers. Thus, a total of 8.4 per cent of the women were raped by men with whom they had intimate relations. Bart's survey also found that 12 per cent of rape victims were raped by dates and 23 per cent were raped by acquaintances. Less than half of the victims (41%) were raped by total strangers. Additional research on rape also reveals a pattern where victims were likely to know the offender or be related to the offender. Of the 250 victims of rape studied by the Center for Rape Concern at Philadelphia General Hospital, 58 per cent of the rape victims under the age of 18 were assaulted by a relative or acquaintance. When the victim is a child, she is likely to be sexually attacked by her father – six of the thirteen children were raped by their fathers (Peters, 1976).

7 'South Dakota became the only state to eliminate spousal exclusion from the statute on rape. The 1975 Rape Law reads: 'Rape is an act of sexual penetration accomplished by any person … Other states, such as Florida, do not specifically except married persons from rape prosecution' (Silverman, 1976, 10).

8 S. Brownmiller, *Against our Will* (New York: Simon and Schuster, 1975); R. T. Gallen, *Wives Legal Rights* (New York: Dell, 1967); S. Griffin, 'The All American Crime', *Ramparts*, (September 1971): 26–35; New York Radical Feminists, *Rape: The First Sourcebook for Women* (New York: New American Library, 1974); M. L. Bernard and T. L. Bernard, 'Violent Intimacy: The Family as a Model for Love Relationships', *Family Relations*, 32 (1983): 283–286; M. Straus, 'Victims and Aggressors in Marital Violence', *American Behavioral Scientist*, 23, no. 5 (1980): 681–704.

9 'If the perpetrator is known to the victim, people are reluctant to label what transpired as rape. In a study of jurors' attitudes, prior association between the victim and the defendant which would make identification more credible had the opposite result of disposing the jurors more favorably toward the

defendant' (LaFree, Reskin, & Visher, 'Jurors' Responses to Victims' Behavior and Legal Issues in Sexual Assault Trials', *Social Problems*, 32, no. 4 (April 1985): 389–407).

10 On this point, Schopenhauer's dilemma of porcupines might be significant.

II.1 Phenomenological research and ethical experience

1 There are, of course, others who claim to be phenomenological methodologists, however none of them, in our estimation, has fully articulated *an empirical research method* in sufficient detail to be considered here as separate and distinct from the context in which the method is used. Wertz (2005), for example, puts forth a method of phenomenology for mental health fields, yet draws heavily on Giorgi's method and in the end the method cannot truly be distinguished from Giorgi's method applied to clinical experiences. There are several who purport to have a new method because it is applied to a new context. This, for us, while valuable and interesting, is one level of abstraction below what we would consider to be an articulation of phenomenological methods derived from Husserl.

2 In all of the major schools of Psychoanalysis and training programmes for clinically oriented psychologists, counsellors and psychotherapists, the ethical obligation to properly metabolize one's own personal and relational history so as to be able to adequately attend to the material of the client or patient without interference from one's own psychological material is emphasized. Most training programmes also allow for the use of intuition to guide the clinician but caution us to develop skills of discernment in deciding which intuitive impulses and ideas will be useful in our interpretations and in service of the client and which should be withheld or are perhaps erroneous or irrelevant for the client in question. This skill is similar to bracketing and requires a great deal of familiarity with the self, including one's unconscious processes and history, to use psychological language. In the case of Moustakas and Colaizzi there is no such rigorous training process to account for the skill development of the researcher in managing what could be considered to be 'psychodynamic forces' (Atwood & Stolorow, 1984).

3 Intersubjectivity and relational psychology has much to say about relational systems (Stolorow, Atwood & Brandschaft, 1987). Researchers may or may not have adequate training, in my opinion, to attend to the layered and nuanced relational experiences of two subjectivities and the relationship between them in order to sufficiently address the descriptive essence of the ethical dilemmas presented in the next chapters (Lyons-Ruth, 1999). While I am a trained psychologist, I am not steeped in psychoanalytic training or intersubjective and relational psychoanalysis in practice to do these justice here or as a researcher in the use of Colaizzi's method, which I suggest, is required in order to make ethical sense of the material.

II.2 A leadership challenge

1. This attitude relates to the three streams of time as discussed in Chapters I.3 and I.4. As the quote from Gebser (2011) says 'time has us because we are not yet aware of its entire reality'. Time seems to be the essence of our soul, yet it is lived as an overriding preoccupation. 'How shocked one would be if he were to realize that he is also saying "I have no soul" and "I have no life"!' So, when our time feels compressed because of work or any draining activity, in some way our soul feels in the same way. This feeling produces a sense of Angst that makes us lose access to the timeless time of the soul and stops us in one stream of time, the linear one; it's as if that Angst takes away from our soul its space to breathe (Ferrarello's note to Chapters I.3 and I.4).
2. From this point of view it seems that leaders are invested of their role because they can access, more easily than others, the egoless world of passive syntheses and assign a meaning to it so to lead others and facilitate their decision-making process. Leaders' ethical strength seems to come from this ability to shift swiftly between the layers of their passive, practical and active intentions. For example, 'the new awareness of the conflict', as Nicolle Zapien writes below, describes exactly the moment of 'irritation', as Husserl calls it, in which the volitional body of the leader is awoken by passive syntheses and is called to make practical decisions that will assign new meanings to empty layers of sense. The irritation comes exactly from the discomfort evoked by passive layers of lived experiences that need new interpretations and accordingly new directions. As Nicolle Zapien discovers from her study, the ethical dilemma leads to the birth of a new sense of self which comes to life exactly in virtue of this rewiring of the three layers of intention in relation to reality, identity and time. That is why an ethical dilemma in leadership is very often transformational, that is, it fosters the renewal and transformation of the identity of the leader. The concreteness of the Being, its layers and our ability to be part of it by assigning an active meaning to it was described in Chapter I.2 (Ferrarello's footnote to Chapter I.2).
3. Ferrarello and Zapien wrote this commentary on the basis of the analysis conducted in chapters I.2 and II.2.

II.3 A parent's ethical dilemma

1. This 'moment-to-moment experience of time' would refer not to linear time but to the timeless sense of time in which the different layers of now are knitted together by the awakening of practical intention. The reflection on these different nows is what produces a reflexive identity; yet these moments are not connected to any precise narrative but only to a passive felt sense that still needs to be recognized and named.
2. If we use Husserl's ethics, reflecting on our identity would represent our active intentionality, while 'simply living our identity' would represent our passive intentionality (Ferrarello's note to Chapter I.2).

3   Since love, among all the sentiments, involves a true awakening (Husserl Ms E III 4, 12b), we can clearly see here how parent's dilemmas stem from the problem of awakening in relation to intimacy. Parents' volitional bodies awake to a shared world (the one shared with their children); the contents and boundaries of this shared world are not clear in the moments preceding the awakening. Their volitional bodies are called to give a shape through their decisions to the passive contents of their lives and the lives of their children. Yet, in this intersubjective context the volitional bodies of their children are not ready to give any consent to the actions the parents are going to take; rather the opposite – the parents are almost called to override the volitional bodies of their children. The dilemma arises because the parents are called to force the space of intimacy with the passive lived experiences of their own children and make decisions on behalf of their volitional bodies without any explicit consent. The decisions they are going to make will be often life-changing in the shape these decisions are going to give to their future world. In Chapter I.6, I used the expression 'brutal love' in order to indicate this form of wakeful love overriding the bodily consent of those who receive the love (Ferrarello's note, see also Chapter I.6).

4   In Chapter I.2, we called these egos psychological, transcendental and practical. The psychological is the one that lives in a natural way without reflecting or questioning its life; the transcendental one is the condition of the possibility of the ego itself; e.g. it is a reflective ego that objectifies the contents of its lived experiences in order to make meanings, and the practical one is the bridge between the two that awakens and pushes the psychological ego towards the decision of whether to take responsibility or not of the whole of natural life experience. The decision passes through the epoché, that is the commitment of the psychological ego to stop and reflect on the passive lived experiences (Ferrarello's note to Chapter I.2).

5   This can also be linked to Ferrarello's discussion of consent, albeit in that case, consent within the sexual realm, in Chapter I.6.

6   Ferrarello and Zapien wrote this commentary on the basis of the analysis conducted in Part I of the book.

II.4 The beginning of an affair

1   Because the experience is a narrative account of events (often several events or acts) through time (e.g. before the affair existed to after the affair existed) there is a sense of narrativity inherent in the accounts. This narrativity includes both notions of the self and other(s) as well as different layers of time as discussed in previous chapters – linear, transcendental and phenomenological time.

2   Interestingly, the pivotal moments that participants describe also map to shifts in the layers of time and therefore perception. Each of these pivotal moments is not remarkable in an absolute sense but rather is remarkable because it provides access to new views of the experience and the self.

3 We can refer to the layers of time as I described them in Chapter I.3, the linear, transcendental and phenomenological time. Each point in time is an opportunity for an awakening that can reshape the meaning of the lived experiences in a moment in time. If that awakening does not take place, then the linear time keeps flowing without any significant shift of meaning – although the passivity of the lived experience keeps building meanings that escape the active understanding of the persons involved (Ferrarello's note to chapters I.3, I.4).

4 As shown in chapters I.5 and I.6 intimacy is a phenomenon that involves the volitional body and its decision to accept to exert active intentionality on the realm of passive syntheses that constitute its lived experience. Ultimately, intimacy is a decision of taking ownership of one's body and give it and its action an actual meaning. In the case of the beginning of an affair a misalignment takes place because the body refuses to actually own the passive syntheses that are occurring (since one does not want to acknowledge what is in fact happening) and there is no active effort of meaning-shaping activity that the partner involved in the affair would undertake in order to give sense to the transition between the two worlds – from the personal to intersubjectively shared world (Ferrarello's note to chapters I.5 and I.6).

5 This commentary was written by Ferrarello and Zapien after comparing the results of the first and second part of the book, in particular chapters I.5, I.6, and II. 4.

Conclusion

1 These chapters illustrated the link between space and time. In fact, the link between space and time has already been demonstrated in physics and mathematics so it should come as no surprise asserted here philosophically. The relationship between our typical daily understandings of space and time includes the idea that if distances (actual or metaphoric) are greater, then more time is needed to cross those distances. In theoretical examples of black holes, or folding across higher dimensions than the 3rd dimension of space, we see clearly the relationship between space and time is not always linear or fixed. What is proposed here is that we, too, can transcend the confines of the linear lived sense of time that is connected to having a body that moves through space linearly (presuming we do not travel through black holes or have access to dimensions of space greater than the 3rd dimension). This transcendence is in our capacity to shift the view volitionally to another view – one that includes a collapse of the metaphoric space between self and other through empathy or self now and self later, for example, or one that allows for a timeless self or a bodiless self, and other, for all time.

2 Parenthetically, this explains why children who experienced a traumatic childhood with protective parents, on average have more difficulty in the process of individuation when they reach adult age.

Bibliography[1]

I. Introduction to Husserl's phenomenology

Bell, D. *Husserl*, London: Routledge, 1990.
Bernet, R., Kern, I., and Marbach, E. *Edmund Husserl: Darstellung seines Denkens*, Hamburg: Felix Meiner Verlag, 1989.
Bernet, R., Kern, I., and Marbach, E. *An Introduction to Husserlian Phenomenology*, Evanston: Northwestern University Press, 1993.
Cairns, D. 'Guide for Translating Husserl', in *Phaenomenologica*, vol. 55, The Hague: Martinus Nijhoff, 1976.
Carr, D. *Interpreting Husserl: Critical and Comparative Studies*, Dordrecht/Boston/London: Kluwer Academic Publishers, 1987.
Catucci, S. *La filosofia critica di Husserl*, Milan: Guerini e Associati, 1995.
Costa, V., Franzini, E., and Spinicci, P. *Fenomenologia*, Florence: Einaudi, 2001.
Drummond, J. J. *Historical Dictionary of Husserl's Philosophy*, Chicago, Lanham, MD: Scarecrow Press, 2008.
Franzini, E. *Fenomenologia. Introduzione tematica al pensiero di Husserl*, Milan: Franco Angeli, 2001.
Hopkins, B. *Husserl in Contemporary Context*, Dordrecht/Boston/London: Kluwer Academic Publishers, 1997.
Hopkins, B. *The Philosophy of Husserl*, London and New York: Routledge, 2011.
Mohanty, J. N. *The Philosophy of Edmund Husserl*, 2 vols, Yale University Press, 2008.
Moran, D. *Introduction to Phenomenology*, London and New York: Routledge, 2000.
Raggiunti, R. *Introduzione ad Husserl*, Roma-Bari: Laterza, 1970.
Schumann, K. *Husserl-Chronik: Denk- und Lebensweg Edmund Husserls*, Dordrecht/Boston/London: Kluwer Academic Publishers, 1997.
Smith, B. and Smith, D. W., eds. *The Cambridge Companion to Husserl*, Cambridge: Cambridge University Press, 1995.
Sokolowski, *Introduction to Phenomenology*, Cambridge: Cambridge University Press, 2000.
Spiegelberg, H. *Phenomenological Movement: A Historical Introduction*, 2 vols, The Hague: Martinus Nijhoff, 1960.

---

[1] This bibliography is intended to be a tool for research. Not all the books that are in the bibliography are explicitly cited in this book, but all of them are equally part of this research. This is the reason why we want to share this tool with all those scholars who need a start for their quest. We sorted out the sources in such a way that those who want to deepen the philosophical over the psychological discourse know where to go. In fact, we organized each item according to the relevance of their subjects.

Spileers, S. *Husserl Bibliography*, Dordrecht/Boston/London: Kluwer Academic Publishers, 1999.
Wetz, F. J. 'Wider den Absolutismus der Welt. Neuere Beiträge zu Edmund Husserl', *Philosophische Rundschau* 38, no. 4 (1991), 286–299.
Zahavi, D. *Husserl's Phenomenology*, Stanford University Press, 2003.

I. A. Edmund Husserl critical assessments

Circumscriptions: Classic Essays on Husserl's Phenomenology, ed. R. Bernet, R. Welton, G. Zavota, London-New York: Routledge, 2005, vol. 1.
The Cutting Edge: Phenomenological Method, Philosophical Logic, Ontology and Philosophy of Science, ed. R. Bernet, R. Welton, G. Zavota, London-New York: Routledge, 2005, vol. 2.
The Nexus of Phenomena: Intentionality, Perception and Temporality, ed. R. Bernet, R. Welton, G. Zavota, London-New York: Routledge, 2005, vol. 3.
The Web of Meaning: Language, Noema and Subjectivity and Intersubjectivity, ed. R. Bernet, R. Welton, G. Zavota, London-New York: Routledge, 2005, vol. 4.
Horizons: Life-world, Ethics, History and Metaphysics, ed. R. Bernet, R. Welton, G. Zavota, London-New York: Routledge, 2005, vol. 5.

II. Husserl's works

II. A. Husserliana (abbreviated in the book as Hua)

Husserliana I
Cartesianische Meditationen und Pariser Vorträge, ed. S. Strasser, The Hague, Netherlands: Martinus Nijhoff, 1973.

Husserliana II
Die Idee der Phänomenologie. Fünf Vorlesungen, ed. W. Biemel, The Hague, Netherlands: Martinus Nijhoff, 1973.

Husserliana III
Ideen zu einer reinen Phänomenlogie und phänomenlogischen Philosophie. Erstes Buch: Allgemeine Einführung in die reine Phänomenologie, ed. W. Biemel, The Hague, Netherlands: Martinus Nijhoff, 1950.

Husserliana III-1
Ideen zu einer reinen Phänomenologie und phänomenologischen Philosophie. Erstes Buch: Allgemeine Einführungin die reine Phänomenologie 1. Halbband: Text der 1.-3. Auflage – Nachdruck, ed. K. Schuhmann, The Hague, Netherlands: Martinus Nijhoff, 1977.

Husserliana III-2
Ideen zu einer reinen Phänomenologie und phänomenologischen Philosophie. Erstes Buch: Allgemeine Einfuhrung in die reine Phänomenologie,

2. Halbband: Ergänzende Texte (1912–1929), ed. K. Schuhmann, The Hague, Netherlands: Martinus Nijhoff, 1988.

Husserliana IV
Ideen zur einer reinen Phänomenologie und phänomenologischen Philosophie. Zweites Buch: Phänomenologische Untersuchungen zur Konstitution, ed. M. Biemel, The Hague, Netherlands: Martinus Nijhoff, 1952.

Husserliana V
Ideen zur einer reinen Phänomenologie und phänomenologischen Philosophie. Drittes Buch: Die Phänomenologie und die Fundamente der Wissenschaften, ed. M. Biemel, The Hague, Netherlands: Martinus Nijhoff, 1971.

Husserliana VI
Die Krisis der europäischen Wissenschaften und die transzendentale Phänomenologie. Eine Einleitung in die phänomenologische Philosophie, ed. W. Biemel, The Hague, Netherlands: Martinus Nijhoff, 1954.

Husserliana VII
Erste Philosophie (1923/4). Erste Teil: Kritische Ideengeschichte, ed. R. Boehm, The Hague, Netherlands: Martinus Nijhoff, 1956.

Husserliana VIII
Erste Philosophie (1923/4). Zweiter Teil: Theorie der phänomenologischen Reduktion, ed. R. Boehm, The Hague, Netherlands: Martinus Nijhoff, 1959.

Husserliana IX
Phänomenologische Psychologie. Vorlesungen Sommersemester. 1925, ed. W. Biemel, The Hague, Netherlands: Martinus Nijhoff, 1968.

Husserliana X
Zur Phänomenologie des inneren Zeitbewusstesens (1893–1917), ed. R. Boehm, The Hague, Netherlands: Martinus Nijhoff, 1969.

Husserliana XI
Analysen zur passiven Synthesis. Aus Vorlesungs- und Forschungsmanuskripten, 1918–1926, ed. M. Fleischer, The Hague, Netherlands: Martinus Nijhoff, 1966.

Husserliana XII
Philosophie der Arithmetik. Mit ergänzenden Texten (1890–1901), ed. E. Lothar, The Hague, Netherlands: Martinus Nijhoff, 1970.

Husserliana XIII
Zur Phänomenologie der Intersubjektivität. Texte aus dem Nachlass. Erster Teil. 1905–1920, ed. I. Kern, The Hague, Netherlands: Martinus Nijhoff, 1973.

Husserliana XIV
Zur Phänomenologie der Intersubjektivität. Texte aus dem Nachlass. Zweiter Teil. 1921–28, ed. I. Kern, The Hague, Netherlands: Martinus Nijhoff, 1973.

Husserliana XV
Zur Phänomenologie der Intersubjektivität. Texte aus dem Nachlass. Dritter Teil. 1929–35, ed. I. Kern, The Hague, Netherlands: Martinus Nijhoff, 1973.

Husserliana XVII
Formale und transzendentale Logik. Versuch einer Kritik der logischen Vernunft, ed. P. Janssen, The Hague, Netherlands: Martinus Nijhoff, 1974.

Husserliana XVIII
Logische Untersuchungen. Erster Teil. *Prolegomena zur reinen Logik.* Text der 1. und der 2. Auflage, Halle: 1900, rev. ed. 1913, ed. E. Holstein, The Hague, Netherlands: Martinus Nijhoff, 1975.

Husserliana XIX
Logische Untersuchungen. Zweiter Teil. *Untersuchungen zur Phänomenologie und Theorie der Erkenntnis*, Halle: 1901; rev. ed. 1922, ed. U. Panzer, The Hague, Netherlands: Martinus Nijhoff, 1984.

Husserliana XX/XXI
Logische Untersuchungen. Ergänzungsband. Erster Teil. Entwürfe zur Umarbeitung der VI. Untersuchung und zur Vorrede für die Neuauflage der Logischen Untersuchungen, ed. U. Melle, The Hague, Netherlands: Kluwer Academic Publishers, 2002.

Husserliana XXII
Aufsätze und Rezensionen (1890–1910), ed. B. Rang, The Hague, Netherlands: Martinus Nijhoff, 1979.

Husserliana XXIV
Einleitung in die Logik und Erkenntnistheorie. Vorlesungen 1906/07, ed. U. Melle, The Hague, Netherlands: Martinus Nijhoff, 1985.

Husserliana XXV
Aufsätze und Vorträge. 1911–1921. Mit ergänzenden Texten, ed. T. Nenon and H. R. Sepp, The Hague, Netherlands: Martinus Nijhoff, 1986.

Husserliana XXVI
Vorlesungen über Bedeutungslehre. Sommersemester 1908, ed. U. Panzer, The Hague, Netherlands: Martinus Nijhoff, 1987.

Husserliana XXVII
Aufsätze und Vorträge. 1922–1937, ed. T. Nenon and H. R. Sepp, The Hague, Netherlands: Kluwer Academic Publishers, 1988.

Husserliana XXVIII
Vorlesungen über Ethik und Wertlehre. 1908–1914, ed. U. Melle, The Hague, Netherlands: Kluwer Academic Publishers, 1988.

Husserliana XXIX
Die Krisis der europäischen Wissenschaften und die transzendentale Phänomenologie. Ergänzungsband. Texte aus dem Nachlass 1934–1937, ed. R. Smid, The Hague, Netherlands: Kluwer Academic Publishers, 1992.

Husserliana XXXI
Aktive Synthesen: Aus der Vorlesung 'Transzendentale Logik' 1920/21 Ergänzungsband zu 'Analysen zur passiven Synthesis', ed. R. Breeur, The Hague, Netherlands: Kluwer Academic Publishers, 2000.

Husserliana XXXIII
Die Bernauer Manuskripte über das Zeitbewusstsein (1917/18), ed. von Rudolf Bernet und Dieter Lohmar, 2001.

Husserliana XXXIV
Zur phänomenologischen Reduktion. Texte aus dem Nachlass (1926–1935), ed. S. Luft, Dordrecht, Netherlands: Kluwer Academic Publishers, 2002.

Husserliana XXXV
Einleitung in die Philosophie. Vorlesungen 1922/23, ed. B. Goossens, Dordrecht, Netherlands: Kluwer Academic Publishers, 2002.

Husserliana XXXVII
Einleitung in die Ethik 1920/1924, ed. H. Peucker, Dordrecht/Boston/London: Kluwer Academic Publishers, 2004.

Husserliana XXXVIII
Wahrnehmung und Aufmerksamkeit. Texte aus dem Nachlass (1893–1912), ed. T. Vongehr, and R. Giuliani, New York: Springer, 2005.

Husserliana XXXIX
Die Lebenswelt. Auslegungen der vorgegebenen Welt und ihrer Konstitution. Texte aus dem Nachlass (1916–1937), ed. Rochus Sowa, New York: Springer, 2008.

Husserliana XL
Untersuchungen zur Urteilstheorie. Texte aus dem Nachlass (1893–1918), ed. Robin Rollinger, New York: Springer, 2009.

Husserliana XLI
Zur Lehre vom Wesen und zur Methode der eidetischen Variation. Texte aus dem Nachlass (1891–1935), ed. Dirk Fonfara, New York: Springer, 2012.

Husserliana XLII
Grenzprobleme der Phänomenologie. Analysen des Unbewusstseins und der Instinkte. Metaphysik. Späte Ethik (Texte aus dem Nachlass 1908–1937), ed. Rochus Sowa and Thomas Vongehr, New York: Springer, 2014.

II. B. Documents

Husserliana: Edmund Husserl Dokumente 3/1–10.
E. Husserl, *Briefwechsel*, ed. K. Schuhmann, The Hague, Netherlands: Kluwer Academic Publishers, 1994.
Band I: Die Brentanoschule
Band II: Die Münchener Phänomenologen
Band III: Die Göttinger Schule
Band IV: Die Freiburger Schüler
Band V: Die Neukantianer
Band VI: Philosophenbriefe
Band VII: Wissenschaftkorrespondenz

Band VIII: Institutionelle Schreiben
Band IX: Familienbriefe
Band X: Einführung und Register

II. C. Manuscripts consulted at 'Les Archives-Husserl' (Paris)

Ms A V 21, Ethisches Leben. Theologie – Wissenschaft (1924–1927).
Ms A V 22, Universale Ethik. Theologie – Wissenschaft (1924–1927).
Ms A VI 3, Gemüt und Wille (1909–1914).
Ms B I 21, Weg in die Philosophie von der Praxis (1917–1918).
Ms B II 2, Absolutes Bewußtsein, Metaphysisches (1907–1908).
Ms E III, Teleologie (1930).
Ms E III 7, Mensch im Schicksal, Religion und Wissenschaft (1934).
Ms E III 8, Kosmologische Weltbesinnung (1934).
Ms E III 9, Instinkt, Wert, Gut, Teleologie, Normstruktur der Personalität (1931–1933).

II. D. Materials

Husserliana: Edmund Husserl Materialienband I
Logik. Vorlesung 1896, ed. Elisabeth Schuhmann, Dordrecht, Netherlands: Kluwer Academic Publishers, 2001.
Husserliana: Edmund Husserl Materialienband II
Logik. Vorlesung 1902/03, ed. Elisabeth Schuhmann, Dordrecht, Netherlands: Kluwer Academic Publishers, 2001.
Husserliana: Edmund Husserl Materialienband III
Allgemeine Erkenntnistheorie. Vorlesung 1902/03, ed. Elisabeth Schuhmann, Dordrecht, Netherlands: Kluwer Academic Publishers, 2001.
Husserliana: Edmund Husserl Materialienband IV
Natur und Geist. Vorlesungen Sommersemester 1919, ed. Michael Weiler, Dordrecht, Netherlands: Kluwer Academic Publishers, 2002.
Husserliana: Edmund Husserl Materialienband V
Urteilstheorie. Vorlesung 1905, ed. Elisabeth Schuhmann, Dordrecht, Netherlands: Kluwer Academic Publishers, 2002.
Husserliana: Edmund Husserl Materialienband VI
Alte und neue Logik. Vorlesung 1908/09, ed. Elisabeth Schuhmann, Dordrecht, Netherlands: Kluwer Academic Publishers, 2003.
Husserliana: Edmund Husserl Materialienband VII
Einführung in die Phänomenologie der Erkenntnis. Vorlesung 1909, ed. Elisabeth Schuhmann, Dordrecht, Netherlands: Kluwer Academic Publishers, 2005.
Husserliana: Edmund Husserl Materialienband VIII
Späte Texte über Zeitkonstitution (1929–1934). Die C-Manuskripte, ed. Dieter Lohmar, New York: Springer, 2006.
Husserliana: Edmund Husserl Materialienband IX
Einleitung in die Philosophie. Vorlesungen 1916–1919, ed. Hanne Jacobs, Dordrecht: Springer, 2012.

III. English translations[2]

Husserl, E. *Analyses Concerning Passive and Active Syntheses: Lectures on Transcendental Logic*, trans. A. J. Steinbock, Dordrecht: Kluwer, 2001. (Husserliana XXXI)
Husserl, E. *Cartesian Meditations*, trans. D. Cairns, Dordrecht: Kluwer, 1989. (Husserliana I)
Husserl, E. *The Crisis of European Sciences and Transcendental Phenomenology*, ed. D. Carr, Evanston: Northwestern Press, 1970. (Husserliana VI)
Husserl, E. *Early Writings in the Philosophy of Logic and Mathematics*, trans. D. Willard, Dordrecht: Kluwer, 1994.
Husserl, E. *Experience and Judgment: Investigations in a Genealogy of Logic*, trans. J. Churchill and K. Ameriks, London: Routledge & Kegan, 1973.
Husserl, E. *Formale und transzendentale Logik*, ed. P. Janssen, The Hague: Martinus Nijhoff, 1974. (Husserliana XVII)
Husserl, E. 'Husserls Randbemerkungen zu Schelers Formalismus'. in H. Leonardy, ed., *Études phénoménologiques*, 1991,13–14, 3–57.
Husserl, E. *Ideas Pertaining to a Pure Phenomenology and to a Phenomenological Philosophy, First Book*, ed. F. Kersten, The Hague: Martinus Nijhoff, 1983. (Husserliana III)
Husserl, E. *Ideas Pertaining to a Pure Phenomenology and to a Phenomenological Philosophy, Second Book*, trans. R. Rojcewicz and A. Schuwer, Dordrecht: Kluwer Academic Publishers, 1989.
Husserl, E. *Logical Investigations*, trans. J. N. Findlay and ed. D. Moran, London and New York: Routledge, 2001.
Husserl, E. *On the Phenomenology of the Consciousness of Internal Time (1893–1917)*, trans. J. B. Brough, Dordrecht: Kluwer, 1990.
Husserl, E. 'Philosophy as Rigorous Science', trans. and ed. Q. Lauer, *Phenomenology and the Crisis of Philosophy*, New York: Harper, 1965.
Husserl, E. 'Renewal: Its Problem and Method', trans. Jeffner Allen, in P. McCormick and F. Elliston, eds, *Husserl: Shorter Works*, University of Notre Dame, 1981. (Husserliana XXVII)

IV. Secondary literature

IV. A. 'Analecta Husserliana'

'Husserlian Phenomenology in a New Key. Intersubjectivity, Ethos, the Social Sphere, Human Encounter, Pathos', Dordrecht/Boston/London: Kluwer Academic Publishers, 1991.
'Apriori and the World, European Contributions to the Husserlian Phenomenology', Dordrecht/Boston/London: Kluwer Academic Publishers, 1981.

---

[2] These translations are abridged in the volume with Hua.

Boehm, R. 'Le phénoménal et le politiche', Boston/Dordrecht/London: Kluwer Academic Publishers, 1991, 125–133.
Holyst, B. 'The Topicality of Husserl's Ethical Antirelativism', Dordrecht/Boston/London: Kluwer Academic Publishers, 1991, 5–15.
Mohanty, J. N. 'Husserl's Formalism in Phenomenology and the Formal Sciences', in M. Hartimo, ed. *Phenomenology and Mathematics*, Dordrecht/Boston/London: Kluwer Academic Publishers, 1991, 44–58.
Sancipriano, M. 'Les Sourses de la vie morale', Dordrecht/Boston/London: Kluwer Academic Publishers, 1988, 13–43.
Spahn, C. 'Der Ethische Impuls der Husserlschen Phanomenologie', Dordrecht/Boston/London: Kluwer Academic Publishers, 1988, 25–81.
Timiniecka, A. 'The Teleologies in Husserlian Phenomenology', in *Analecta Husserliana* IX, Dordrecht/Boston/London: Kluwer Academic Publishers, 1979.

IV. B. *'Alter'*

Afeissa, H. S. 'Empirisme, association, et réduction: à propos de la lecture husserlienne de Hume', *Alter* 11 (2003), 51–78.
Barbaras, R. 'Pulsion et perception', *Alter* 9 (2001), 12–27.
Bégout, B. 'Esquisse d'une théorie phénoménologique de l'habitude', *Alter* 12 (2004), 173–190.
Bégout, B. 'Pulsion et socialisation', *Alter* 9 (2001), 27–63.
Benoist, J. 'Dire les phénomènes', *Alter* 9 (2001), 273–280.
Bouckaert, A. 'Solitude et purete du sujet phenomenologique. Hypotheses au sujet de l'origine historique de la reduction du sujet empirique', *Alter* 9 (2001), 403–413.
Brainard, M. 'Reducing the Reduction: Husserl's Many Ways to the One Reduction', *Alter* 11 (2003), 79–90.
Fink, E. 'Redoing the Phenomenology of the World in the Freiburg Workshop, 1930–1934', *Alter* 6 (1998), 39–118.
Flajoliet, A. 'L'habitude entre psychologie et phénoménologie', *Alter* 12 (2004), 27–45.
Houillon, V. 'L'épochè de la vie', *Alter* 11 (2003), 135–164.
Joumier, L. 'Le renouvellement éthique chez Husserl', *Annales de Phénoménologie*, 2004.
Kern, I. 'Les trois voies de la reduction phénoménolgoique transcendantale dans la philosophie de Edmund Husserl', *Alter* 11 (2003), 285–322.
Kokoszka, W. 'Habitualité et genèse: le devenir de la monade', *Alter* 12 (2004), 57–77.
Kühn, R. 'Pulsion et passibilité radicale', *Alter* 12 (2004), 153–170.
Landgrebe, L. 'Le problème de la constitution passive', trad. ed. N. Depraz, *Alter* 12 (2004), 235–248.
Lavigne, J. F. 'La reduction phénoménologique dans les recherches logiches selon leur première edition, 1901', *Alter* 11 (2003), 23–47.
Lohmar, D. 'L'idée de la réduction. Les réductions de Husserl – et leur sens méthodique commun', *Alter* 11 (2003), 91–110.
Nam-In Lee, 'La phénomélogie des tonalites affectives chez Edmund Husserl', *Alter* 7 (1999), 243–250.

Perreau, L. 'La double visée de l'éthique husserlienne: intentionnalité et téléologie', *Alter* 13 (2005), 32–89.
Rodrigo, P. 'La dynamique de l'hexis chez Aristote', *Alter* 12 (2004), 11–25.
Steinbock, J. A. 'Limit-Phaenomena and the Liminality of Experience', *Alter* 6 (1998), 275–296.
Yamaguchi, I. 'Triebintentionalität als Uraffektive passive Synthesis in der genetischen Phänomenologie', *Alter* 9 (2001), 219–240.

IV. C. *'Fenomenologia e societá'*

Ales Bello, A. 'L'etica nelle analisi fenomenologiche di E. Husserl', *Fenomenologia e società* 14 (1991), 21–44.
Ales Bello, A. 'Fenomenologia e politica. Esposizione ed analisi dei testi husserliani', *Fenomenologia e società* 9, no. 12 (1986), 35–54.
Ales Bello, A. 'Il recupero dell'intersoggettività in E. Husserl', *Fenomenologia e società* 1 (1978), 290–301.
Held, K. 'Per una fondazione fenomenologica della filosofia politica', trad. it. G. Pirola, in *Fenomenologia e società* 9, no. 12 (1986), 55–68.

IV. D. *'Husserl Studies'*

Bergmann, W. & Hoffmann, G. 'Selbstreferenz und Zeit: Die dynamische Stabilität des Bewusstseins.' *Husserl Studies* 6, no. 2 (1989), 155–175.
Bruzina, R. 'The Transcendental Theory of Method in Phenomenology: The Meontic and Deconstruction', *Husserl Studies* 14, no. 2 (1997), 75–94.
De Palma, V. 'Die Fakta leiten alle Eidetik', *Husserl Studies* 30, no. 3 (2014), 195–223.
Depraz, N. 'Phenomenological Reduction and Poltical', *Husserl Studies* 1 (1995), 1–17.
Drummond, J. 'Moral Objectivity: Husserl's Sentiments of the Understanding', *Husserl Studies* 12 (1995), 165–183.
Leung, K-W 'Meaning and Intuitive Act in the Logical Investigations', *Husserl Studies* 27 (2011), 125–142.
Hart, J. 'The Entelechy and Authenticity of Objective Spirit: Reflections on Husserliana XXVII', *Husserl Studies* 9 (1992), 91–110.
Hart, J. 'Genesis, Instinct and Reconstruction: Nam-In Lee's Edmund Husserl's Phänomenologie der Instincte', *Husserl Studies* 15 (1998), 101–120.
Hart, J. 'Husserl and Fichte: With Special Regard to Husserl's Lectures on "Fichte's Ideal of Humanity"', *Husserl Studies* 12, no. 2 (1995), 135–163.
Hart, J. 'Michel Henry's Phenomenological Theology of Life: A Husserlian Reading of C'est moi, la vérité', *Husserl Studies* 15, no. 3 (1998), 183–230.
Heffernan, G. 'A Study of the Sedimented Origin of Evidence in Husserl and His Contemporaries Engaged in a Collective Essay in the Phenomenology and Psychology of Epistemic Justification', *Husserl Studies* 16 (1999), 83–181.
Kohàk, E. 'Knowing Good and Evil', *Husserl Studies* 10 (1993), 31–41.
Melle, U. 'Edmund Husserl. Wert des Lebens. Wert der Welt. Sittlichkeit und Glückseligkeit', *Husserl Studien* (1997), 201–235.

Melle, U. 'Signitive und Signifikative Intentionen', *Husserl Studies* 3, no. 15 (1998), 167–181.
Mensch, J. 'Instincts–A Husserlian Account', *Husserl Studies* 14, no. 3 (1998), 219–237.
Mensch, J. R. 'Freedom and Selfhood', *Husserl Studies* 1, no. 14 (1997), 41–59.
Mishara, A. 'Husserl and Freud: Time, Memory and the Unconscious', *Husserl Studies* 7 (1990), 29–58.
Null, G. T. 'The Ontology of Intentionality I: The Dependence Ontological Account of Order: Mediate and Immediate Moments and Pieces of Dependent and Independent Objects', *Husserl Studies* 23, no. 1 (2007), 33–69.
Nam-In Lee, 'Experience and Evidence', *Husserl Studies* 23 (2007), 229–246.
Nam-In Lee, 'Practical Intentionality and Transcendental Phenomenology as a Practical Philosophy', *Husserl Studies* 17 (2000), 49–63.
Nam-In Lee, 'Static-Phenomenological and Genetic-Phenomenological Concept of Primordiality in Husserl's Fifth Cartesian Meditation', *Husserl Studies* (2002), 179–182.
Sakakibara, T. 'Das Problem des Ich', *Husserl Studies* 1, no. 14 (1997), 21–39.
Schmid, H. B. 'Apodictic Evidence', *Husserl Studies* 17 (2001), 217–237.
Soffer, G. 'The Other as the Alter Ego: A Genetic Approach', *Husserl Studies* 3, no. 15 (1998), 151–166.
Tengelyi, L. 'Lebensgeschichte als Selbstkonstitution bei Husserl', *Husserl Studies* 1, no. 13 (1997), 157–167.
Toadvine, T. 'Phenomenological Method in Merleau-Ponty's Critique of Gurwitsch', *Husserl Studies* 17 (2001), 195–205.
Walton, R. J. 'World-experience. World-representation, and the World as an Idea', *Husserl Studies* 1, no. 14 (1997), 1–20.
Welsh, J. R. 'E. Husserl. Vorlesungen über Ethik und Wertlehre', *Husserl Studies* 8 (1991–92), 221–232.

IV. E. *'Phaenomenologica'*

Biemel, A. 'Die Welt des Menschen', *Phaenomenologica* 76, The Hague: Martinus Nijhoff, 1972.
Brownmiller, S. *Against Our Will*, New York: Simon and Schuster, 1975.
Cairns, D. 'Guide for Translating Husserl', *Phaenomenologica* 55, The Hague: Martinus Nijhoff, 1976.
Carr, D. 'The Problem of the Non-Empirical Ego: Husserl and Kant', *Phaenomenologica* 106, The Hague: Martinus Nijhoff, 1987.
Carroll, S. *From Here to There*, New York, 2010.
Costa, V. 'Transcendental Aesthetic and the Problem of Transcendentality', *Phaenomenologica* 148, Dordrecht/Boston/London: Kluwer Academic Publishers, 1998, 9–28.
Depraz, N. 'Imagination and Passivity. Husserl and Kant: A Cross-relationship, Alterity and Facticity', *Phaenomenologica* 148, Dordrecht/Boston/London: Kluwer Academic Publishers, 1998, 29–56.
Dodd, J. 'Attitude, Facticity, Philosophy', *Phaenomenologica* 148, Dordrecht/Boston/London: Kluwer Academic Publishers, 1998, 57–85.
Dodd, J. 'Crisis and Reflection', *Phaenomenologica* 174, Dordrecht/Boston/London: Kluwer Academic Publishers, 2004.

Dodd, J. 'Idealism and Corporeity. An Essay on the Problem of the Body in Husserl's Phenomenology', *Phaenomenologica* 148, Dordrecht/Boston/London: Kluwer Academic Publishers, 1998.
Drummond, J. J. 'Exceptional love', *Phenomenologica* 216, Dordrecht/Boston/London: Kluwer Academic Publishers, 2015, 51–69.
Fuchs, W. A. 'Phenomenology and the Metaphysics of Presence', *Phaenomenologica* 115, The Hague: Martinus Nijhoff, 1989.
Hart, J. 'I, We and God: Ingredients of Husserl's Theory of Community', *Phaenomenologica* 115, Dordrecht/Boston/London: Kluwer Academic Publishers, 1990.
Hart, J. 'The Person and the Common Life', *Phaenomenologica* 148, Dordrecht/Boston/London, Kluwer Academic Publishers, 1998.
Held, K. 'Lebendige Gegenwart', *Phaenomenologica* 23, The Hague: Kluwer Acedemic Publishers, 1966.
Henry, M. 'Rèflexions sur la cinquième Méditation cartésienne de Husserl', *Phanomenologica* 115, Dordrecht/Boston/London: Kluwer Academic Publishers, 1990.
McIntyre, R. 'Husserl and Intentionality', *Phaenomenologica* 11, Dordrecht/Boston /London: Kluwer Academic Publishers, 1982.
Marbach, E. 'Das Problem des Ich in der Phänomenologie Husserls', *Phaenomenologica* 59, Dordrecht/Boston/London: Kluwer Academic Publishers, 1974.
Marbach, E. 'Mental Representation and Consciousness. Towards a Phenomenological Theory of Representation and Reference', *Phaenomenologica* 128, Dordrecht/Boston/London: Kluwer Academic Publishers, 1993.
Mertens, K. 'Husserl's Phenomenology of Will in His Reflections on Ethics', *Phaenomenologica*, 148, Dordrecht/Boston/London: Kluwer Academic Publishers, 1998.
Nam-In Lee, 'Edmund Husserl's Phenomenology of Mood', *Phaenomenologica* 148, Dordrecht/Boston/London: Kluwer Academic Publishers, 1998.
Pazanin, A. 'Wissenschaft und Geschichte in der Phänomenologie Edmund Husserls', *Phänomenologica* 46, The Hague: Martinus Nijhoff, 1972.
Rang, B. 'Kausalität und Motivation', *Phaenomenologica* 53, Dordrecht/Boston/London: Kluwer Academic Publishers, 1973.
Roth, A. 'Edmund Husserls ethische Untersuchungen: dargestellt anhand seiner Vorlesungmanuskripte', *Phaenomenologica, numero* 7, The Hague: Martinus Nijhoff, 1960.
Soffer, G. 'Husserl and the Question of Relativism', *Phaenomenologica* 122, Dordrecht/Boston/London: Kluwer Academic Publishers, 1991.
Sokolowski, R. 'Displacement and Identity in Husserl's Phenomenology', *Phaenomenologica* 115, Dordrecht/Boston/London: Kluwer Academic Publishers, 1990, 172–184.
Steeves, H. P. 'Founding Community', *Phaenomenologica* 143, Dordrecht/Boston/London: Kluwer Academic Publishers, 2004.
Steinbock, J. 'A. Sprit and Generativity: The Role and Contribution of the Phenomenologist in Hegel and Husserl', *Phaenomenologica* 148, Dordrecht/Boston/London: Kluwer Academic Publishers, 1998.
Strasser, S. 'Welt in Wiederspruch', *Phaenomenologica* 120, Dordrecht/Boston/London: Kluwer Academic Publishers, 1991.

Ubiali, M., and Wherle, M. 'Feeling and Value, Willing and Action', *Phenomenologica* 216, Dordrecht/Boston/London: Kluwer Academic Publishers, 2015.

IV. F. Psychological and philosophical sources

Fenomenologia e l'Europa, Naples: Vivarium, 1999.
Neurofenomenologia. Le scienze della mente e la sfida dell'esperienza cosciente, Milan: Mondadori, 2006.
Phenomenology and Marxism, trad. ed. C. Evans, London/ Boston/ Melbourne/ Henley: Routledge & Kegan Paul, 1990.
Razionalità fenomenologica e destino della filosofia, Potenza: Marietti, 1998.
Ales Bello, A. *Analisi fenomenologica della volontà. E. Husserl ed E. Stein*, in *Per la filosofia*, Milan: Adif, 1994.
Ales Bello, A. 'Un approccio fenomenologico al problema della società', *Vita sociale* 1(1974), 58–61.
Ales Bello, A. *The Divine in Husserl*, Dordrecht: Springer, 2009.
Ales Bello, A. *Edmund Husserl. Pensare Dio. Credere in Dio*, Rome: EMP, 2005.
Ales Bello, A. *Husserl e le scienze*, Rome: La Goliardica editrice, 1980.
Ales Bello, A. *L'oggettività come pregiudizio*, Rome: La Goliardica editrice, 1982.
Ales Bello, A. 'Teleology as "the Form of All Forms" and the inexhaustability of Research', in A. Tymieniecka, ed., *The Teleology in Husserlian Phenomenology*, 1979, 337–351.
Ales Bello, A. 'Una via d'uscita nella crisi dell'Occidente', *Vita sociale* 3 (1983), 199–206.
Anderson, W. T. *Reality Isn't What It Used to Be*, New York: Harper & Row, 1990.
Applebaum, M. 'Amedeo Giorgi and Psychology as a HumanScience', *NeuroQuantology* [Online], 9.3 (2011): n. pag. Web. 17 April 2018.
Aportone, A., Aronadio, F., and Spinicci, P. *Il problema dell'intuizione*, Naples: Bibliopolis, 2002.
Arisaka, Y. 'The Nishida Enigma: "The Principle of the New World" ', *Monumenta Nipponica* 51, no. 1 (1996), 1–21.
Arisaka, Y. 'System and Existence: Nishida's Logic of Place', *Logique du lieu et depassement de la modernite. Augustin Berque*, Brussels: Ousia, 1999.
Atwood, R., and Stolorow, G. 'Psychoanalytic Phenomenology: Toward a Science of Human Experience', *Psychoanalytic Models* 4, no. 1 (1984), 87–105.
Atwood, R., and Stolorow, G. *Structures of Subjectivity: Explorations of Psychoanalytic Phenomenology*, New York, NY: The Analytic Press, 1984.
Avram, W. 'On the Priority of "Ethics" in the Work of Levinas', *The Journal of Religious Ethics* 24, no. 2 (1996), 261–284.
Baccarini, E. *La fenomenologia come vocazione*, Rome: Studium, 1981.
Baranger, M. 'The Intrapsychic and the Intersubjective in Contemporary Psychoanalysis', *International Forum of Psychoanalysis* 21, no. 3–4 (2012), 130–135.
Bart, P. B. 'Rape as a Paradigm of Sexism in Society: Victimization and Its Discontents', *Women's Studies International Quarterly* 2, no. 3 (1979), 347–357.
Bartley, W. W. *Morality and Religion*, Macmillan: London and New York, 1971.

Bauman, Z. *Modernity and Ambivalence*, Ithaca, NY: Cornell University Press, 1991.
Bauman, Z. *Paradoxes of Assimilation*, New Brunswick, NJ: Transaction, 1990.
Bégout, B. *La Généalogie de la Logique. Husserl, l'antéprédicatif et le categorical*, Paris: Vrin, 2000.
Benítez Reyes, F. *Paraíso manuscrito*, Sevilla, Spain: Calle del Aire, 1982.
Benjamin, C. 'What Is Empirical Philosophy?' *The Journal of Philosophy* 36, no. 19 (1939), 517–525.
Benoist, J. *L'Apriori conceptuel. Bolzano, Husserl, Schlick*, Paris: Vrin, 1999.
Benoist, J. *Autour de Husserl. L'Ego e la raison*, Paris: Vrin, 1994.
Benoist, J. 'La fenomenologia e i limiti dell'oggettivazione: il problema degli atti non obiettivanti', in *Fenomenologia della ragione pratica*, Naples: Bibliopolis, 2004, 153–174.
Benoist, J. 'Fenomenologia e teoria del significato', *Leitmotiv* 3 (2003), 133–142.
Benoist, J. 'The Question of Grammar in Logical Investigations, With Special Reference to Brentano, Marty, Bolzano and Later Developments in Logic', in A. Tymieniecka, ed., *Phenomenology World-Wide*, Dordrecht: Kluwer, 2003, 94–97.
Bergson, H. *Duration and Simultaneity*. Indianapolis: Bobbs-Merrill, 1965.
Bernard M. L., and Bernard, T. L. 'Violent Intimacy: The Family as a Model for Love Relationships', *Family Relations* 32 (1983): 283–286.
Bernet, R. *La vie du sujet. Recherches sur l'interprétation de Husserl dans la phénoménologie*, Paris: P. U. F., 1994.
Bernstein, R. J. *Beyond Objectivism and Relativism: Science, Hermeneutics, and Praxis*. Philadelphia: University of Pennsylvania Press, 1983.
Bertolini, S., and Fabbianelli, F. 'Ontologie fenomenologiche: individualità, essenza, idea', *Discipline Filosofiche*, 2016.
Bianchi, I. A. *Etica husserliana. Studio sui manoscritti inediti degli anni 1920–1934*, Milan: Franco Angeli, 1999.
Bianchi, I. A. *Fenomenologia della volontà*, Milan: Franco Angeli, 2003.
Biceaga, V. *The Concept of Passivity in Husserl's Phenomenology*, London and New York: Springer, 2010.
Blankenburg, W. 'First Steps toward a Psychopathology of "Common Sense", (trans. A. L. Mishara), *Philosophy, Psychiatry, and Psychology* 8 (2001), 303–315.
Borgatta, E. F., and Borgatta, M. L., eds, *Encyclopedia of sociology* (Vol. 4), New York: Macmillan, 1992.
Bosio, F. 'Costituzione statica e costituzione genetica', *Archivio di filosofia* 1 (1960), 73–89.
Bowlby, J. *The Making and Breaking of Affectional Bonds*, New York, NY: Routledge, 1979.
Brand, G. *Welt, Geschichte, Mythos und Politik*, Berlin: W. de Gruyter, 1971.
Brentano, F. *The Foundation and Construction of Ethics*, ed. H. E. Schneewind, London: Routledge, 1973.
Brentano, F. *Die Lehre vom richtigen Urteil*, ed. F. Mayer-Hillebrand, Bern, 1956.
Brentano, F. *Psychology from the Empirical Standpoint*, trans. Rancurello, Terrell, and McAlister, London, Routledge, 1973.
Brentano, F. *Über Wahrheit und Evidenz*, ed. O. Kraus, Hamburg, 1930/1958.
Brentano, F. *Vom Ursprung sittlicher Erkenntnis*, ed. O. Kraus, Hamburg, 1969.

Bruzina, R. *Edmund Husserl and Eugen Fink: Beginnings and Ends in Phenomenology, 1928–1938*, New Haven, London: Yale University Press, 1995.
Bukhard, F. P. 'Edmund Husserl: Vorlesungen über Ethik und Wertlehre (1908–14)', *Brentano Studien* 3 (1990–91), 265–266.
Burns, J. *Leadership*, New York, NY: Harper Perennial Political Classics, 1978.
Byers, D. *Intentionality and Transcendence*, Seattle: Noesis Press, 2002.
Cairns, D. 'Nine Fragments on Psychological Phenomenology', *Journal of Phenomenological Psychology* 41 (2010), 1–27.
Campbell Garnett, A. 'Relativism and Absolutism in Ethics', *Ethics* 54, no. 3 (1944), 186–199.
Carlson, D., and Perrewe, P. 'Institutionalization of Organizational Ethics through Transformational Leadership', *Journal of Business Ethics* 14, no. 1 (1995), 829–838.
Carman, Taylor (1999). 'The Body in Husserl and Merleau-ponty'. *Philosophical Topics* 27, no. 2, 205–226.
Carney, T. F. *Collaborative Inquiry Methodology*, 1st edn, Windsor, ON, Canada: University of Windsor, Division for Instructional Development, 1990.
Caruso, P. 'L'io trascendentale come "durata esplosiva". Intenzionalità e tempo nella fenomenolgia di Husserl', *Archivio di filosofia* 1 (1960), 49–73.
Cassirer, E. *Vita e dottrina di Kant*, Florence: La Nuova Italia, 1997.
Centi, B., and Gigliotti, G. *Fenomenologia della ragion pratica*, Naples: Bibliopolis, 2004.
Cermolacce, M., Naudin, J., and Parnas, J. 'The 'Minimal Self' in Psychopathology: Re-examining the Self-disorders in the Schizophrenia Spectrum', *Consciousness and Cognition* 16 (2007), 703–714.
Chan, D., Fox, N. C., Scahill, R., Crum, W. R., Whitwell, J. L., Leschziner, G, Rossor, A. M., Stevens, J. M., Cipolotti, L., Rossor, M. N., "Patterns of Temporal Lobe Atrophy in Semantic Dementia and Alzheimer's Disease', *Ann Neurol* 49, no. 4 (2001 April), 433–42.
Chang, R. *Physical Chemistry for the Biosciences*, Sausalito California: University Science Books, 2005.
Cheal, D. *Family: Critical Concepts in Sociology*, Routledge, 2003.
Chittick, C. *Sufism: A Beginner's Guide*, Oneworld Publications, 2007.
Cho, K. K. 'Mediation and Immediacy for Husserl', in *Phenomenology and Natural Existence*, Albany: New York Press, 1973.
Chukwu, P. *Competing Interpretation of Husserl's Noema*, New York: Peter Lang, 2009.
Churchill, S. D. 'Intercorporeality, Gestural Communication, and the Voices of Silence: Towards a Phenomenological Ethology – Part Two', *Somatics* XIII, no. 2 (2001), 40–45.
Colaizzi, P. 'Psychological Research as the Phenomenologist Views It', in R. Valle and M. King, eds, *Existential Phenomenological Alternatives for Psychology*, New York, NY: Oxford University Press, 1978.
Collen, A. *Systemic Change Through Praxis and Inquiry*, Vol. 11, *Praxiology: The International Annual of Practical Philosophy and Methodology*, New Brunswick, NJ: Transaction Publishers, 2003.
Conrad, K. *Die beginnende Schizophrenie. Versuch einer Gestaltanalyse des Wahns*, Bonn: Edition Das Narrenschiff im Psychiatrie-Verlag, 2002.

Cooper, B. 'Constructivism in Social Work, *British Journal of Social Work* 31, 721–738.
Correia, F. 'Husserl on Foundation', *Dialectica* 58, no. 3 (2004), 349–367.
Creswell, J. W. *Qualitative Inquiry and Research Design: Choosing among Five Approaches*, 2nd edn, Thousand Oaks, CA: Sage, 2007.
Cristin, R. *La rinascita dell'Europa*, Rome: Donzelli Editore, 2001.
Cristin, R., and Fontana, S. *Europa al plurale*, Venezia: Marsilio, 1997.
Crowell, S. *Normativity and Phenomenology in Husserl and Heidegger*, Cambridge University Press, 2013.
Daly, C. *An Introduction to Philosophical Methods*, Broadview Press, 2010.
D'Ecclesia, A. *Le sfide della fenomenologia husserliana*, Foggia: Bastoni Editrice Italiana, 2005.
De Monticelli, R. *La conoscenza personale*, Milan: Guerini studio, 2002.
Dennett, D. *Contenuto e coscienza*, Bologna: il Mulino, 1995.
Dennet, D. *Sweet Dreams. Illusioni filosofiche sulla coscienza*, Milan: Cortina Raffaello, 2006.
De Palma, V. *Il soggetto e l'esperienza. La critica di Husserl a Kant e il problema fenomenologico del trascendentale*, Bologna: Quodlibet, 2001.
De Palma, V. 'La forma e la sostanza', *La Cultura*, XLII (2004), 1–19.
Depraz, N. 'The Phenomenological Reduction as Praxis', *Journal of Consciousness Studies, The View from Within* 6, no. 2–3 (1999), 95–110.
Depraz, N. 'En quête d'une métaphysique phénoménologique: La référence henryenne à Maître Eckhart', in A. David and J. Greisch, eds, *Michel Henry, L'Epreuve de la Vie*, Paris, France: Les Éditions Cerf, 2001, 255–280.
Derrida, J. *Introduzione a Husserl, l'origine della geometria*, Milan: Jaca Book, 1987.
Derrida, J. *Il problema della genesi nella filosofia di Husserl*, Milan: Jaca Book, 1992.
Devitt, M. *Realism and Truth*, 2nd edn, Englewood Cliffs, NJ: Prentice Hall, 1991.
Diemer, A. *Edmund Husserl. Versuch einer systematischen Darstellung seiner Phaenomenologie*, Hain: Meisenheim am Glan, 1956.
Dilworth, D. A., and Silverman, H. 'A Cross-Cultural Approach to the De Ontological Self Paradigm', *The Monist* 16, no. 1 (1978), 91.
Di Pinto, L. *Impronte kantiane in Edmund Husserl*, Bari: Cacucci Editore, 1988.
Donnici, R. *Intenzioni d'amore di scienza e d'anarchia*, Naples: Bibliopolis, 1996.
Donnici, R. 'Le lezioni di Husserl sull'etica e sulla teoria del valore', *Giornale critico della filosofia italiana* 1 (1991), 109–129.
Donohoe, J. *Husserl on Ethics and Intersubjectivity*, Amherst, NY: Humanity Books, 2004.
Dreyfus, H. *Husserl, Intentionality and the Cognitive Science*, Massachussetts: MIT, 1982.
Dreyfus, H. 'Sinn and Intentional Object', in C. R. Solomon, ed., *Phenomenology and Existentialism*, New York: Harper and Row, 1972, 241–50.
Drummond, J. J. *Husserlian Intentionality and Non-Foundational Realism: Noema and Objects*, Boston: Kluwer Academic Publishers, 1990.
Dummet, M. *The Logical Basis of Metaphysics*, Cambridge, MA: Harvard University Press, 1991.
Dupond, P., and Cournaire, L. *Phénoménologie, un siècle de philosophie*, Paris: Ellipses, 2002.

Earle, W. 'Phenomenology of Mysticism', *The Monist*, 59, no. 4 (1976), 519–531.
Edie, J. M. 'Transcendental Phenomenology and Existentialism', in J. J. Kockelmans, ed., *Phenomenology*, New York: Doubleday, 1965.
Ehrenfels, C. 'Ueber Gestaltqualitaeten', *Vierteljahrsschrijt für Philosophie* 14 (1890), 249–292.
Elwood, B. D. 'The Problem of the Self in the Later Nishida and in Sartre', *Philosophy East and West* 44, no. 2 (1994), 303–316.
Englander, M. 'Empathy Training from a Phenomenological Perspective', *Journal of Phenomenological Psychology* 45, no. 1 (2014), 5–26.
Englander, M. 'The Interview: Data Collection in Descriptive Phenomenological Human Science Research', *Journal of Phenomenological Psychology* 43, no. 1 (2012), 13–35.
English, J. 'Que signifie l'idée d'une téléologie universelle chez le dernier Husserl', *Recherches Husserliennes* 9 (1998), 3–36.
English, J. *Le vocabulaire de Husserl*, Paris: Ellipses, 2002.
Ey, H. *Consciousness: A Phenomenological Study of Being Conscious and Becoming Conscious*, trans. J. H. Flodstrom, Bloomington; London: Indiana University Press, 1978.
Ey, H. *Traite des hallucinations*, Tome I et II, Paris: Masson, 1973.
Falcioni, D. 'Il pensiero dello stato in Husserl; recenti problemi critici', *Rivista internazionale di filosofia del diritto* 67 (1990), 296–301.
Farber, M. *Prospettive della fenomenologia*, Florence: Sansoni, 1989.
Feenberg, A., and Arisaka, Y. 'Experiential Ontology: The Origins of the Nishida Philosophy in the Doctrine of Pure Experience', *International Philosophical Quarterly* 30, no. 2 (1990).
Ferrarello, S. *Husserl's Ethics and Practical Intentionality*, London, 2015.
Ferraro, G. *La verità dell'Europa e l'idea di comunità*, Naples: Filema, 1998.
Ferres, U. S. *Connocer y actuar. Dimensions fenomenologia, lógica, ética y política*, Salamnc, San Estebàn, 1992.
Findler, R. S. 'Kant's Phenomenological Ethics', *Research in Phenomenology* 27 (1997), 167–184.
Fink, E. 'Husserl's Philosophy and Contemporary Criticism', in R. O. Elveton, ed. *The Phenomenology of Husserl*, Chicago: Quadrangle, 1970, 73–147.
Fink, E. 'The Problem of the Phenomenology of Edmund Husserl', trans. R. M. Harlan, in W. McKenna, R. M. Harlan and L. E. Winters, eds, *Apriori and World: European Contributions to Husserlian Phenomenology*, The Hague: Martinus Nijhoff, 1981.
Fink, Eugen. VI. *Cartesianische Meditation*. Teil 2,. ed. Guy Van Kerckhoven, Dordrecht: Kluwer, 1988.
Fink, E. *Sixth Cartesian Meditation: The Idea of a Transcendental Theory of Method*, Indiana University Press, 1995.
Finlay, L. 'Debating Phenomenological Research Methods', *Phenomenology & Practice* 3, no. 1 (2009), 6–25.
Fisette, D. 'Love and Hate: Brentano and Stumpf on Emotions and Sense Feelings', *Gestalt Theorie* 31, no. 2 (2009), 115–127.
Føllesdal, D. 'Husserl's Notion of Noema', in H. L. Dreyfus, ed., *Husserl, Intentionality and the Cognitive Sciences*, Cambridge: MIT Press, 1982, 73–81.

Foucault, M. *History of Sexuality*, vol. 1, trans. R. Hurley, New York: Random House, 1984.
Frege, G. (1892). 'On Sense and Reference', in P. Geach and M. Black, eds and trans., *Translations from the Philosophical Writings of Gottlob Frege*, Oxford, Blackwell, 1980.
Friesen, N., Henrickson, C., and Saevi, T., eds, *Hermeneutic Phenomenology in Education: Method and Practice*, Boston, MA: Sense Publishers, 2012.
Fulton, J. S. 'The Cartesianism of Phenomenology', in M. Natanson, ed., *Essays in Phenomenology*, The Hague: Martinus Nijhoff, 1969, 59, 61.
Gadamer, H. G. *Philosophical Apprenticeships*, trans. Robert R. Sullivan, Cambridge, MA: MIT Press, 1985.
Gaffney, J. 'Newman on the Common Roots of Morality and Religion', *The Journal of Religious Ethics* 16, no. 1 (1988), 143–159.
Gallen, R. T. *Wives Legal Rights*, New York: Dell, 1967.
Gallese, V. 'The Roots of Empathy: The Shared Manifold Hypothesis and the Neural Basis of Intersubjectivity', *Psychopathology* 36 (2003), 171–180.
García Montero, L. *Poemas*, Madrid, Spain: Visor, 2001.
Garelli, J. *Rythmes et mondes*, Grenoble: Jerôme Millon, 1991.
Gebser, J. *Ursprung und Gegenwart. Zweiter Teil: Die Manifestationen der aperspektivischen Welt*, Flensburg Fjord: Novalis Verlag, 2011.
Gelles, R. 'Power, Sex, and Violence: The Case of Marital Rape', *The Family Coordinator* 26, no. 4 (1977): 339–347.
Gendlin, E. T. *Focusing*, New York: Bantam, 1982.
Gérard, V. *L'analogie entre l'éthique formelle et la logique formelle chez Husserl*, in *Fenomenologia della ragione pratica*, Naples: Bibliopolis, 2002, 115–151.
Ghigi, N. *La Storia della filosofia e la sua finalitá*, Rome: Citta Nuova, 2004.
Ghosal, S. and Ghosa, S. 'Socio-political Dimensions of Rape', *The Indian Journal of Political Science*, 70, no. 1 (2009): 107–120.
Giddens, A. *The Transformation of Intimacy*, Stanford, CA: Stanford University Press, 1992.
Gigliotti, G. *Avventure e disavventure del trascendentale*, Naples: Guida editori, 1989.
Giorgi, A. *The Descriptive Phenomenological Method in Psychology: A Modified Husserlian Approach*, Pittsburg, PA: Duquesne University Press, 2009.
Giorgi, A. *Psychology As a Human Science: A Phenomenologically Based Approach*, New York: Harper & Row, 1970.
Giorgi, A., ed. *Phenomenology and Psychological Research*, Pittsburgh, PA: Duquesne University Press, 1985.
Greening, T. *American Politics and Humanistic Psychology*, San Francisco, CA: Saybrook, 1984.
Griffin, S. 'The All American Crime', *Ramparts*, September 1971, 26–35.
Groenwald, T. 'A Phenomenological Research Design Illustrated', *International Journal of Qualitative Methods* 3, no. 1 (2004), 42–55.
Gurwitsch, A. *Phenomenology and the Theory of Science*, Evanston, IL: Northwestern University, 1974.
Hart, J. 'We, Representation and War-resistance: Some Para-Husserlian Reflections', *Zeitschrift für philosophische Forschung* 13 (1959), 127–141.

Hart, J. *Who One Is: Meontology of the I: A Transcendental Phenomenology*, Springer, 2009.
Hartman, R. S. 'The Logic of Description and Evaluation', *Review of Metaphysics* 14 no. 2 (1960), 191–230.
Hartmann, E. *Das Unbewusste vom Standpunkt der Physiologie und Deszendenzlehre*, Berlin, 1872.
Hartmann, N. *Ethics*, vol. 1, Berlin: De Gruyter, 2002.
Hartmann, N. *Teleologisches Denken*, Berlin: De Gruyter, 2010 (first published 1951).
Heidegger, M. *The Basic Problems of Phenomenology*, Indiana University Press, 1975.
Heidegger, M. *Being and Time*, trans. J. Macquarrie and E. Robinson, Oxford: Blackwell, 2007.
Held, K. 'Eigentliche Existenz und Welt', in K. Held and W. Hennigfeld, eds, *Kategorien der Existenz. Ferschrift für Wohlfang Janke*, Würzburg: Könnigshausen & Neumann, 1993, 395–412.
Henckmann, W. *Max Scheler*, Munich: Verlag, 1998.
Henckmann, W. 'Schelers Lehre vom Apriori', in W. Baumgartner, ed., *Gewissen und Gewissheit*, Wuerzburg, 1987, 117–140.
Henkel, M. 'Professional Competence and Higher Education', in M. Yelloly and M. Henkel, eds, *Learning and Teaching in Social Work*, London: Jessica Kingsley Publication, 1995.
von Hermann, F. W. 'Husserl et Descartes', *Revue de Métaphysique et Morale* 1 (1992), 4–24.
Heyting, A. 'Intuitionism in Mathematics', in *La philosophie contemporaine*, Florence: La nuova Editrice Italia, 1968, 316–324.
Hickerson, R. *The History of Intentionality*, London and New York: Continuum Press, 2007.
Higgins, C. 'A Plea for Moderation in Educational Policy and Research', *Educational Theory* 59 (2009), 499–502.
Hill, C. O. *Word and Object in Husserl, Frege, and Russell*, Athens, OH: Ohio University Press, 1991.
Hintikka, J. 'Logic and Philosophy', in *La philosophie contemporaine*, Florence: La nuova Editrice Italia, 1968, 3–30.
Housset, E. *Personne et sujet selon Husserl*, Paris: Presses Universitaires de France, 1997.
Howard, G. S. 'Can Research in the Human Sciences Become More Relevant to Practice?' *Journal of Counseling and Development* 63 (1985), 539–544.
Huni, H. *Wie kommt Phänomenologie zur Geschichte?* in *Phänomenologische Forschung*, 1999, 203–212.
Hurlbert, D., Apt, C., Gasar, S., Wilson, N., and Murphy, Y. Sexual Narcissism: A Validation Study, *Journal of Marriage and Family Therapy* 20, no. 1 (2008), 24–34.
Ingarden, R. *On the Motives Which Led Husserl to Transcendental Idealism*, Dordrecht: Kluwer, 1975.
Issac, D., and Rowe, C. *Empathic Attunement: The Technique of Psychoanalytic Self Psychology*, Lanham, MD: Rowman & Littlefield, 2000.
Jeffner, A. 'Husserl's Communal Spirit: A Phenomenological Study of the Fundamental Structure of Society', *Philosophy and Social Criticism* 5, no. 1 (1978), 68–82.

Johnson, S. *Love Sense: The Revolutionary New Science of Romantic Relationships*, New York, NY: Little Brown, 2014.
Kaufman, F. 'Phenomenology and Logical Empiricism', in M. Farber, ed., *Philosophical Essays in Honor of Edmund Husserl*, Cambridge: Harvard University Press, 1940.
Kelly, C. 'The Interrelationship of Ethics and Power in Today's Organizations', *Organizational Dynamics* 16, no. 2 (1987), 5–18.
Kelly, G. A. *The Psychology of Personal Constructs*, New York: Norton, 1955.
Kern, I. 'Trinity: Theological Reflections of a Phenomenologist', in S. W. Laycock and J. G. Hart, eds, *Essays in Phenomenological Theology*, New York: State University of New York Press, 1986.
Kersten, F. 'Universals', *Research in Phenomenology* 4 (1974), 29–33.
Kim, S. K. *Phenomenological and Political Philosophy. A Study of the Political Implications of Husserl's Account of the Life World*, Athens: University of Georgia, 1979.
Kjosavik, F. 'Husserl's View of the Life-World and the World of Science', *Revue Internationale de Philosophie* 2 (2003), 194–200.
Klemke, E. D. 'On the Alleged Inseparability of Morality and Religion', *Religious Studies* 11, no. 1 (1975), 37–48.
Klibansky, R. *La philosophie contemporaine*, Florence: La nuova Editrice Italia, 1968.
Kockelmans, Joseph J. *Edmund Husserl's Phenomenological Psychology. A Historico-critical Study*, Duquesne University Press, 1967.
Koestenbaum, P. *Existential Sexuality*, Englewood Cliffs, NJ: Prentice Hall, 1974.
Kohak, E. *Jan Patocka, Philosophical Readings and Selected Writings*, Chicago Press, 1989, 26.
Kohut, H. *The Analysis of the Self: A Systematic Approach to Psychoanalytic Treatment of Narcissistic Personality Disorders*, Chicago, IL: University of Chicago Press, 1971/2009.
Kohut, H. 'Forms and Transformations of Narcissism', in A. P. Morrison, ed., *Essential Papers on Narcissism*, New York, NY: The Free Press, 1986 (original work published 1966), 61–87.
Kohut, H. *Self Psychology and the Humanities*, New York, NY: WW Norton, 1985.
Kopf, G. 'Temporality and Personal Identity in the Thought of Nishida Kitaro', *Philosophy East and West* 52, no. 2 (2002), 224–245.
Kopf, G. and Park, J. Y. *Merleau-Ponty and Buddhism*, London: Lexington Books, 2009.
Kozyra, A. 'Nishida Kitarō's Logic of Absolutely Contradictory Self-Identity and the Problem of Orthodoxy in the Zen Tradition', *Japan Review* 20 (2008), 69–110.
Krueger, J. W. *The Varieties of Pure Experience: William James and Kitaro Nishida on Consciousness and Embodiment. William James Studies*, vol. 1, 2006, 1–37.
Kuhn, T. S. *The Structure of Scientific Revolution*, Chicago Press: Chicago, 1964.
Künne, W. *Abstrakte Gegenstände. Semantik und Ontologie*, Frankfurt a.M., Suhrkamp, 1983.
Ladrière, J. 'Physical Reality. A Phenomenological Approach', *Dialectica* 43, no. 1-2 (1989), 125–139.
Landgrebe, L. 'Husserl's Departure from Cartesianism', in Donn Welton, ed., *The Phenomenology of Edmund Husserl*, Ithaca: Cornell University Press, 1981.

Landgrebe, L. *Itinerari della fenomenologia*, trad. ed. G. Piacenti, Turin: Einaudi, 1975.
Landgrebe, L. 'Regions of Being and Regional Ontologies in Husserl's Phenomenology', in *Apriori and World*, The Hague: Martinus Nijhoff, 1981, 132–151.
Landucci, S. *Sull'etica di Kant*, Milan: Guerini e Associati, 1994.
Lanfredini, R. *Husserl. La teoria dell'intenzionalità*, Bari: Laterza, 1994.
Lasch, C. *Haven in a Heartless World: The Family Besieged*, New York: Basic Books, 1977.
Levere, T. H. *A History of Chemistry from Alchemy to the Buckyball*, Johns Hopkins University Press, 2001.
Levin, D. M. *Reason and Evidence in Husserl's Phenomenology*, Evanston, IL: Northwestern University, 1970.
Levinas, E. *Autrement qu-être ou au-delà de l'essence*, Dordrecht: Martinus Nijhoff, 1974.
Levinas, E. *Entre Nous*, ed. M. B. Smith and B. Harshav, New York: Columbia University Press, 1998.
Levinas, E. *The Theory of Intuition in Husserl's Phenomenology*, Evanston, IL: Northwestern University, 1995.
Lohmar, D. 'Die phänomenologische Methode der Wesensschau und ihre Präzisierung als eidetische Variation', *Phänomenologische Forschungen* (2005), 65–91.
Lohmar, D. *On Time. New Contributions to the Husserlian Phenomeology of Time*, Dordrecht-Boston-London: Springer, 2010.
Lo Lee-chun, 'Weltteleologie und Gottesidee: Die Bedeutung Gottes in der Phänomenologie Edmund Husserls', *New Studies in Phenomenology* 1 (2002), 195–210.
Lotze, R. H. *Logik*, Leipzig, 1874.
Lotze, R. H. *Metaphysics*, Leipzig: Hirzel, 1879.
Lotze, R. H. *Mikrokosmus*, Leipzig: Hirzel, vol. 3, 1856, 1858, 1864.
Luft, S. *Epistemology, Archaeology, Ethics: Current Investigations of Husserl's Corpus*, New York: Continuum, 2010.
Luo, T. ' "Marrying My Rapist?!" The Cultural Trauma among Chinese Rape Survivors', *Gender & Society* 14 (2000), 581–597.
Lyons-Ruth, K. 'The Two-person Unconscious: Intersubjective Dialogue, Enactive Relational Representation, and the Emergence of New Forms of Relational Organization', *Psychoanalytic Inquiry* 19, no. 4 (1999), 576–617.
McCall, T. *Which Trinity? Whose Monotheism?*, Cambridge: Eerdmans, 2010.
McDowell, J. *Mind and World*, Cambridge, MA: Harvard University Press, 1996.
Maesschalck, M. 'L'éthique des convictions et le rapport à la vie originaire. Critique de la lecture habermassienne de Husserl', in *La voix des phénomènes: Contribution à une phenomenologie du sens et des affects*, Brussels: Università di Saint-Louis, 1995, 331–357.
Mahoney, M. J. 'Constructive Metatheory: I. Basic Features and Historical Foundations', *International Journal of Personal Construct Psychology* 1, no. 1 (1988), 1–35.
Maraldo, John C., 'Translating Nishida', *Philosophy East and West* 39, no. 4 (1989), 465–496.

Marbach, E. 'On Bringing the Consciousness into the House of Sciences – With the Help of Husserlian Phenomenology', *Angelaky* 10, no. 1 (2005), 145–162.
Marini, A. *Husserl, Heidegger. Libertà Europa*, Milan: Mimesis, 2002.
Marion, J.-L. *Givennes and Revelation*, Oxford University Press, 2016.
Marion, J.-L. *Réduction et donation: recherches sur Husserl, Heidegger et la phenomenologie*, Paris: Presses Universitaires de France, 2002.
Martin, J. 'Life Positioning Analysis: An Analytic Framework for the Study of Lives and Life Narratives', *Journal of Theoretical and Philosophical Psychology* 33, no. 1 (2013), 1–17.
Mayr, E. 'Idea of Teleology', *Journal of the History of Ideas* 53, no.1 (1992), 117–135.
Meinong, A. *Logik: Philosophische Propädeutik*, Erster Teil, ed. F. Tempsky, and G. Freytag, Leipzig: Felix Meiner Verlag, 1890.
Melandri, E. *Logica ed esperienza in Husserl*, Bologna: Il Mulino, 1960.
Melle, U. 'The Development of Husserl's Ethik', *Etudes Phénoménologiques* 13–14 (1991), 115–135.
Melle, U. 'Edmund Husserl, From Reason to Love', in J. Drummond, and L. Embree, eds, *Phenomenological Approaches to Moral Philosophy*, Dordrecht: Kluwer, 2002.
Melle, U. 'Ethics in Husserl', in *Encyclopedia of Phenomenology*, Dordrecht/Boston/London: Kluwer Academic Publishers, 1997, 180–184.
Melle, U. 'Husserls Phänomenologie des Willens', *Tijdschrift voor Filosopfie* 54, no. 2 (1992), 280–305.
Melle, U. 'Husserls Personalistiche Ethik', in B. Centi and G. Gigliotti, eds, *Fenomenologia della ragion pratica*, Naples: Bibliopolis, 2004, 344–346.
Melle, U. 'Schelersche Motive in Husserls Freiburger Ethik', in G. Pfafferott, ed. *Vom Umsturz der Werte in der modernen Gesellschaft*, Bonn, 1997.
Melle, U. *Zu Brentano und Husserls Ethikansatz: die Analogie zwischen den Vernuftenarten* in *Brentano Studien*, 1, 1998, 109–120.
Menachem, A. *Victim Precipitated Forcible Rape* 58 *J. Crim. Law & Criminology* 493 (1968).
Mensch, J. R. *Postfoundational Phenomenology: Husserlian Reflections on Presence and Embodiment*, University Park, PA: The Pennsylvania State University Press, 2001.
Merleau-Ponty, M. 'The Child's Relations with Others', trans. W. Cobb, in M. Merleau-Ponty, *The Primacy of Perception*, ed. J. Edie, Evanston: Northwestern University Press, 1964 (original work published, 1961), 96–155.
Merleau-Ponty, M. *Phenomenology of Perception*, trans. C. Smith, London and New York: Routledge, 1962.
Merleau-Ponty, M. (1968). *The Visible and the Invisible*, trans. A. Lingis, Evanston: Northwestern University Press, 1968 (original work published, 1964).
Mertens, K. 'Husserl's Phenomenology of the Will in His Reflections on Ethics', in N. Depraz and D. Zahavi, eds, *Alterity and Facticity: New Perspectives on Husserl*, Dordrecht: Kluwer, 1998, 121–138.
Mertens, K. 'Zwischen Letztbegründung und Skepsis. Kritische Untersuchungen zum Selbstverständnis der transzendentalen Phänomenologie Edmund Husserls', *British Society for Phenomenology* 42, no. 1 (2011), 53–77.

Merz, J. T. *European Scientific Thought in the Nineteenth Century*, New York: Dover Publications, 1965.
Minkowski, E. 'Findings in a Case of Schizophrenic Depression', trans. Barbara Bliss in: *Existence: A New Dimension in Psychiatry and Psychology*, New York, NY: Basic Books, 1958, 127–138.
Mohanty, J. M. *Phenomenology and Ontology*. The Hague, Martinus Nijhoff, 1970.
Montavont, A. *De la passivité dans la phénoménologie de Husserl*, Paris: PUF, 1990.
Moore, T. *Dark Eros*, Thompson, CT: Spring Publications, 1998.
Moran, D. 'Edmund Husserl's Phenomenology of Habituality and Habitus', *Journal for the British Society of Phenomenology* 42 (2011), 53–77.
Moustakas, C. *Phenomenological Research Methods*, Thousand Oaks, CA: SAGE, 1994.
Myhill, J. 'The Formalization of Intuitionism', in R. Klibansky, ed., *La philosophie contemporaine*, Florence: La Nuova Editrice Italia, 1968, 324–342.
Nakamura, Y. 'Nishida, le … Au dela de la logique du lieu', in Augustin Berque, ed. *Logique du lieu et le depassement de la modernite*, Brussels, 1983.
Nelson, B., Parnas, J., and Sass, L. A. 'Disturbance of Minimal Self (Ipseity) in Schizophrenia: Clarification and Current Status', **Schizophrenia Bulletin**, 40 (2014), 479–482.
Nieswiadomy, R. M. *Foundations of Nursing Research*, 2nd edn, Norwalk, CT: Appleton & Lange, 1993.
Nishida K. (1945), 'The Logic of Topos and the Religious World-view', Part 1, trans. Yusa Michiko, *The Eastern Buddhist*, NS, 19, no. 2 (1986), 1–29.
Nishida Kitarō Zenshū, 4th edn 1987–1989, Tokyo: Iwanami Shoten.
Nishitani, K. *Nishida Kitarō*, University of California Press, 1991.
Noll, R. 'Shamanism and Schizophrenia: A State-Specific Approach to the "Schizophrenia Metaphor" of Shamanic States', *American Ethnologist*, 10, no. 3 (1983), 443–459.
Noor, A. 'Individualité et volonté', *Études Phénoménologiques* 13–14 (1991), 146–162.
Nordgaard, J., and Parnas, J. 'Self-disorders and Schizophrenia Spectrum: A Study of 100 First Hospital Admissions', *Schizophrenia Bulletin* 40 (2014), 1300–1307.
Oiler, C. J. 'Phenomenology: The Method', in P. L. Munhall and C. J. Oiler, eds, *Nursing Research: A Qualitative Perspective*, Norwalk, CT: Appleton-CenturyCrofts, 1986, 69–82.
Olivieri, A. *Prima lezione di neuroscienze*, Rome-Bari: Laterza, 2004.
O'Neill, J. 'Situation and Temporality', *Philosophy and Phenomenological Research* 28 (1968), 413–422.
Ong, W. *Orality and Literacy*, London and New York: Routledge, 1982, 1988.
Orth, W. 'Lebenskrisis and Lebensbedeytsamkeit as Motives in Husserl's Phenomenology of Culture', in *Phenomenology of Interculturality and Life-World*, Münich, 1998, 54–71.
Overgaard, S. 'How To Do Things with Brackets: The Epoché Explained', *Continental Philosophy Review* 48 (2015), 179–195.
Overvold, G. 'Husserl on Reason and Justification in Ethics', in Don Ihde and H. J. Silverman, eds, *Description*, Albany: New York State University, 1985, 248–255.

Paci, E. 'I Paradossi della fenomenologia e l'ideale di una società razionale', *Giornale critico della filosofia italiana* 40 (1961), 411–442.
Pap, A. 'Different Kinds of Apriori', *Philosophical Review* 53, no. 5 (1944), 465–484.
Parnas, J., and Henriksen, M. G. 'Mysticism and Schizophrenia: A Phenomenological Exploration of the Structure of Consciousness in the Schizophrenia Spectrum Disorders', *Consciousness and Cognition* 43 (2016), 75–88.
Parnas, J., and Sass, L. A. 'The Structure of Self-Consciousness in Schizophrenia', in S. Gallagher, ed., *The Oxford Handbook of the Self*, Oxford: Oxford University Press, 2011, 521–546.
Pattinson, S. D. 'Consent and Informational Responsibility', *Journal of Medical Ethics* 35, no. 3 (2009), 176–179.
Patočka, J. *Introduction à la phenomènologie de Husserl*, Paris: Millon, 1992.
Peat, F. D. *Synchronicity: The Bridge between Matter and Mind*, New York: Bantam, 1987.
Peirce, C. S. *Philosophical Writings*, vol. 1, New York: Dover, 1995.
Perreau, L. *Le monde social selon Husserl*, Dordrecht: Springer, 2013.
Peters, J. J. 'Children Who Are Victims of Sexual Assault and the Psychology of Offenders', *The American Journal of Psychotherapy* 30 (1976), 398–421.
Piazza, T. *Esperienza e sintesi passiva. La costituzione percettiva nella filosofia di Edmund Husserl*, Milan: Guerini e Associati, 2001.
Piché, C. 'La phénoménologie de l'expérience moral chez Kant', *Kairos* 22 (2003), 123–150.
Ploug, T., and Soren, H. 'Informed Consent and Routinisation', *Journal of Medical Ethics* 39, no. 4 (2013), 214–218.
Polkinghorne, D. E. 'Incarnate Phenomenological Reflection', *Theoretical & Philosophical Psychology* 9, no. 1 (1989), 46–51.
Ponsetto, A. 'La dimensione politica della fenomenologia husserliana', *Fenomenologia e società* 9, no. 12 (1986), 7–38.
Ponsetto, A. 'Edmund Husserl, dalla critica alla società alla domanda intorno a Dio', *Civiltà Cattolica* 121, no. 4 (1970), 233–239.
Ponsetto, A. 'Fenomenologia e politica. Le implicanze politiche dei concetti husserliani di intersoggettività e di Leib', in *Edmund Husserl. La 'crisi delle scienze europee' e la responsabilità storica dell'Europa*, Milan: Franco Angeli, 1985, 248–263.
Price, T. 'The Ethics of Authentic Transformational Leadership', *The Leadership Quarterly* 14, no. 1 (2003), 67–81.
Pugliese, A. *La dimensione dell'intersoggettività*, Palermo, Mimesis, 2004.
Putnam, H. *Reason, Truth, and History*, Cambridge, MA: Cambridge University Press, 1981.
Raggiunti, R. *Introduzione a Husserl*, Bari: Laterza, 1998.
Rein, M., and Schön, D. A. 'Problem Setting in Policy Research', in C. H. Weiss, ed., *Using Social Research in Public Policy Making*, Lexington, MA: Lexington Books, 1977, 235–251.
Reinach, A. 'Concerning Phenomenology', *Kant Studien* 1918, 349–370.
Richir, M. *La crise du sens et la phénoménologie: autour de la Krisis de Husserl; suivi de Commentaire de L'Origine de la géométrie*, Grenoble: Millon, 1990.

Richir, M. 'Discontinuités et rythmes des durées: Abstraction et concretion de la conscience du temps', in Pierre Sauvanet and Jean-Jacques Wunenburger, eds, *Rythmes et philosophie*, Paris: Kimé, 1996.
Richir, M. 'Lebenswelt et épochè phénoménologique transcendentale', *Kairos* 22 (2003), 151–164.
Richir, M. 'Synthèse passive et temporalisation/spatialization', in Eliane Escoubas, and Marc Richir, eds, *Husserl*, Grenoble: Jerôme Million, 1989.
Rickert, H. *Der Gegenstand der Erkenntnis*, Tübingen: Mohr, 1892.
Ricoeur, P. 'Hermeneutics and Phenomenology', *Nous* 9, no. 1 (1975), 85–102.
Ricoeur, P. *Husserl, An Analysis of His Phenomenology*, Evanston, IL: Northwestern University, 1967.
Ricoeur, P. *A Key to Husserl's Ideas*, Marquette University Press, 1996.
Ricoeur, P. *Memory, History, Forgetting*, Chicago: Chicago University Press, 2004.
Ricoeur, P. 'Narrative Identity', *Philosophy Today* 35, no. 1 (1991), 160–187.
Ricoeur, P. *Oneself as Another*, trans. K. Blamey, Chicago: Chicago University Press, 1992.
Riemer, M. 'Remarks in "Anisotropy of time" ', *Consciousness and Cognition* 38 (15 December 2015), 191–197.
Rorty, R. *Objectivity, Relativism, and Truth*, vol. 1 of *Philosophical Papers*, Cambridge, MA: Cambridge University Press, 1991.
Roth, A. *Edmund Husserl Ethische Untersuchungen*, The Hague, Martinus Nijhoff, 1960.
Ruch, L. O., and Chandler, S. M. 'Sexual Assault Trauma during the Acute Phase: An Exploratory Model and Multivariate Analysis', *Journal of Health and Social Behavior* 24 (1983), 174–185.
Ruggennini, M. 'Krisi. La ragione nella storia e la crisi della fenomenologia', *Genos* 5 (2000), 165–179.
Ryle, G. *Phenomenology: Proceedings of the Aristotelian Society* 11 (1932), 68–83.
Sancipriano, M. *Edmund Husserl. L'etica sociale*, Tilgher-Genova, 1988.
Sartre, J.-P. *Being and Nothingness*, trans. Hazel E. Barnes, New York: Philosophical Library, 1942.
Sauvanet, P. *Le Rythme et la raison*, Paris: Kimé, 2000.
Schlick M. *Allgemeine Erkenntnislehre: Naturwissenschaftliche Monographien und Lehrbücher*, vol. I, Berlin: Springer, 1979.
Schlick, M. *General Theory of Knowledge*, trans. A. Blumberg, Wien-New York: Verlag-Springer, 1974.
Schreber, D. P. *Memoirs of My Nervous Illness*, trans. I. Macalpine and R. A. Hunter, New York: New York Review of Books, 2000.
Schuhmann, K. 'Husserl and Twardoski', in F. Coniglione, R. Poli and J. Wolenski, eds, *Polish Scientific Philosophy*, Amsterdam: Rodopi, 1993.
Schuhmann, K. *Husserls Staatsphilosophie*, Freiburg/München: Karl Alber, 1988.
Schuhmann, K. 'Probleme der Husserlschen Wertlehre', *Philosophisches Jahrbuch* 98 (1991), 106–113.
Schumann, P. 'A Moral Principles Framework for Human Resource Management Ethics', *Human Resource Management Review* 11, no. 1–2 (2001), 93–111.
Schütz, A. 'Type and Eidos in Husserl's Late Philosophy', *Philosophy and Phenomenological Research* 20, no. 2 (1959), 147–165.
Searle, J. *The Construction of Social Reality*, New York: Free Press, 1995.

Seidman, I. *Interviewing as Qualitative Research*, New York, NY: Teacher's College Press, 1998.
Sellars, W. *Empiricism and the Philosophy of Mind*, Harvard University Press, 1997.
Sennett, R. *The Fall of Public Man*, Cambridge, MA: Cambridge University Press, 1977.
Sepp, H. R. *Edmund Husserl und die phänomenologische Bewegung. Zeugnisse in Text und Bild*, Freiburg: Verlag Karl Alber, 1988.
Sepp, H. R. *Husserl über Erneuerung Ethik mit Schnittfeld von Wissenschaft und Sozialität*, in H. M. Gerlach and H. R. Sepp, eds, *Husserl in Halle*, Frankfurt: Peter Lang, 1994, 109–130.
Seron, D. *Object et Signification*, Paris: Vrin, 2003.
Shelton, J. 'Schlick and Husserl on the Foundation of Phenomenology', *Philosophy and Phenomenological Research* 48, no. 3 (1988), 557–561.
Silverman, J. 'Shamans and Acute Schizophrenia', *American Anthropologist* 69, no. 1 (1967), 21–31.
Simeonov, P. L. 'Yet Another Time about Time. Part I: An Essay on the Phenomenology of Physical Time', *PubMed* 119, no. 3 (2015), 271–287.
Smith, J. *Interpretive Phenomenological Analysis*, Thousand Oaks, CA: Sage, 2009.
Smith, J. A., and Eatough, V. 'Interpretative Phenomenological Analysis', in G. Breakwell, C. Fife-Schaw, S. Hammond and J. A. Smith, eds, *Research Methods in Psychology*, 3rd edn, London: Sage, 2006.
Sowa, R. 'Wesen und Wesensgesetze in der deskriptiven Eidetik Edmund Husserls', *Phenomenologische Forschungen* 2007, 5–37.
Spiegelberg, H. 'Indubitables in Ethics: A Cartesian Meditation', *Social Research* 1947, 35–50.
Spiegelberg, H. 'Husserl's and Peirce's Phenomenologies: Coincidence or Interaction', *Philosophy and Phenomenological Research* 17, no. 2 (1956), 164–185.
Spinicci, P. *I pensieri dell'esperienza*, Florence: La Nuova Italia, 1985.
Stace, W. T. *Mysticism and Philosophy*, London: MacMillan, 1960.
Stapleton, T. *Husserl and Heidegger. The Question of a Phenomenological Beginning*, Albany: State University of New York, 1983.
Steeves, H. P. 'Constituing the Trascendental Community: Some Phenomenological Implications of Husserl's Social Ontology', in *Phenomenology, Interpretation and Community*, Albany: University of New York, XXIII, 1996, 83–100.
Steinbock, A. J. 'Affection and Attention: On the Phenomenology of Becoming Aware', *Continental Philosophy Review* 37 (2004), 28–31.
Steinbock, A. J. 'Facticité et intuition dans la problématique du monde de la vie', *Kairos* 22 (2003), 189–211.
Steinbock, A. J. *Home and Beyond: Generative Phenomenology after Husserl*, Northwestern University Press, 1995.
Steinbock, A. J. *Phenomenology and Mysticism*, Indiana University Press, 2007.
Stewart, David, and Mickunas, Algis, *Exploring Phenomenology: A Guide to the Field and Its Literature*, Ohio University Press, 1990.
Stieb, J. 'Rorty on Realism and Constructivism', *Metaphilosophy*, 36, no. 3 (2006), 272–294.

Stifler, K. et al., 'An Empirical Investigation of the Discriminability of Reported Mystical Experiences among Religious Contemplatives, Psychotic Inpatients, and Normal Adults', *Journal for the Scientific Study of Religion*, 32, no. 4 (1993), 366–372.

Stogler, R. *Das ästhetische Apriori des Alter Ego. Untersuchungen zur transzendentalen Intersubjektivitäts-Theorie in der Phänomenologie Edmund Husserls*, Würzburg: Königshausen & Neumann, 1994.

Stolorow, R., Atwood, B. and Brandchaft, G. *Psychoanalytic Treatment: An Intersubjective Approach*, Hillsdale, NJ: Analytic Press, 1987.

Strasser, S. 'Grundgedanken der Sozialontologie Edmund Husserls', *Zeitschrift für Philosophische Forschung* 1 (1975), 3–33.

Straus, M. 'Victims and Aggressors in Marital Violence', *American Behavioral Scientist* 23, no. 5 (1980): 681–704.

Ströker, E. *Husserls transzendentale Phänomenologie*, Frankfurt am Main, 1987.

Stumpf, C. *Über den psychologischen Ursprung der Raumvorstellung*, Leipzig: S. Hirzel, 1873.

Swingewood, A. *A Short History of Sociological Thought*, New York: St. Martin's, 1991.

Tesch, R. *The Contribution of a Qualitative Method: Phenomenological Research*, Unpublished manuscript, Qualitative Research Management, Santa Barbara, CA, 1988.

Theunissen, M. *The Other*, Cambridge: MIT Press, 1984.

Thierry, Y. *Conscience et humanité selon Husserl. Essai sur le sujet politique*, Paris: Presses Universitarie de France, 1995.

Thomas, E. E. *Lotze's Theory of Reality*, Kessinger, 2010.

Tiryakian, E. A. 'Existential Phenomenology and the Sociological Tradition', *American Sociological Review* 30 (1965).

Tomas, R. 'Mathématisation indirecte et monde de la vie un commentare de la section 9 C de la Krisis', *Kairos* 22 (2003), 213–224.

Toulemont, R. *L'Essence de la société selon Husserl*, Paris: Presses Universitaires, 1962.

Tugendhat, E. 'Phenomenology and Linguistic Analyisis', in F. Elliston and P. McCormick, eds, *Husserl: Expositions and Appraisals*, Indiana: University Notre Dame Press, 1973.

Tugendhat, E. 'Der Wahrheitsbegriff bei Husserl und Heidegger' *Phänomenologische Forschungen* 1967, 5–37.

Turner, N., Barling, J. Epitropaki, O., Butcher, V. and Milner, C. 'Transformational Leadership and Moral Reasoning', *Journal of Applied Psychology* 87, no. 2 (2002), 304–311.

Vandevelde, P. *Review to Husserl's Ethics and Practical Intentionality*, Notre Dame Philosophical Reviews, 2016.

Van Manen, M. *Researching Lived Experience: Human Science for an Action Sensitive Pedagogy*, New York, NY: State University of New York Press, 1990.

Vygotsky, L. 'The Historical Meaning of the Crisis in Psychology: A Methodological Investigation', in *The Collected Works of Vygotsky*, New York: Plenum Press, 1927.

Wallace, W. *Hegel's Philosophy of Mind*, Pantianos Classics, 1894.

Walsh, R. 'Phenomenological Mapping and Comparisons of Shamanic, Buddhist, Yogic, and Schizophrenic Experiences', *Journal of the American Academy of Religion* 61, no. 4 (1993), 739–769.

Walton, J. 'La consideración interior de la historia en la fenomenología transcendendental', *Escritos de la filosofía*, Buenos Aires, 16, 1997.

Ward et al., 'Interactions of Timing and Motivational Impairments in Schizophrenia', in A. Vatakis and M. Allman, eds, *Time Distortions in Mind*, Brill, 168–89.

Warren, B. *Philosophical Dimensions of Personal Construct Psychology*, London: Routledge, 1998.

Warren, N. 'Husserl et la question du monde', *Kairos* 22 (2003), 165–187.

Warren, N. *Husserl and the Promise of Time*, Cambridge University Press, 2009.

Welman, J., and Kruger, S. *Research Methodology for the Business and Administrative Sciences*, Johannesburg, South Africa: International Thompson, 1999.

Wertz, F. 'Phenomenological Research Methods for Counseling Psychology', *Journal of Counseling Psychology* 52, no. 2 (2005), 167–177.

Wertz, F. J. 'The Qualitative Revolution and Psychology: Science, Politics, and Ethics', *The Humanistic Psychologist* 39 (2011), 77–104.

Willard, D. 'The Paradox of Logical Psychologism: Husserl's Way Out', *American Philosophical Quarterly* 9, no. 1 (1972), 94–100.

Winnicott, D. *Playing and Reality*, New York, NY: Routledge, 1953.

Zahavi, D. 'Inner Time-consciousness and Pre-reflective Self-awareness', in D. Welton, ed., *The New Husserl: A Critical Reader*, Bloomington: Indiana University Press, 2003, 157–180.

Zahavi, D. 'Self-awareness and Affection', in N. Depraz and D. Zahavi, eds, *Alterity and Faciticity*, Dordrecht: Kluwer, 1998.

Zahavi, D. *Self and Other: Exploring Subjectivity, Empathy, and Shame*, Oxford University Press, 2014.

Zapien, N. 'The Beginning of an Extra-marital Affair: A Phenomenological Study and Clinical Implications', *The Journal of Phenomenological Psychology* 47, no. 2 (2016), 134.

Zapien, N. *Clinical Treatment Directions for Infidelity: A Phenomenological Framework for Understanding*, New York, NY: Routledge, 2017.

Zapien, N. and M. Levand 'Sexual Consent as Transcendence', *International Journal of Transpersonal Studies*, in press.

Index

Note: Page numbers followed by "n" refer to endnotes.

absolute, triadic structures and
    meontic 34–6
affair, beginning of an 161–2
    examples 162–72
    explication of constituents 177–9
    findings 172–7
    limitations and directions 179–80
    philosophical commentary 180–1
affair, extramarital 161
'amo et odi' 87
Analysen zur passiven Synthesis
    (1918–1926) 197 n.15
Analyses Concerning Active and
    Passive Syntheses (Husserl) 40,
    57–8
An Inquiry into the Good 200 n.4
Applebaum, M. 4, 14
Ariska, Y. 51, 52, 200 n.4, 205 n.37
Aristotle 13, 199 n.24
Ashworth 120
attitude, natural 31, 33, 197 n.12
Atwood and Stolorow (1984) 159

Bart, Pauline 214 n.6
Bauman, Z. 106
Being and Nothingness (Sartre) 97
Bergson 45
Bernet, R. 21
Bernstein 24
bias, phenomenology 36–7
Biceaga, V. 21
body–mind and intentionalities 39–41

Cairns, D. 14
Carman 39
Chandler, S. M. 102
Chittick, C. 69, 72
Churchill, S. D. 14

Clingan 27
Colaizzi, P. 14, 17, 112, 114, 115
common sense 74
Conrad, K. 78
consciousness
    intentionality of 15
    sexualization of 97
consent
    and ambiguity 87–8
    wakefulness and 85–7
constituents, explication of
    beginning of an affair 177–9
    leadership challenge 134–7
    parent's ethical dilemma 153–7
construens pars 23
Crowell, S. 22

Davalos, Deana B. 206 n.3
decision-making, ethical 4
descriptive method for psychology 117
descriptive phenomenological method
    14–15
Dodd, J. 45
Donohoe, J. 198 n.17
Drummond, J. J. 191 n.6, 192 n.16,
    193 n.19

ego 41, 90, 91
    independently of 42
    primordial 42
    psychical 86
    psychological 33, 34–5, 73, 197 n.12
    reflexive 34
    transcendental 31, 35
    triadic structure of 34
    wakefulness 31
Elwood, B. D. 200 n.4
Englander, M. 14

epistemology, Husserl's phenomenological 14
epoché 30–2, 112
  motivation for 31–2
  psychological 33
  and reduction 34, 112
eroticism 176, 177, 202 n.21
eternity 62
ethical decision-making 4
ethical dilemma, parent 141–2
  explication of constituents 153–7
  exploration 157–8
  findings 149–51
  within intersubjective system 158–9
  philosophical commentary 158–9
  verbatim responses 142–9
ethical leadership 133
Ethics and Practical Intentionality (Husserl) 58
ethics and triadic structure of being 37–9
existential sexuality 95–6
Ey, H. 79

Feenberg, A. 205 n.37
Ferrarello, S. 185
Fink, E. 30–6, 195 n.3, 196 n.9
Finlay, L. 190 n.4
Focusing (Gendlin) 99
forced intimacy 100–4, 214 n.6
Formal and Transcendental Logic 197 n.15

Gadamer, H. G. 23
García, Alvaro 99
Gebser, J. 78, 199 n.27, 215 n.1
Geistiges 79
Gemeinschaft 106
Gendlin, E. T. 99
General Systems Approach 194 n.27
genetic analysis, investigations 21
genuine phenomenological inquiry 31
Giddens, A. 96, 104, 105
Giorgi, A. 14, 16, 112, 115, 116, 121, 134, 138, 141, 149, 153, 159, 162, 181, 184, 190 n.4, 195 n.7, 197 n.14, 215 n.1
  descriptive phenomenological method 14, 117

phenomenological method 15, 17
phenomenological psychological research study 124
phenomenological research method 10–11
good enough mother 149
Greek culture 19
Greening, T. 26

Halling, Steen 191 n.4
Hart, J. 75, 85, 88, 205 n.34
Hartmann, E. 61
Hartmann, N. 50, 60
Heidegger, M. 13
Henriksen, M. G. 68
Higgins, C. 27
homogeneity 58
Husserl, Edmund 13, 50, 62, 63–4, 67, 75, 82, 84, 86, 88, 89, 91, 96, 111, 117, 184, 187–8, 192 n.14, 193 n.24, 194 n.28, 196 n.10, 197 n.15, 204 n.30
  affirms in *Logical Investigations I* 19
  Analysen zur passiven Synthesis (1918–1926) 197 n.15
  Analyses 53
  analysis 5
  archontic thesis 13
  detractors read *Ideas* 30
  ethics 12, 184
  ethics and triadic structure of being 37–9
  genetic and static approach 183
  holistic conception of science 17
  imaginative variation 15
  investigations 21
  investigations of subjectivity 14
  Logical Investigations 15, 195 n.2
  phenomenological epistemology 14
  phenomenological motto 30
  phenomenological theory 13
  phenomenology 14, 25–7, 99, 112–13
  phenomenology of ethics 5
  science and reactivation of meanings in 17–20
  scientific inquiry 19, 20
  simplification 14
  Späte Texte über Zeitkonstitution 203 n.24

teleology in 60–2
theory of intentionality 57–8
trinitarian relationship of the world 58–60
western and eastern interpretation of reality 51
Husserl on Ethics and Intersubjectivity 198 n.17

Ideas (Husserl) 30–1, 57
infidelity, instance of 172
in fieri – I 38
inquirer 22
inquiry
   determination of scope of 116–17
   genuine phenomenological 31
   phenomenological 113
'instinct' 89
Institutional Review Board (IRB) 117
intentionality
   active 184
   body–mind and 39–41
   forms of 35, 41
   Husserl's theory of 57–8
   passive 40
   practical 38, 45, 184
   transcendental-act 35
   triggers 89
intentions, triad of time and 43–6
interconnectedness 17
interpretative phenomenological analysis (IPA) 16, 190 n.4
intersubjective system, ethical dilemma within 158–9
intimacy
   forced 100–4
   transcendental 98–100
   transformation of 105
IPA, *see* interpretative phenomenological analysis (IPA)
IRB, *see* Institutional Review Board (IRB)

James, William 200 n.4, 210 n.29
jetzigen Wahl 43

Kant 13, 24, 189 n.1
Keen, Ernest 191 n.4
Kern, I. 202 n.22

Kockelmans, Joseph 189 n.2
Koestenbaum, P. 95–8
Kohut, H. 142
Kopf, G. 53, 54, 201 n.14
körperlichen Auge 79
Kruger, S. 117
Kuhn, T. S. 26
Kunz, George 191 n.4

Ladrière, Jean 194 n.1
Lambert, Johann Heinrich 13
language 20
La Noche Junto al Á lbum (2001) 99
Lasch, C. 106
lawfulness 84
laws, Nazi-promulgated 30
leadership 123
   dilemmas 125, 132–4
   ethical 133
   identity of 133
   and work environments 123
leadership challenge 125–32
   explication of constituents 134–7
   findings 132–4
   philosophical commentary 137–8
   unexpected 132
'*lebendige Gegenwart*' 59
Leibniz 199 n.24
Levere, T. H. 199 n.28
Logical Investigations (Husserl) 15, 19, 30, 31, 57, 195 n.2, 197 n.15
'Logic of Topos *(basho)* and the Religious Worldview' (Nishida) 51–2
The Logic of Topos and the Religious Worldview (Kitaro) 50
Lotze, R. H. 205 n.36
love 87–92
Luo, T. 102

MacLeod, Robert 191 n.4
Marion, J. L. 202 n.22
Mayr, E. 203 n.29
McDowell, J. 96
Menachem, Amir 214 n.6
meontology 44
Merleau-Ponty, M. 13, 67, 72
Mickunas, Algis 15
Minkowski, E. 75, 76

Mohanty, J. N. 191 n.6
Montero, García 98–9
Moore, T. 105
morality
　and religion 56–7, 63–4
　and sexual plasticity 104–6
　teleology and 56–7
Moran, D. 22, 82
motivation 82, 83–4
Moustakas, C. 14–16, 112, 114, 115, 192 n.9
mystics 73

Narcissistic Personality Disorder 157
natural attitude 31, 33, 197 n.12
natural self-evidence 74
Nazi-promulgated laws 30
negation of negation 53, 56
Newton 199 n.24, 210 n.28
nihilism 5
Nishida, K. 50, 53, 55, 57, 58–9, 62–4, 67, 75, 79, 116, 202 n.16, 205 n.37
　'Logic of Topos (*basho*) and the Religious Worldview' 51–2
　western and eastern interpretation of reality 51
Nishitani, K. 200 n.4

Opper, Jamie 206 n.3
our sense of reality? 6

Paraíso Manuscrito (1982) 99
parenting dilemmas, empirical study of 186
parent's ethical dilemma 141–2
　areas for further exploration 157–8
　explication of constituents 153–7
　findings 149–51
　philosophical commentary 158–9
　verbatim responses 142–9
Parnas, J. 68, 73, 79
pars construens 23
pars destruens 50
passive intentionality 40
passive syntheses 42–3, 74
Peirce, C. S. 13, 189 n.2
phenomenological inquiry 113
phenomenological method
　descriptive 14–15
　philosophical tools in 15
　in psychology 14–17
　theoretical approach 20–3
phenomenological motto 30
phenomenological research method 117–20
　selection 112–16
phenomenological science 19
phenomenology 14, 25–7, 112–13
　as 'a revolution of thought' 30
　bias 36–7
　defined 13
　of ethics 5
　and psychology 32–4
　reduction in 30–2
Pilisuk 26
Piovesana, Gino 200 n.4
Plastic sexuality (Giddens) 104
presuppositionless 17, 21
presuppositionlessness science 19
presuppositionless science 15
primordial ego 42
Prolegomena 26
psychical ego 86
psychoanalysis 215 n.2
psychological distress, moments of 49
psychological ego 197 n.12
psychologism 18, 33
psychology
　descriptive method for 117
　ego 33
　phenomenological methods in 14–17
　phenomenology and 32–4
　reduction 33
　research methods in 23
psychotic disorders 206 n.3
psychotic episode 78

quaestio juris of scientific analysis 17
qualitative research, theoretical and empirical approach in 23–4

Rape Law (1975) 214 n.7
real and reel 30–2
reality 5, 36, 42, 137, 183
　access to other 68–70
　intentional 31
　'Into the Heart of Reality'

analogies 70–3
  differences 73–5
  multilayered 34
  psychological grasp of 18
  of schizophrenics 37
  western and eastern interpretation of 51
reduction
  epoché and 34, 112
  motivation for 31–2
  in phenomenology 30–2
  psychological 33
Rein, M. 26
relativism 5
religion
  morality and 56–7, 63–4
  and topos of logic 56–7
research methods, in psychology 23
Reyes, Benítez 99
rhythmatizations 43
Ricoeur, P. 199 n.26
Riemer, M. 210 n.27
Romanyshyn, Robert 191 n.4
Ruch, L. O. 102

Sardello, Robert 191 n.4
Sartre, J.-P. 13, 96–8
schizophrenia 74, 75, 206 n.3, 209 n.21
schizophrenics 73–7, 80
  reality of 37
schizophrenics and mystics 70
Schön, D. A. 26
Schreber, D. P. 79
scientific inquiry 19, 20
scientism 15
Second World War 30
self-awareness 56
self-consciousness 36
self-distancing attitude 72
self-evidence, natural 74
self-familiarity 74
self-forming being 56
self-intimacy 74
self-presence 74
self-realization 52, 53
self-reflection 72
self-transformation 72
Sennett, R. 106
sensuous association 40

sensuousness 89
sexual activity 96–7
sexual existence, recursive structure of 96–8
sexual identity 96
sexuality, existential 95–6
sexualization, of consciousness 97
sexual plasticity, morality and 104–6
sexual violations 88
Simenov 45, 199 n.27
Sinnlichkeit 40
Sixth Cartesian Meditation *(SCM)* 195 n.3
Smith, S. 14, 16, 190 n.4
  interpretative phenomenological analysis (IPA) 16
Späte Texte über Zeitkonstitution 203 n.24
Spiegelberg, H. 14
Sprachleib 20
Stace, W. T. 71
Steinbock, A. J. 68, 72
Stewart, David 15
stigmatizing time 75–7

Teleologisches Denken 60
teleology
  forms of 60, 61
  Hartmann's critique of 60
  hidden 85
  in Husserl 60–2
  and morality 56–7
  and time 62–3
Temporality and Personal Identity in the Thought of Nishida Kitaro 201 n.14
'*The moral order of the world*' 56
theorein 22
theoretical sense 18
time
  defending 78–80
  stigmatizing 75–7
  teleology and 62–3
topos of logic, religion and 56–7
transcendental-act intentionality 35
transcendental dimension 33
transcendental ego 31
transcendental intimacy 98–100
transcendental realm 33

The Transformation of Intimacy 96
triggers, instinctive intentionality 89
'The Trinitarian relationship of the world' 50–1, 58–60
Trinitarian view of world and time 53–6
Tsun-Yin Luo 102

Van Breda, Hermann 195 n.3
Vandevelde, P. 64
Van Kaam 190 n.4
van Manen, Max 14, 15, 112, 113, 115
    phenomenological research 16
    phenomenology 16
violation, sexual 88
'volitional body' 38, 40, 82, 91, 216 n.3

wakefulness and consent 85–7
Walter Ong 57
Welman, J. 117
Wertz, F. J. 14, 191 n.4, 215 n.1
Willard, D. 205 n.36
work environments, leadership and 123

Yûjirô, N. 202 n.16

Zahavi, D. 68
Zapien, Nicolle 4, 96, 105, 184, 187, 198 n.22, 204 n.31, 209 n.24, 212 n.13, 216 n.2
Zen practice 51

www.ingramcontent.com/pod-product-compliance
Lightning Source LLC
Chambersburg PA
CBHW051806230426
43672CB00012B/2653